W9-CCN-546

Trees of North America
and Europe

For Elsie Phillips

Trees of North America and Europe

by Roger Phillips

assisted by Sheila Grant
edited by Tom Wellsted
line drawings by John White

Random House New York

Acknowledgements

It was only possible to consider doing this book when I had been offered help and cooperation by the organizations in charge of our wonderful arboretae. I would particularly like to thank the following:

The Royal Botanic Gardens, Kew.
The Forestry Commission at:
Alice Holt Lodge, Surrey;
Bedgebury National Pinetum, Kent;
Westonbirt Arboretum, Gloucestershire.
The Royal Horticultural Society, Wisley.
Hillier Arboretum, Hampshire.
University of Cambridge Botanic Garden, Cambridge.
United States National Arboretum, Washington D.C.
English Eucalyptus Garden Centre, Kent.

I am indebted to a great many people for the work they have done in identification, specimen collection, tree climbing, typing, tracing and all the other tasks needed to complete the work. Thank you: John Albers, Peter Barnes, Beverley Clark, Jenny Deakin, Nicky Foy, Hatton Gardner, Sally Jellis, John Jobling, Jim Keesing, Clive King, Isobyl & Eric Lacroix, Roy Lancaster, Gus Macartney Filgate, Ruth Messom, Lindsey Mitchel, Sam Phillips, Martyn Rix, Malcolm Scott, Beverley Stokes, Lucy Su, Tim the Tree climber, Uncles and Summers, V. A. Waldren, Alf Westall, John White, R. M. Wickham, Felicity Youett.

In addition I would especially like to thank Alf Westall and Malcolm Scott for their work in checking the text and photographs of the conifer entries.

Copyright ©1978 by Roger Phillips
All rights reserved under International and Pan-American Copyright Conventions.
This work was originally published in 1978 by Random House, Inc., New York in the United States and by Pan Books Ltd., London in Great Britain as Trees of North America and Europe

Library of Congress Cataloging in Publication Data
Phillips, Roger.
Trees of North America and Europe.
1. Trees — Identification. 2. Trees — United States — Identification. 3. Trees — Europe — Identification. 4. Trees — Canada — Identification. I. Title.
QK477.2.I4P45 582'.1609'7 78-57103
ISBN 0-394-50259-0
ISBN 0-394-73541-2 pbk.

Printed and bound in Singapore
by Toppan Printing Co., (Singapore) Pte., Ltd.

8 9 7

Contents

Introduction	6
How to use the book	7
Glossary	9
The leaf index	10
The illustrations and text	60
Bark photographs	216
Index	221

Introduction

Of all the flowering plants I have come to know from doing my wild flower book, the ones I have become most fond of and intrigued by are the trees. But I soon found that though there are many fine textbooks none was designed to help people like myself, who have no academic training, to make accurate identification of trees. Having arrived at a clear analysis of what it was I myself needed, I set about actually producing it. The first thing I have done is establish a leaf index. Traditionally a tree book begins with a key that requires the reader to make yes/no decisions about the characteristics of leaves, flowers and other aspects of the tree. The problem with this method is that it involves learning and understanding the specialized vocabulary which botanists have evolved to describe the minute and precise differences between leaves. My innovation is to do visually what they have done verbally: if you can see the leaf you do not need to know whether it is lanceolate or oblong lanceolate, you just look at it and compare it with the photograph, and if it is too broad or too narrow you pass on to the next leaf or page of leaves. Then check with the text. Bear in mind that I have illustrated a selection of over 500 of the most common and important trees that can be found in temperate climatic regions. If the leaf fits none of those shown you may have come up with a species or variety that I have not been able to include in the book.

I have used the word 'index' to describe what would traditionally, I suppose, be called a 'key' because all you have to do is turn the pages looking for the leaf that matches the one of the tree you wish to identify.

The second thing I have set out to do is consistently illustrate three aspects of each of the main trees in the book with the following: a photograph of the flowers; a photograph of the fruit; and a drawing of the adult tree shape. I have retained this formula for two reasons. First, it is very frustrating to use a book which is inconsistent in the information given entry by entry and secondly, it has enabled me to show many aspects of trees which have not been adequately illustrated in photography before.

How to use the book

The book is in two main sections, first the fifty page leaf index and then the larger section with the trees arranged alphabetically by Latin name.

The Leaf Index

512 leaves and foliage samples have been grouped according to shape. The following table shows the thinking behind the layout.

10–23: Conifers
- 10–11: Scale-like leaves, including cypresses.
- 11–12: Needle-like leaves at all angles round the stem, including junipers.
- 13–18: Needle-like leaves in 2 rows; silver firs, spruces, hemlocks, etc.
- 19–20: Needle-like leaves in bunches of 2; pines.
- 21: Needle-like leaves in bunches of 3; pines.
- 21–22: Needle-like leaves in bunches of 5; pines.
- 23: Needle-like leaves in bunches of more than 5; cedars and larches.

24–49: Broad-leaves (Simple)
- 24–42: Narrow leaves (willows), grading to broad (magnolias and cherries) to heart-shaped (limes).
- 43–47: Palmately lobed; including maples.
- 47–49: Pinnately lobed, including oaks.

50–59: Broad-leaves (Compound)
- 50: 3 leaflets.
- 51–52: Palmate; horse chestnuts.
- 53–58: Pinnate; including ashes.
- 59: Bipinnate.

Each leaf has its Latin botanical name, common name(s) and the page number for the main text. The leaves in this section were all photographed from mid July to mid August. Each page carries a scale, the circle represents a diameter of 1 centimetre and the horizontal line represents 1 inch.

If you wish to make an identification of a tree you have found, whether in the wild or planted in a street, park or garden, compare the leaf with those shown in the leaf index and note which trees it closely resembles, and then look them up and compare details of shape, height, environment, flowers, fruit and bark. Do take into account that leaves can vary a great deal; they develop and grow and change colour during the year, often the leaves from suckers are much larger than those on the main branches of the same tree, and they may also vary from tree to tree.

The text photographs

In the majority of cases the photograph on the left shows the flower and that on the right the fruit. In cases where one or other has been unavailable or insignificant we have shown a detail of the bark as a further aid. Do not forget to observe the leaves on these photographs, often the flower photograph will show the young spring leaves and the fruit photograph the mature autumnal leaves. In addition to the general photographs there are two spreads of autumn leaves; pages 76, 77, 188, 189 and a small section of bark pages 216 to 220 inclusive.

The drawings

John White of the Forestry Commission has done simple line drawings of each tree, designed to show you first whether it is evergreen; drawn with a full canopy of leaves, semi-evergreen; drawn with a partial covering of leaves; or deciduous, drawn without leaves. But the main function of the drawings is to give an indication of the shape of the mature tree. Remember when comparing your tree to the drawing to consider the conditions under which it is growing; the drawings below are to remind you how the shape and size of a tree may be altered by age and position. All the drawings are based on live specimens.

Scots Pine *Pinus sylvestris* left an old tree, centre a fairly mature middle aged tree, right a young specimen.

Oak *Quercus* three examples of a tree roughly one hundred years old, on the left a tree growing in normal woodland, tall and thin because it is competing for light, centre a tree grown in the open without undue exposure to wind, right a tree grown in the open but in a position very exposed to strong winds.

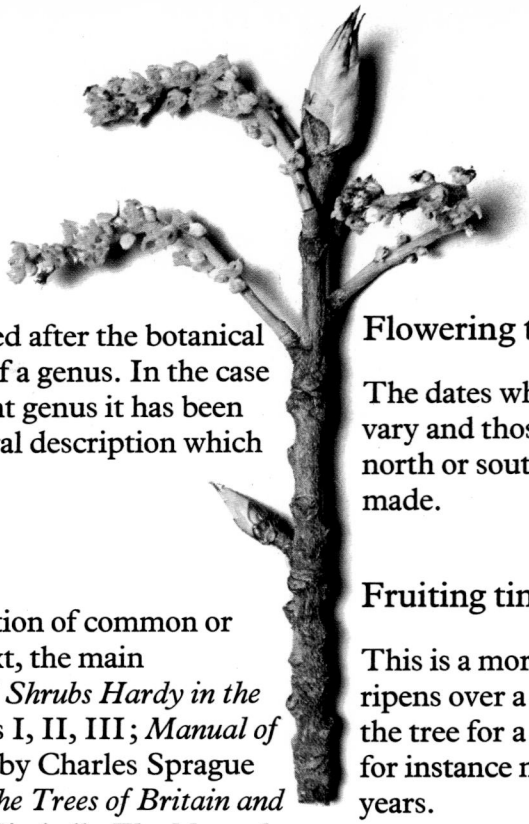

Family Name

The family name is included after the botanical name of the first member of a genus. In the case of a large or more important genus it has been included in the short general description which precedes the detailed text.

Common Names

I have included a full selection of common or vernacular names in the text, the main authorities being *Trees and Shrubs Hardy in the British Isles* W. J. Bean vols I, II, III; *Manual of the Trees of North America* by Charles Sprague Sargent; *A Field Guide to the Trees of Britain and Northern Europe* by Alan Mitchell; *The Manual of Cultivated Plants* by L. H. Bailey.

Botanical Names

The botanical or Latin names are set in italics. They have been drawn from the same books as the common names above except for in one or two cases where I have had to make reference to *Flora Europaea*. Occasionally, when there has been a recent name change or where there is some dispute as to which is the correct name to use, I have included a synonym. The botanical name is followed by an initial, a group of initials or an abbreviated name, which refers to the botanist responsible for giving it that name.

Origin

I have started the text with the details of the country of origin of the tree.

Height

The height given is that of a normal mature specimen. When comparing a tree, take into consideration the factors which control its growth: its age, the quality of the soil, whether or not it is exposed to high winds, the altitude, and whether or not it has had to reach up for light in a wooded position.

Flowering time

The dates when the tree is likely to flower will vary and those given are average; if you are far north or south allowance must therefore be made.

Fruiting time

This is a more vague figure as the fruit forms and ripens over a period and in many cases stay on the tree for a considerable time; some pine cones for instance may stay on the trees for many years.

Scale

Although the leaf index photographs have a scale indication, no scale is included on the main text photographs but relevant measurements are stated in centimetres and (inches) in the text.

The photographs

The photographs in the leaf index were taken on 5 x 4″ size, Daylight Ektachrome E6 using a De Vere camera and a 210mm lens, with aperture f.64 The small photographs in the text that were taken in the studio – that is those on plain backgrounds – were taken on a Pentax 6 x 7cm camera using close-up lenses, with an aperture of f.22. The film stock was Kodak either E.P. 120 (E3 processing) or E.P.R. 120 (E6 processing). The bark photographs were taken on a Nickormat using Kodak E.P.D. 135. In the studio the light source was a 2 x 3ft Fish Fryer head and strobe boxes with an output up to 13,000 Joules.

Glossary

Alternate Of leaves, arranged successively up the stem or branch, neither OPPOSITE, nor in WHORLS.
Annual A plant which completes its life-cycle within one year.
Anther The part of the flower on the STAMEN which produces POLLEN.
Berry Fleshy fruit, usually containing many seeds.
Bipinnate A leaf which has PINNATE divisions.
Bract A leaf, or modified leaf which bears a flower in its axil.
Capsule A dry fruit which consists of more than one CARPEL and splits to release its seeds.
Carpel A modified leaf, one or more of which make up the female parts of a plant.
Catkin A hanging spike of small, usually rather insignificant flowers.
Chimaera A plant formed from the tissues of 2 different forms or species, usually originating at the point where one form has been grafted onto the other, and showing parts of each parent. A graft-hybrid.
Clone A group of identical plants derived asexually from a single plant.
Compound Made up of several similar parts; a leaf made up of several LEAFLETS.
Coniferous Cone-bearing.
Coppicing Cutting back a tree to a stump to encourage growth of slender sprouts which have traditionally been used in basket and fence making.
Cultivar A cultivated plant distinct from others in any of its characteristics and which remains distinct when reproduced.
Deciduous A tree which sheds all its leaves annually.
Entire Referring to leaf margins, means not toothed or lobed.
Evergreen A tree which is in leaf throughout the year. Semi-evergreen—A tree which loses some of its leaves in autumn retaining some until new leaves form in the spring.
Glabrous Hairless.
Graft-hybrid See CHIMAERA.
Hardy Able to withstand cold.
Hermaphrodite Containing both sexes, i.e. functional OVARY and STAMENS.
Husk The thin dry covering on some fruits and seeds.
Hybrid A plant originating from the fertilization of one species by another.
Kernel A seed within a hard shell or the edible part of a nut.
Leaflet One of the divisions of a COMPOUND leaf.
Lenticel A warty or corky mark on the surface of branches or stems which provides a pore for air to reach the tissues beneath the bark layer.
Native Not known to be introduced.
Nut A hard dry fruit.
Nutlet A small dry one-seeded fruit: the stone of a fleshy one.
Opposite Of leaves; arising at the same point on either side of a stem or branch.
Ovary The part of the flower which encloses the OVULES.
Ovule The female part which, on fertilization, forms the seed.
Palmate Having lobes or leaflets arising from one point in a hand shape.
Panicle A branched flowerhead.
Pinnate Referring to a COMPOUND leaf with 2 rows of LEAFLETS on either side of a central stem.
Pistil The female parts of a flower.
Pollen The fertilizing (male cells) powder formed in the ANTHERS.
Pubescent Covered with soft, short hairs.
Receptacle The enlarged end of a stem which bears the parts of a flower. Also the fleshy part which encloses the OVARIES in some types of plant.
Semi-evergreen See EVERGREEN.
Sessile Unstalked.
Simple Not COMPOUND.
Shrub A woody plant, much branched and smaller than TREES. (Often taken as less than 4.5m (15 ft) tall).
Sucker A shoot arising from roots eventually forming a new plant.
Tree A large plant with a single woody trunk. (Often taken as taller than 4.5 m (15 ft)).
Whorls Leaves or flowers arranged at the same level around the branch or stem.

Abbreviations used in the text:

cv.	cultivar
var.	variety
X	denotes a hybrid
+	denotes a graft-hybrid or a bigeneric-hybrid

Further Reading

Trees & Shrubs Hardy in the British Isles Vols I-III, by W. J. Bean (John Murray, eighth edition)

A Field Guide to the Trees of Britain and Northern Europe, by Alan Mitchell (Collins)

Manual of the Trees of North America Vols I, II, by Charles Sprague Sargent (Dover)

The Manual of Cultivated Plants, by L. H. Bailey

Trees of North America, by C. Frank Brockman (Golden Press)

Hilliers' Manual of Trees & Shrubs. Fourth edition

Conifers in the British Isles, by A. F. Mitchell (Forestry Commission Booklet No. 33)

Trees for Your Garden, by Roy Lancaster (Floraprint Ltd.)

Field Recognition of British Elms, by J. Jobling and A. F. Mitchell (Forestry Commission Booklet No. 42)

Trees and Bushes of Europe, by Oleg Polunin and Barbara Everard (Oxford)

The International Book of Trees, by Hugh Johnson (Mitchell Beazley)

The Oxford Book of Trees, by B. E. Nicholson and A. R. Clapham (Oxford)

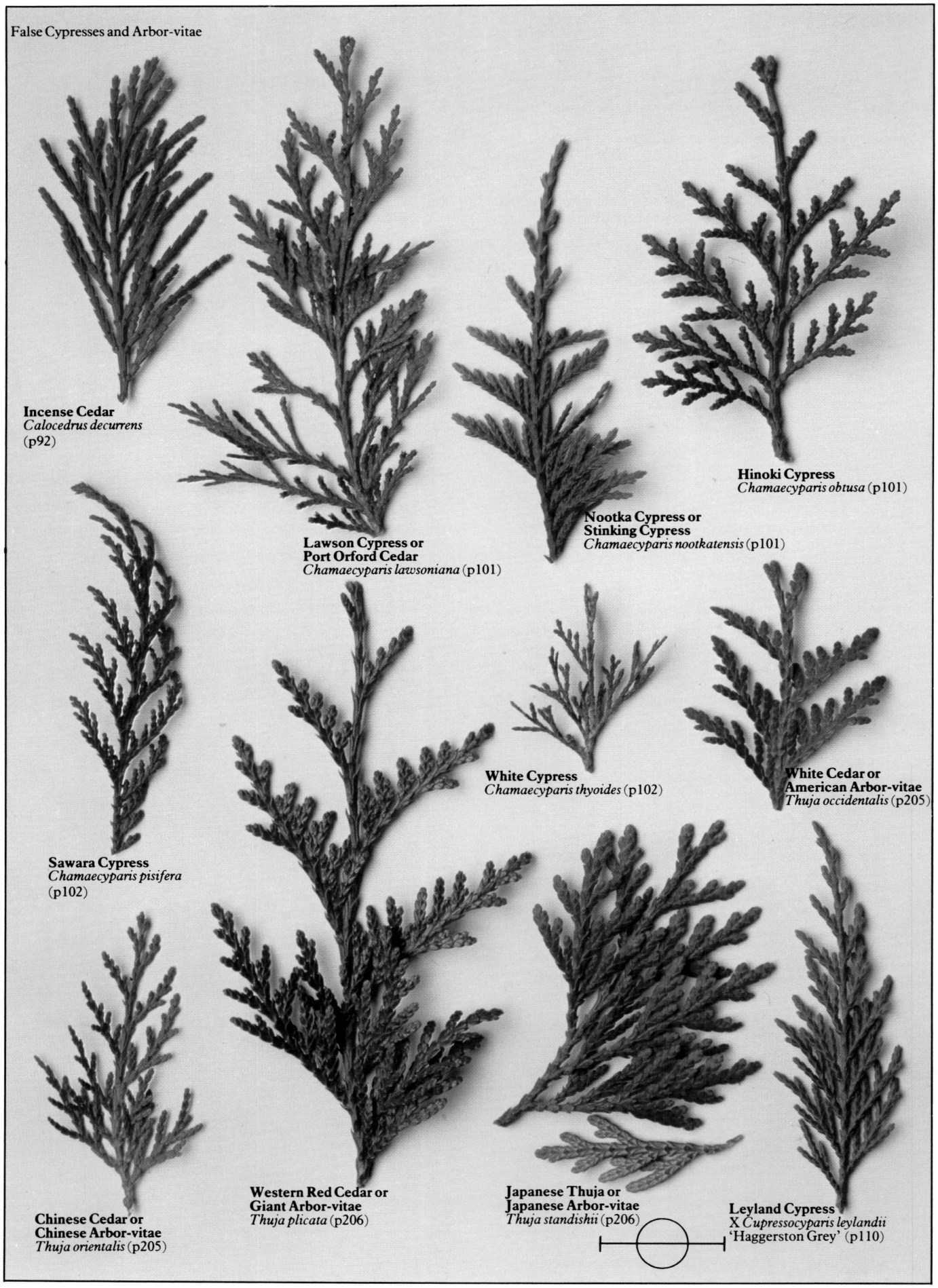
False Cypresses and Arbor-vitae
Incense Cedar
Calocedrus decurrens
(p92)
Lawson Cypress or
Port Orford Cedar
Chamaecyparis lawsoniana (p101)
Nootka Cypress or
Stinking Cypress
Chamaecyparis nootkatensis (p101)
Hinoki Cypress
Chamaecyparis obtusa (p101)
Sawara Cypress
Chamaecyparis pisifera
(p102)
White Cypress
Chamaecyparis thyoides (p102)
White Cedar or
American Arbor-vitae
Thuja occidentalis (p205)
Chinese Cedar or
Chinese Arbor-vitae
Thuja orientalis (p205)
Western Red Cedar or
Giant Arbor-vitae
Thuja plicata (p206)
Japanese Thuja or
Japanese Arbor-vitae
Thuja standishii (p206)
Leyland Cypress
X Cupressocyparis leylandii
'Haggerston Grey' (p110)

Hiba Arbor-vitae
Thujopsis dolbrata (p206)
Chilean Cedar
Austrocedrus chilensis (p88)
Patagonian Cypress
Fitzroya cupressoides (p118)
Italian Cypress or
Mediterranean Cypress
Cupressus sempervirens (p111)
Smooth Arizona Cypress
Cupressus glabra (p110)
Monterey Cypress
Cupressus macrocarpa (p111)
Rough-barked Arizona Cypress
Cupressus arizonica (p110)
Summit Cedar
Athrotaxis laxifolia (p87)
Smooth Tasmanian Cedar
Athrotaxis cupressoides (p87)
King William Pine
Athrotaxis selaginoides (p87)

Mostly Junipers
Japanese Cedar
Cryptomeria japonica (p109)
Taiwania cryptomerioides (p203)
Wellingtonia or
California Big Tree
Sequoiadendron giganteum (p197)
Chinese Juniper
Juniperus chinensis (p125)
Common Juniper
Juniperus communis (p126)
Syrian Juniper
Juniperus drupacea (p126)
Mexican Juniper
Juniperus flaccida (p126)
One-seed Juniper or
Cherrystone Juniper
Juniperus monosperma (p126)
Drooping Juniper or
Himalayan Juniper
Juniperus recurva (p127)
Temple Juniper or
Needle Juniper
Juniperus rigida (p127)
Pencil Cedar or
Eastern Redcedar
Juniperus virginiana (p127)

Nutmegs, Redwoods and others
Japanese Nutmeg
Torreya nucifera (p209)
California Nutmeg
Torreya californica (p209)
Monkey Puzzle or
Chile Pine
Araucaria araucana (p85)
Cephalotaxus
harringtonia
(p100)
Chinese Fir
Cunninghamia lanceolata (p109)
Cow's Tail Pine or
Japanese Plum Yew
Cephalotaxus harringtonia
var. drupacea (p100)
Chinese Plum Yew
Cephalotaxus fortunei (p99)
Coast Redwood
Sequoia sempervirens (p196)
Dawn Redwood
Metasequoia glyptostroboides (p140)
Swamp Cypress or
Bald Cypress
Taxodium distichum (p203)
Plum-fruited Yew or
Chilean Yew
Podocarpus andinus (p165)
Prince Albert's Yew
Saxegothaea conspicua (p196)

Common Yew or
English Yew
Taxus baccata (p204)
Golden Irish Yew
Taxus baccata
cv. 'Fastigiata
Aureomarginata' (p204)
Pacific Yew or
Western Yew
Taxus brevifolia (p204)
Chinese Yew
Taxus celebica (p204)
Japanese Yew
Taxus cuspidata (p204)
Eastern Hemlock or
Canadian Hemlock
Tsuga canadensis (p209)
Carolina Hemlock
Tsuga caroliniana (p210)
Chinese Hemlock
Tsuga chinensis (p210)
Northern Japanese Hemlock
Tsuga diversifolia (p210)
Western Hemlock
Tsuga heterophylla (p211)
Mountain Hemlock
Tsuga mertensiana (p211)
Southern Japanese Hemlock
Tsuga sieboldii (p211)

European Silver Fir or Common Silver Fir
Abies alba (p60)

Red Silver Fir or Pacific Silver Fir
Abies amabilis (p60)

Santa Lucia Fir
Abies bracteata (p60)

Greek Fir
Abies cephalonica (p61)

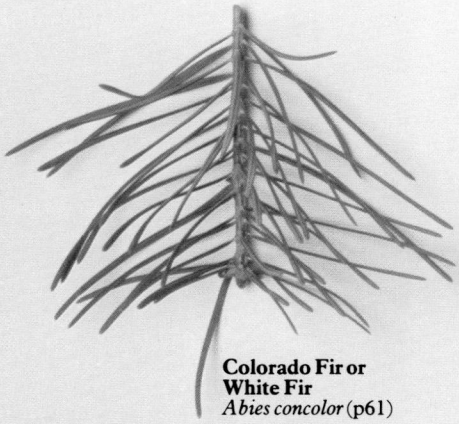

Colorado Fir or White Fir
Abies concolor (p61)

Delavay's Silver Fir
Abies delavayi var. *georgei* (p61)

Momi Fir or Japanese Fir
Abies firma (p62)

Grand Fir or Giant Fir
Abies grandis (p62)

Nikko Fir
Abies homolepis (p62)

Alpine Fir
Abies lasiocarpa (p63)

Red Fir
Abies magnifica (p63)

Caucasian Fir
Abies nordmanniana (p64)

Algerian Fir
Abies numidica (p64)

Noble Fir
Abies procera (p64)

Veitch's Silver Fir
Abies veitchii (p65)

Blue Douglas Fir
Pseudotsuga menziesii var. *glauca* (p178)

Large-coned Douglas Fir
Pseudotsuga macrocarpa (p177)

Douglas Fir or Green Douglas Fir
Pseudotsuga menziesii (p177)

Norway Spruce
Picea abies (p145)
Dragon Spruce
Picea asperata (p145)
Sargent Spruce
Picea brachytyla (p145)
Blue Engelmann Spruce
Picea engelmannii glauca (p146)
White Spruce
Picea glauca (p146)
Koyama's Spruce
Picea koyamai (p147)
Brewer's Weeping Spruce
Picea breweriana (p146)
Hondo Spruce
Picea jezoensis var. hondoensis (p147)
Likiang Spruce
Picea likiangensis (p147)
Black Spruce
Picea mariana (p148)

Spruces and Umbrella Pine
Siberian Spruce
Picea obovata (p148)
Serbian Spruce
Picea omorika (p148)
Oriental Spruce or
Caucasian Spruce
Picea orientalis (p149)
Tiger-tail Spruce
Picea polita (p149)
Colorado Spruce
Picea pungens (p149)
Blue Spruce
Picea pungens glauca (p150)
Red Spruce
Picea rubens (p150)
Sitka Spruce
Picea sitchensis (p150)
Sikkin Spruce or
East Himalayan Spruce
Picea spinulosa (p151)
Picea wilsonii (p151)
Morinda Spruce or
West Himalayan Spruce
Picea smithiana (p151)
Umbrella Pine
Sciadopitys verticillata (p196)

Two-needled Pines
Jack Pine
Pinus banksiana (p154)
Shore Pine or
Beach Pine
Pinus contorta (p155)
Lodgepole Pine
Pinus contorta var. latifolia (p155)
Aleppo Pine
Pinus halepensis (p156)
Bosnian Pine
Pinus heldreichii var. leucodermis (p157)
Bishop Pine
Pinus muricata (p158)
Austrian Pine
Pinus nigra (p158)
Crimean Pine
Pinus nigra var. caramanica (p159)
Corsican Pine
Pinus nigra var. maritima (p159)

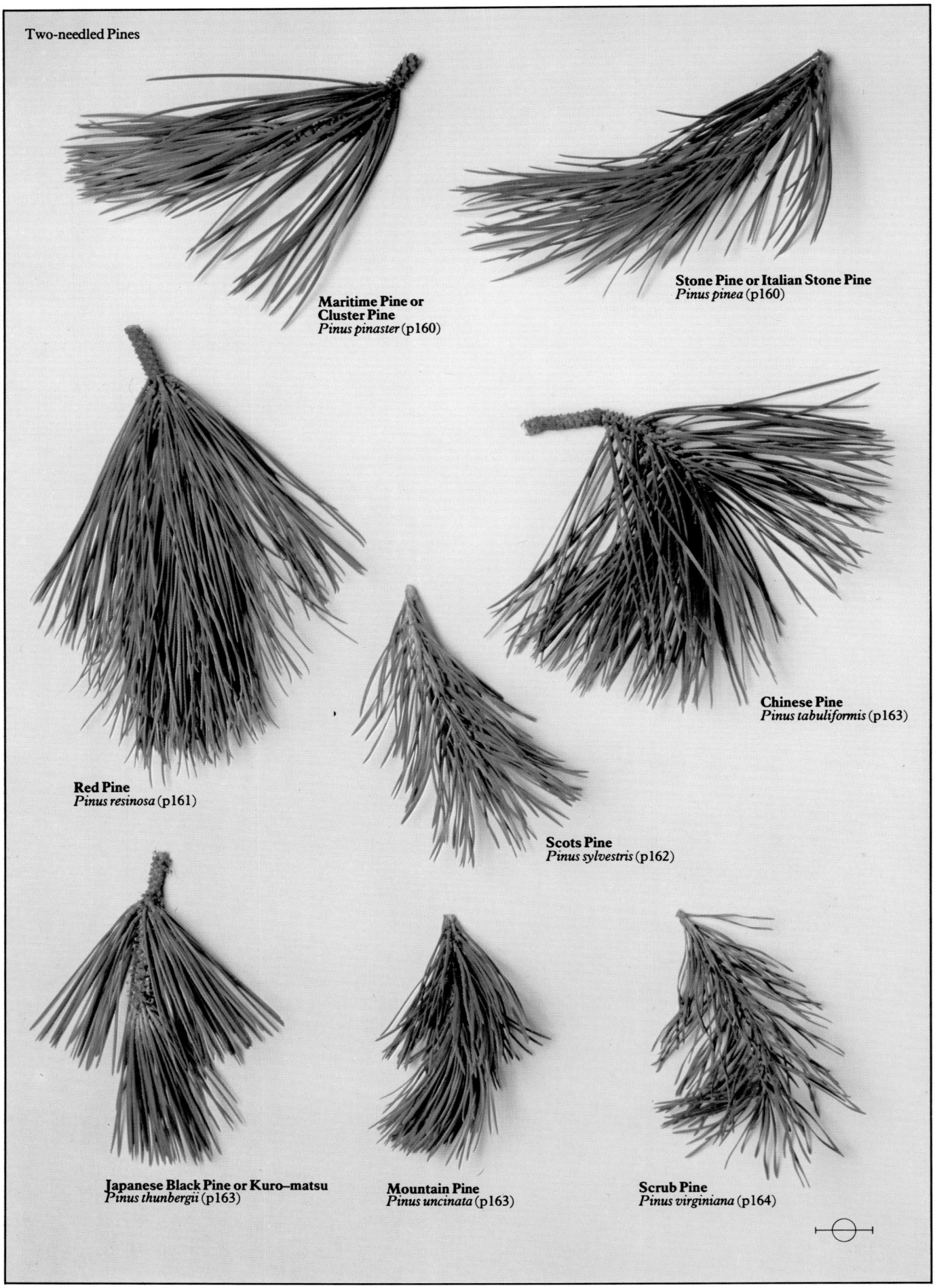
Two-needled Pines
Maritime Pine or Cluster Pine
Pinus pinaster (p160)
Stone Pine or Italian Stone Pine
Pinus pinea (p160)
Red Pine
Pinus resinosa (p161)
Chinese Pine
Pinus tabuliformis (p163)
Scots Pine
Pinus sylvestris (p162)
Japanese Black Pine or Kuro–matsu
Pinus thunbergii (p163)
Mountain Pine
Pinus uncinata (p163)
Scrub Pine
Pinus virginiana (p164)

Three-needled Pines
Knobcone Pine
Pinus attenuata (p153)
Lacebark Pine
Pinus bungeana (p154)
Big-cone Pine
Pinus coulteri (p156)
Pinyon,
Mexican Nut Pine or
Mexican Stone Pine
Pinus cembroides (p155)
Jeffrey Pine
Pinus jeffreyi (p157)
Western Yellow Pine
Pinus ponderosa (p161)
Monterey Pine
Pinus radiata (p161)
Five-needled Pines
Northern Pitch Pine
Pinus rigida (p162)
Whitebark Pine
Pinus albicaulis (p152)
Bristle-cone Pine
Pinus aristata (p152)

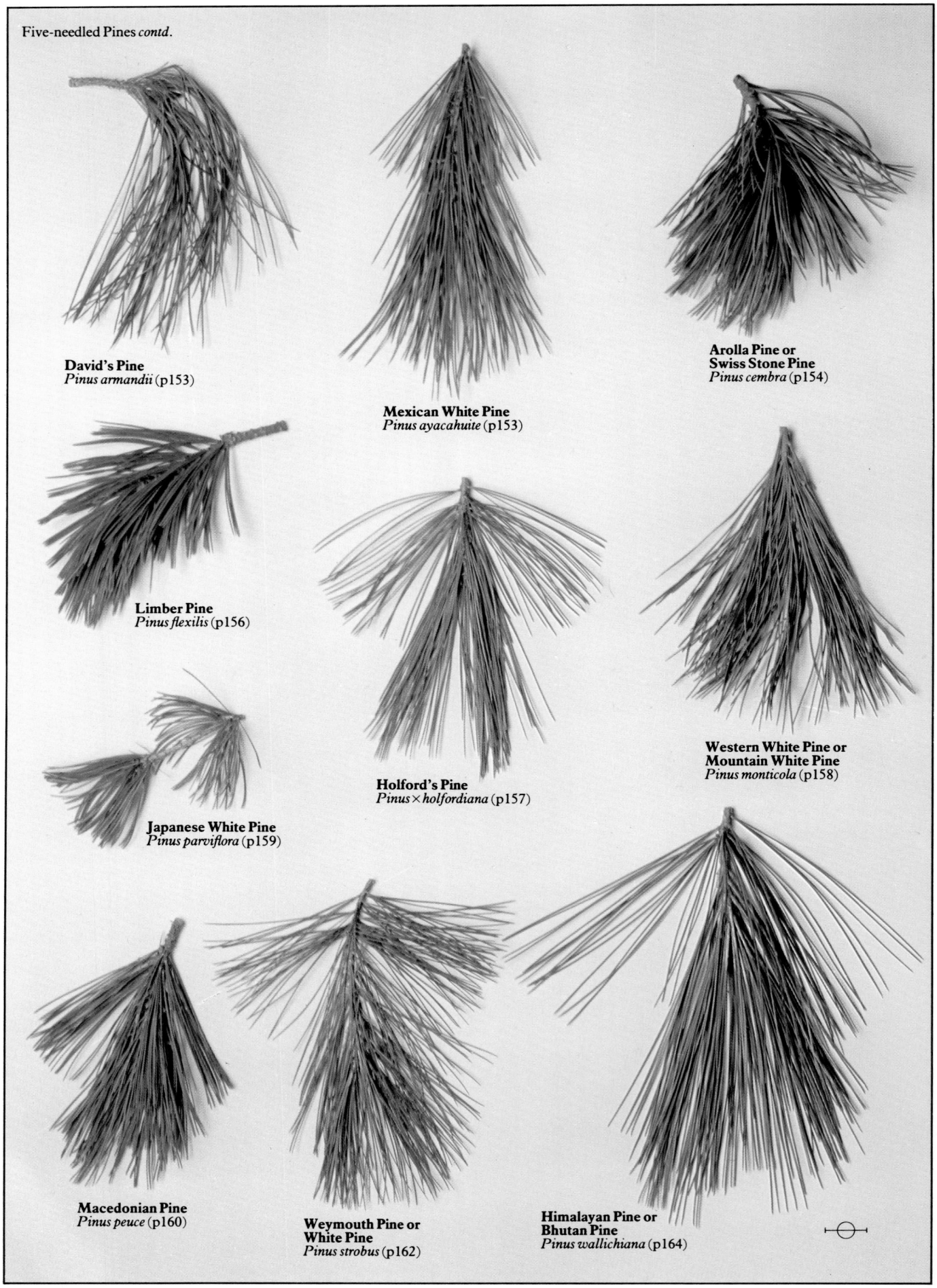
Five-needled Pines *contd.*
David's Pine
Pinus armandii (p153)
Mexican White Pine
Pinus ayacahuite (p153)
Arolla Pine or Swiss Stone Pine
Pinus cembra (p154)
Limber Pine
Pinus flexilis (p156)
Holford's Pine
Pinus × holfordiana (p157)
Western White Pine or Mountain White Pine
Pinus monticola (p158)
Japanese White Pine
Pinus parviflora (p159)
Macedonian Pine
Pinus peuce (p160)
Weymouth Pine or White Pine
Pinus strobus (p162)
Himalayan Pine or Bhutan Pine
Pinus wallichiana (p164)

Cedars and Larches
Atlas Cedar
Cedrus atlantica (p97)
Blue Cedar
Cedrus atlantica
var. glauca (p97)
Cyprus Cedar
Cedrus libani var.
brevifolia (p98)
Deodar
Cedrus deodara (p97)
Cedar of Lebanon
Cedrus libani (p98)
European Larch or
Common Larch
Larix decidua (p129)
Dunkeld Larch
Larix × eurolepis (p130)
Dahurian Larch
Larix gmelinii (p130)
Japanese Larch
Larix kaempferi (p130)
Tamarack,
American Larch or
Hackmatack
Larix laricina (p131)
Western Larch or
West American Larch
Larix occidentalis (p131)
Tibetan Larch
Larix potaninii (p131)

Very Narrow Leaves
Osier
Salix viminalis (p195)
Oleaster
Eleagnus angustifolia (p113)
Willow-leaved Pear
Pyrus salicifolia (p180)
Willow-leaved Magnolia
Magnolia salicifolia (p135)
Canyon Live Oak or
Maul Oak
Quercus chrysolepis (p182)
Golden Chestnut
Chrysolepis chrysophylla (p102)
Laurel Oak
Quercus laurifolia (p184)
Chilean Fire Bush
Embothrium coccineum (p114)
Willow Oak
Quercus phellos (p186)
Winter's Bark
Drimys winteri (p113)
Spinning Gum
Eucalyptus perriniana (p115)
Snow Gum
Eucalyptus niphophila (p114)
Cider Gum
Eucalyptus gunnii (p114)

Mostly Willows
White Willow
Salix alba (p193)
Crack Willow or
Brittle Willow
Salix fragilis (p194)
Contorted Willow
Salix matsudana 'Tortuosa' (p194)
Golden Weeping Willow
Salix × chrysocoma (p194)
Grey Sallow
Salix cinerea (p194)
Almond-leaved Willow or
French Willow
Salix triandra (p195)
Bay Willow or
Laurel-leaved Willow
Salix pentandra (p195)
Southern Nettle-tree
Celtis australis (p98)
Pin Cherry or
Wild Red Cherry
Prunus pensylvanica (p173)
Peach
Prunus persica (p173)
Tibetan Cherry
Prunus serrula (p174)

Japanese Stewartia or
Deciduous Stewartia
Stewartia pseudocamellia (p202)
Chinese Stewartia
Stewartia sinensis (p202)
Portugal Laurel
Prunus lusitanica (p172)
Hornbeam Maple
Acer carpinifolium (p66)
Mountain Snowdrop Tree or
Silver Bell
Halesia monticola (p121)
Medlar
Mespilus germanica (p140)
Hybrid Strawberry Tree
Arbutus × andrachnoides (p85)
Bamboo-leaved Oak
Quercus myrsinifolia (p185)
Cherry Laurel
Prunus laurocerasus (p172)
Strawberry Tree
Arbutus unedo (p86)
Sweet Chestnut or
Spanish Chestnut
Castanea sativa (p95)
Lebanon Oak
Quercus libani (p184)
Tanbark Oak
Lithocarpus densiflorus (p133)
Chestnut-leaved Oak
Quercus castaneifolia (p181)

Date Plum
Diospyros lotus (p112)
Common Persimmon
Diospyros virginiana (p112)
Evergreen Magnolia, Southern Magnolia or Bull Bay
Magnolia grandiflora (p135)
Kohuhu
Pittosporum tenuifolium (p164)
Madrona
Arbutus menziesii (p86)
Cyprus Strawberry Tree or Eastern Strawberry Tree
Arbutus andrachne (p85)
Sorrel Tree or Sour Wood
Oxydendrum arboreum (p143)
Sugarberry or Mississippi Hackberry
Celtis laevigata (p99)
Wilson's Magnolia
Magnolia wilsonii (p136)
Northern Japanese Magnolia
Magnolia kobus (p135)
Magnolia × soulangiana (p135)

Japanese Big-leaf Magnolia
Magnolia hypoleuca (p135)
Cucumber Tree
Magnolia acuminata (p134)
Umbrella Tree
Magnolia tripetala (p136)
Shingle Oak
Quercus imbricaria (p183)
Veitch's Hybrid Magnolia
Magnolia × veitchii (p136)
Papaw
Asimina triloba (p86)
Fraser Magnolia or
Ear-leaved Umbrella Tree
Magnolia fraseri (p134)
Campbell's Magnolia
Magnolia campbellii (p134)

Californian Live Oak or Encina
Quercus agrifolia (p180)
Hackberry or Nettle-tree
Celtis occidentalis (p99)
Roblé Beech
Nothofagus obliqua (p142)
Cork Oak
Quercus suber (p190)
Dombey's Southern Beech or Coigüe
Nothofagus dombeyi (p141)
Antarctic Beech or Ñirre
Nothofagus antarctica (p141)
Raoul or Rauli
Nothofagus procera (p142)
Pontine Oak or Armenian Oak
Quercus pontica (p186)
Holm Oak or Holly Oak
Quercus ilex (p183)
Caucasian Elm
Zelkova carpinifolia (p215)
English Elm
Ulmus procera (p213)
Wych Elm or Scotch Elm
Ulmus glabra (p212)
Keaki or Japanese Zelkova
Zelkova serrata (p215)

Ornamental Cherries
Great White Cherry
Prunus 'Tai-Haku'
(p176)
Prunus
'Pink Perfection' (p175)
Prunus
'Shirofugen' (p175)
Prunus
'Hokusai' (p174)
Prunus
'Shirotae' (p175)
Prunus
'Amanogawa' (p174)
Prunus
'Kanzan' (p175)
Prunus 'Ukon' (p176)
Prunus 'Accolade'
(*Prunus sargentii* × *P. subhirtella*) (p170)
Prunus
'Mikurama-gaeshi' (p175)
Yoshino Cherry
Prunus × *yedoensis* (p177)

Other Cherries
Cherry Plum or Myrobalan
Prunus cerasifera (p171)
Pissard Plum
Purple-leaved Plum
Prunus cerasifera 'Pissardii' (p171)
Sloe or Blackthorn
Prunus spinosa (p176)
American Red Plum
Prunus americana (p170)
Manchurian Cherry
Prunus maackii (p172)
St Lucie Cherry
Prunus mahaleb (p172)
Black Cherry or Rum Cherry
Prunus serotina (p174)
Spring Cherry or Rosebud Cherry
Prunus subhirtella (p176)
Choke Cherry
Prunus virginiana (p176)
Bird Cherry
Prunus padus (p173)
Sargent Cherry
Prunus sargentii (p173)
Prunus 'Hillieri' (p171)
Gean, Wild Cherry or Mazzard
Prunus avium (p170)

Quince
Cydonia oblonga (p111)
Persian Ironwood or
Iron Tree
Parrotia persica (p144)
American Smoketree
Cotinus obovatus (p105)
Box
Buxus sempervirens
(p92)
Balearic Box
Buxus balearica (p92)
Tree Privet or
Glossy Privet
Ligustrum lucidum (p132)
Bay or
Laurel
Laurus nobilis (p132)
Californian Laurel,
California Bay or
Headache Tree
Umbellularia californica (p214)
Himalayan Tree-cotoneaster
Cotoneaster frigidus (p105)
Magnolia × loebneri
'Leonard Messel' (p135)
Goat Willow or
Pussy Willow
Salix caprea (p193)
Yellow Cucumber Tree
Magnolia cordata (p134)

Common Beech or
European Beech
Fagus sylvatica (p116)
Purple Beech
Fagus sylvatica purpurea
(p117)
Oriental Beech
Fagus orientalis (p116)
Eucommia ulmoides (p115)
American Elm,
White Elm or
Water Elm
Ulmus americana (p212)
Rock Elm or
Cork Elm
Ulmus thomasii
(p214)
Single-leaved Ash
Fraxinus excelsior diversifolia
(p119)
American Hornbeam or
Blue Beech
Carpinus caroliniana (p93)
European Hop Hornbeam
Ostrya carpinifolia (p143)
Eastern Hop Hornbeam or
Ironwood
Ostrya virginiana (p143)
European Hornbeam or
Common Hornbeam
Carpinus betulus (p93)
Japanese Hornbeam
Carpinus japonica (p93)

Smooth-leaved Elm
Ulmus minor (p213)
Wych Elm or
Scotch Elm
Ulmus glabra (p212)
Huntingdon Elm or
Chichester Elm
Ulmus × hollandica 'Vegeta' (p212)
European White Elm or
Fluttering Elm
Ulmus laevis (p213)
Dutch Elm
Ulmus × hollandica
'Hollandica' (p212)
Whitebeam
Sorbus aria (p197)
Red Alder or
Oregon Alder
Alnus rubra (p84)
Sorbus 'Wilfred Fox' (p202)
Grey Alder or
European Alder
Alnus incana (p83)
Père David's Maple
Acer davidii
'George Forrest' (p68)
Père David's Maple
Acer davidii
'Ernest Wilson' (p68)

Table Dogwood
Cornus controversa (p103)
Cornelian Cherry
Cornus mas (p104)
Nuttall's Dogwood or
Pacific Dogwood
Cornus nuttalli (p104)
Flowering Dogwood
Cornus florida (p103)
Alternate-leaf Dogwood or
Pagoda Dogwood
Cornus alternifolia (p103)
Snowbell Tree
Styrax japonica (p203)
Osage Orange
Maclura pomifera (p133)
Tupelo,
Black Gum or
Pepperidge
Nyssa sylvatica (p142)
Sweet Bay
Magnolia virginiana
(p136)

Hollies
Holly-leaved Cherry
Prunus ilicifolia (p171)
American Holly
Ilex opaca (p124)
Perny's Holly
Ilex pernyi (p124)
Hedgehog Holly
Ilex aquifolium 'Ferox' (p123)
Ilex aquifolium
'Recurva' (p123)
Common Holly or
English Holly
Ilex aquifolium (p122)
Ilex aquifolium
'Aurea Marginata' (p123)
Ilex aquifolium
'Argentea Marginata' (p123)
Ilex × *altaclarensis*
'Wilsonii' (p122)
Ilex × *altaclarensis*
'Golden King' (p122)
Ilex × *altaclarensis*
'Hendersonii' (p122)
Ilex × *altaclarensis*
'Hodginsii' (p122)
Ilex × *altaclarensis*
'Camelliifolia' (p121)
Himalayan Holly
Ilex dipyrena (p124)

Snowy Mespilus or Allegheny Serviceberry
Amelanchier laevis (p84)
Common Pear
Pyrus communis (p179)
Siberian Crab
Malus baccata (p136)
Magdeburg Crab
Malus 'Magdeburgensis' (p138)
Japanese Crab
Malus floribunda (p137)
Crab Apple or Wild Crab
Malus sylvestris (p139)
Oregon Crab
Malus fusca (p138)
Purple Crab
Malus × purpurea (p139)
Hybrid Cockspur Thorn
Crataegus × lavallei (p108)
Broad-leaved Cockspur Thorn or Frosted Hawthorn
Crataegus × prunifolia (p109)
Cockspur Thorn
Crataegus crus-gallii (p106)
Prairie Crab Apple
Malus ioensis (p138)
Sweet Crab Apple or Garland Tree
Malus coronaria (p137)

Black Hawthorn
Crataegus douglasii (p106)
Scarlet Hawthorn
Crataegus pedicellata (p108)
Western Birch
Betula occidentalis (p89)
Downy Hawthorn
Crataegus mollis (p108)
Himalayan Birch
Betula utilis (p91)
River Birch or
Red Birch
Betula nigra (p89)
Yellow Birch
Betula lutea (p89)
Downy Birch
Betula pubescens (p91)
Silver Birch or
European White Birch
Betula pendula (p90)
Grey Birch or
White Birch
Betula populifolia (p90)
Blue Birch
Betula coerulea-grandis (p88)
Hawthorn-leafed Maple
Acer crataegifolium (p67)
Cherry Birch,
Sweet Birch or
Black Birch
Betula lenta (p88)
Paper Birch or
Canoe Birch
Betula papyrifera (p90)

Common Hazel or Cobnut
Corylus avellana (p104)
Turkish Hazel
Corylus colurna (p105)
Lime-leafed Maple
Acer distylum (p68)
Tartar Maple
Acer tataricum (p78)
Italian Alder
Alnus cordata (p83)
Common Alder or Black Alder
Alnus glutinosa (p83)
Big Leaf Storax
Styrax obassia (p203)
Judas Tree
Cercis siliquastrum (p100)
Katsura Tree
Cercidiphyllum japonicum (p100)
Paper Mulberry
Broussonetia papyrifera (p91)
White Mulberry
Morus alba (p140)
Common Mulberry or Black Mulberry
Morus nigra (p141)

Poplars
Downy Black Poplar or Manchester Poplar
Populus nigra var. betulifolia (p168)
Lombardy Poplar
Populus nigra 'Italica' (p168)
Cottonwood or Necklace Poplar
Populus deltoides (p167)
Hybrid Black Poplar or Railway Poplar
Populus × canadensis 'Regenerata' (p166)
Hybrid Black Poplar
Populus × canadensis 'Robusta' (p167)
Balsam Poplar or Tacamahac
Populus balsamifera (p166)
American Aspen or Quaking Aspen
Populus tremuloides (p169)
Western Balsam Poplar or Black Cottonwood
Populus trichocarpa (p169)
Big-toothed Aspen
Populus grandidentata (p167)
Grey Poplar
Populus canescens (p167)
Aspen or European Aspen
Populus tremula (p169)

Limes
Dove Tree or
Handkerchief Tree
Davidia involucrata (p112)
Silver Lime or
White Lime
Tilia tomentosa (p209)
American Lime,
American Linden or
Basswood
Tilia americana (p207)
Oliver's Lime
Tilia oliveri (p208)
Weeping Silver Lime or
Weeping White Linden
Tilia petiolaris (p208)
Caucasian Lime or
Crimean Linden
Tilia × euchlora (p207)
Large-leaved Lime
Tilia platyphyllos (p208)
Small-leaved Lime
Tilia cordata (p207)
Common Lime or
European Linden
Tilia × europea (p208)

Heart-shaped and almost lobed leaves
Yellow Catalpa
Catalpa ovata (p96)
Foxglove-tree
Paulownia tomentosa (p144)
Chinese Necklace Poplar
Populus lasiocarpa (p168)
Western Catalpa
Catalpa speciosa (p97)
Hybrid Catalpa
Catalpa × erubescens (p96)
Indian Bean or
Southern Catalpa
Catalpa bignonioides (p96)
Spur Leaf
Tetracentron sinense (p205)

Two- and Three-lobed Leaves
Moose-bark, Moosewood or Striped Maple
Acer pensylvanicum (p74)
Grey-budded Snake-bark Maple
Acer rufinerve (p75)
Red Snake-bark Maple
Acer capillipes (p66)
Hers's Maple
Acer grosseri var. hersii (p70)
Red Maple or Scarlet Maple
Acer rubrum (p75)
Montpelier Maple
Acer monspessulanum (p72)
Forrest's Maple
Acer forrestii (p68)
Cretan Maple
Acer sempervirens (p78)
Amur Maple
Acer ginnala (p69)
Tulip Tree or Whitewood
Liriodendron tulipifera (p133)
Chinese Tulip Tree
Liriodendron chinense (p133)
Maidenhair Tree
Gingko biloba (p120)

Three- and Five-lobed Leaves
Black Maple
Acer nigrum (p72)
Cappadocian Maple
Acer cappadocicum
(p66)
Miyabe's Maple
Acer miyabei (p71)
Rock Maple or
Dwarf Maple
Acer glabrum (p69)
Chalk Maple
Acer leucoderme (p71)
Italian Maple
Acer opalus
(p73)
Fig
Ficus carica
(p117)
Sweet Gum
Liquidamber styraciflua
(p132)
Prickly Castor-oil Tree
Kalopanax pictus var. maximowiczii
(p128)
Oriental Sweet Gum
Liquidamber orientalis (p132)

Five-lobed Maples
Sugar Maple
Acer saccharum (p78)
Oregon Maple
Acer macrophyllum (p71)
Mountain Maple
Acer spicatum (p78)
Miyabe's Maple
Acer miyabei (p71)
Heldreich's Maple
Acer heldreichii (p70)
Balkan Maple
Acer hyrcanum (p70)
Sycamore or
Sycamore Maple
Acer pseudoplatanus (p74)
Acer pseudoplatanus
'Atropurpureum' (p74)
Van Volxem's
Maple
Acer velutinum var.
vanvolxemii (p79)
Field Maple or
Hedge Maple
Acer campestre (p65)
Zoeschen Maple
Acer × zoeschense (p79)
Norway Maple
Acer platanoides (p74)
Acer platanoides
'Goldsworth Purple' (p74)
Acer platanoides
'Schwedleri' (p74)

Five or more lobes

Japanese Maple
Acer palmatum (p73)

Acer palmatum
'Atropurpureum (p73)

Silver Maple
Acer saccharinum (p75)

London Plane
Platanus acerifolia (p165)

Oriental Plane
Platanus orientalis (p165)

Bigtooth Maple
Acer grandidentatum
(p69)

Downy Japanese Maple or Fullmoon Maple
Acer japonicum (p70)

Vine Maple
Acer circinatum (p67)

Cut-leaved Beech or
Fern-leaved Beech
Fagus sylvatica 'Asplenifolia' (p117)
Pyrenean Whitebeam
Sorbus mougeottii (p200)
Hawthorn-leaved Crab Apple
Malus florentina (p137)
Service Tree of Fontainebleau
Sorbus latifolia (p200)
Common Hawthorn
Crataegus monogyna (p108)
Midland Hawthorn,
May or
English Hawthorn
Crataegus laevigata
(p107)
Wild Service Tree
Sorbus torminalis (p201)
Bastard Service Tree
Sorbus × thuringiaca (p201)
Oriental Thorn
Crataegus laciniata (p107)
Swedish Whitebeam
Sorbus intermedia (p199)
Sassafras
Sassafras albidum
(p196)
White Poplar or
Abele
Populus alba (p166)

Oaks
Cut-leaved Oak
Quercus robur
'Filicifolia' (p187)
English Oak or
Pedunculate Oak
Quercus robur (p187)
Sessile Oak or
Durmast Oak
Quercus petraea (p186)
Lucombe Oak
Quercus × hispanica
'Lucombeana' (p183)
Pyrenean Oak
Quercus pyrenaica (p187)
Purple English Oak
Quercus robur
purpurascens (p187)
Downy Oak
Quercus pubescens (p187)
(Specimens not typical;
should be more deeply lobed)
Black Oak or
Quercitron Oak
Quercus velutina (p191)
(Specimen not typical;
should be symmetrical
and more deeply lobed)
Red Oak
Quercus rubra (p190)
Ludwig's Oak
Quercus × ludoviciana (p184)
White Oak
Quercus alba (p180)
Scarlet Oak
Quercus coccinea
(p182)
Shumard Oak
Quercus shumardii
(p190)
Pin Oak
Quercus palustris
(p185)
Californian Black Oak
Quercus kelloggii
(p184)

Oaks
Caucasian Oak
Quercus macranthera (p185)
Mirbeck's Oak or
Algerian Oak
Quercus canariensis (p181)
Daimio Oak
Quercus dentata (p182)
Macedonian Oak
Quercus trojana (p191)
Turkey Oak
Quercus cerris (p181)
Basket Oak or
Chestnut Oak
Quercus prinus (p186)
Mirbeck's Oak or
Algerian Oak
Quercus canariensis (p181)
Turner's Oak
Querus × turneri (p191)
Swamp White Oak
Quercus bicolor (p181)
Black Jack Oak
Quercus marilandica (p185)
Hungarian Oak
Quercus frainetto (p182)
Burr Oak or
Mossy Cup Oak
Quercus macrocarpa (p185)
Lea's Hybrid Oak
Quercus × leana (p184)

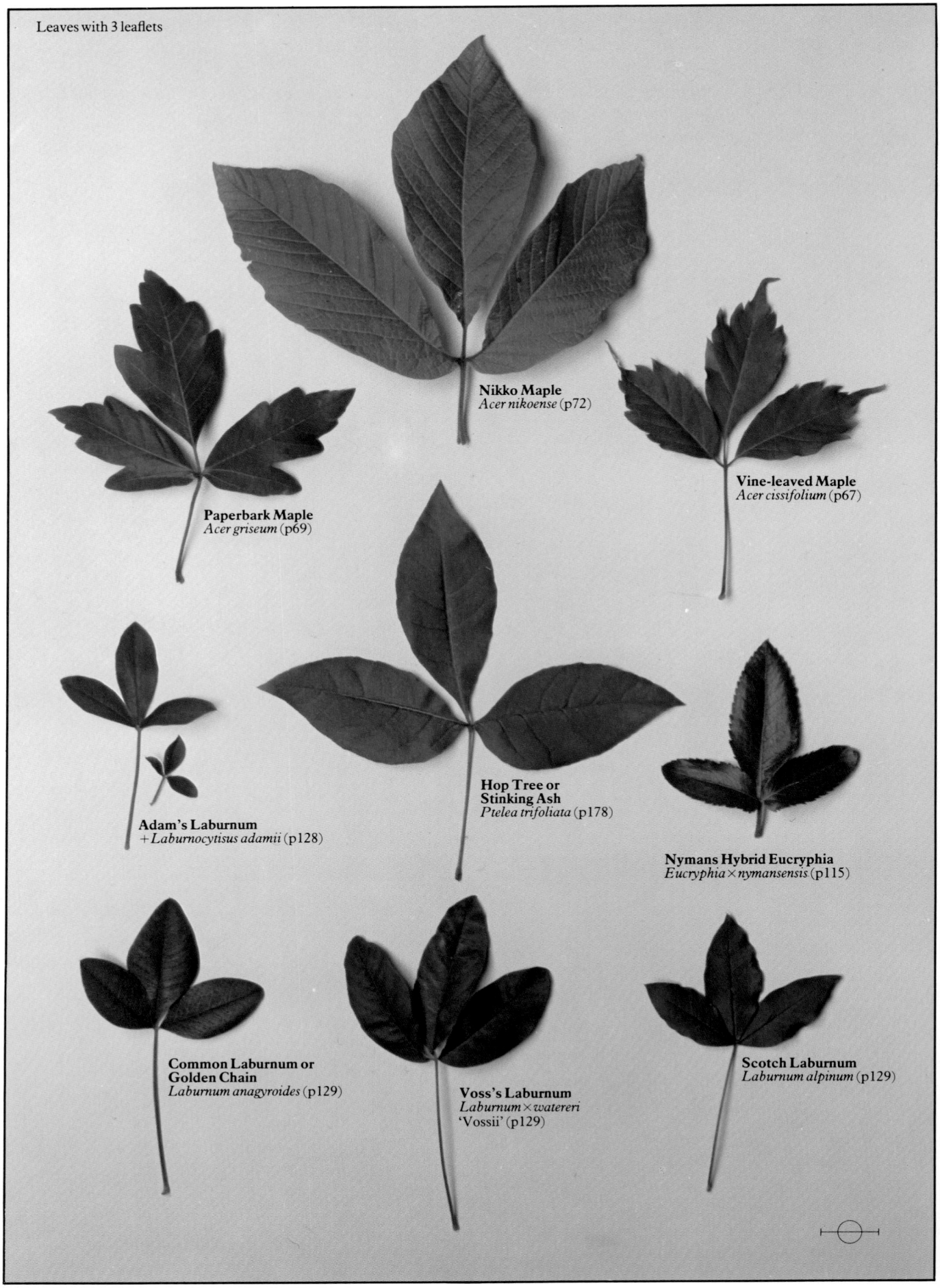
Leaves with 3 leaflets
Nikko Maple
Acer nikoense (p72)
Paperbark Maple
Acer griseum (p69)
Vine-leaved Maple
Acer cissifolium (p67)
Adam's Laburnum
+Laburnocytisus adamii (p128)
Hop Tree or
Stinking Ash
Ptelea trifoliata (p178)
Nymans Hybrid Eucryphia
Eucryphia × nymansensis (p115)
Common Laburnum or
Golden Chain
Laburnum anagyroides (p129)
Voss's Laburnum
Laburnum × watereri
'Vossii' (p129)
Scotch Laburnum
Laburnum alpinum (p129)

Yellow Buckeye or
Sweet Buckeye
Aesculus flava (p80)
California Buckeye
Aesculus californica (p79)
Ohio Buckeye
Aesculus glabra (p80)
Red Horse Chestnut
Aesculus × carnea (p80)

Common Horse Chestnut
Aesculus hippocastanum (p81)
Indian Horse Chestnut
Aesculus indica (p81)
Japanese Horse Chestnut
Aesculus turbinata (p82)
Red Buckeye
Aesculus pavia (p81)

Pignut Hickory
Carya glabra (p94)
Velvet Ash or
Arizona Ash
Fraxinus velutina (p120)
Manna Ash or
Flowering Ash
Fraxinus ornus (p119)
Box Elder
Acer negundo (p72)
White Ash
Fraxinus americana (p118)
Shagbark Hickory or
Little Shellbark Hickory
Carya ovata (p95)
Elder
Sambucus nigra
(p195)
Yellow Wood
Cladrastis lutea (p103)
Red Ash or
Green Ash
Fraxinus pennsylvanica (p120)
Korean Euodia
Euodia daniellii (p116)
Oregon Ash
Fraxinus latifolia (p119)

Mockernut,
Big Bud Hickory or
White Heart Hickory
Carya tomentosa (p95)
Big Shellbark Hickory,
Bottom Shellbark
Hickory or King-nut
Carya laciniosa (p94)
White Ash
Fraxinus americana
(p118)
Bitternut or
Swamp Hickory
Carya cordiformis (p94)
English Walnut or
Persian Walnut
Juglans regia (p125)
Caucasian Wing-nut
Pterocarya fraxinifolia (p178)
Oregon Ash
Fraxinus latifolia (p119)
Hybrid Wing-nut
Pterocarya × rehderiana
(p179)

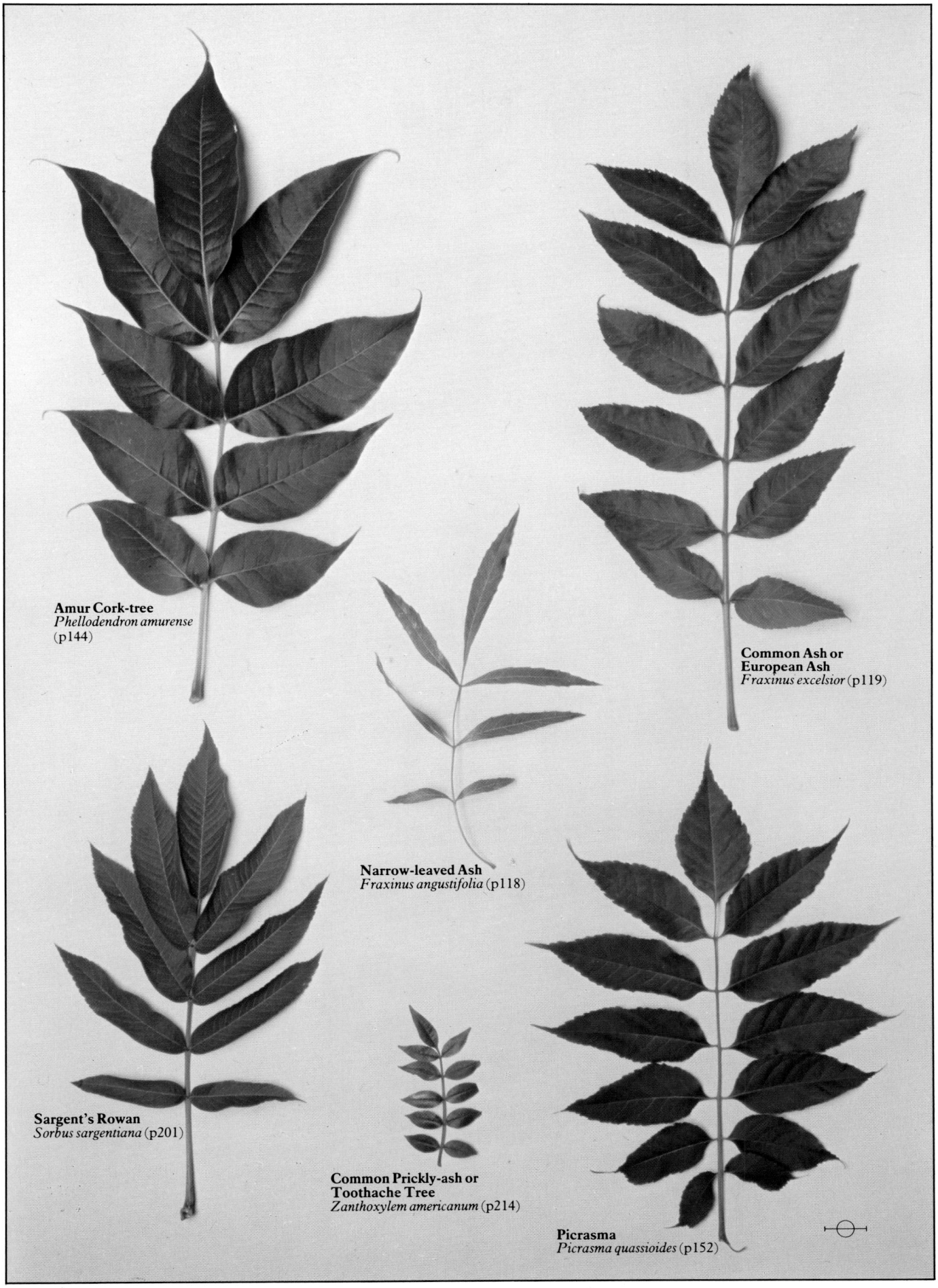
Amur Cork-tree
Phellodendron amurense
(p144)
Common Ash or
European Ash
Fraxinus excelsior (p119)
Narrow-leaved Ash
Fraxinus angustifolia (p118)
Sargent's Rowan
Sorbus sargentiana (p201)
Common Prickly-ash or
Toothache Tree
Zanthoxylem americanum (p214)
Picrasma
Picrasma quassioides (p152)

Japanese Rowan
Sorbus commixta (p198)
Chinese Scarlet Rowan
Sorbus 'Embley' (p199)
Service Tree
Sorbus domestica (p198)
Sorbus
'Joseph Rock' (p200)
Honey Locust
Gleditsia triacanthos (p121)
American Rowan or
American Mountain Ash
Sorbus americana (p197)
Rowan,
Mountain Ash or
European Mountain Ash
Sorbus aucuparia (p198)
Hupeh Rowan
Sorbus hupehensis (p199)

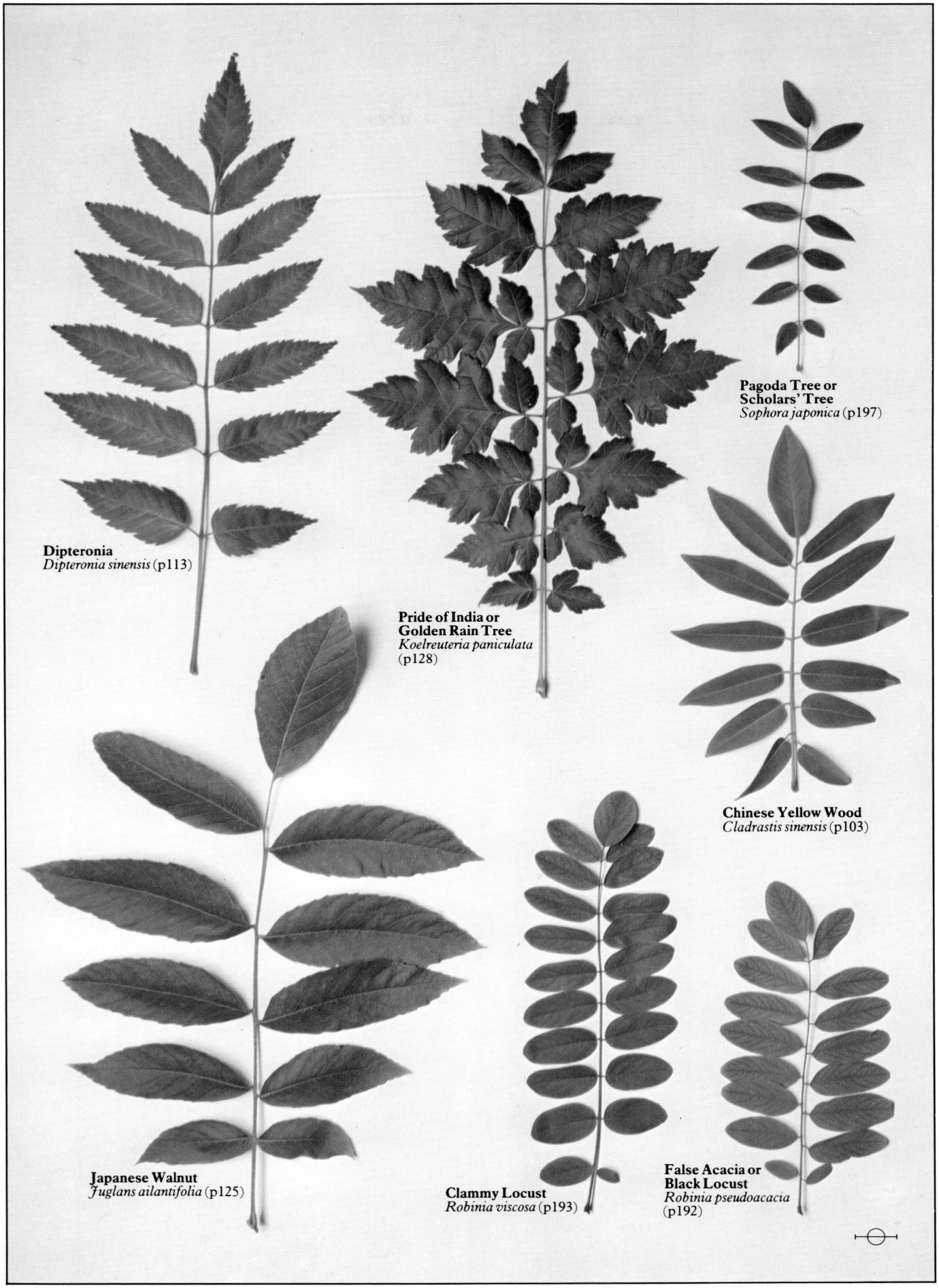
Dipteronia
Dipteronia sinensis (p113)
Pride of India or
Golden Rain Tree
Koelreuteria paniculata
(p128)
Pagoda Tree or
Scholars' Tree
Sophora japonica (p197)
Chinese Yellow Wood
Cladrastis sinensis (p103)
Japanese Walnut
Juglans ailantifolia (p125)
Clammy Locust
Robinia viscosa (p193)
False Acacia or
Black Locust
Robinia pseudoacacia
(p192)

Chinese Cedar
Cedrela sinensis (p97)
Stag's Horn Sumac
Rhus typhina (p192)
Varnish Tree
Rhus verniciflua (p192)
Tree of Heaven
Ailanthus altissima (p82)
Butternut or
White Walnut
Juglans cinerea (p125)
Black Walnut
Juglans nigra (p125)

Kentucky Coffee-tree
Gymnocladus dioica (p121)
Devil's Walkingstick,
Hercules' Club or
Angelica Tree
Aralia spinosa (p84)
Mimosa or
Silver Wattle
Acacia dealbata (p65)

Abies family Pinaceae, **Silver Fir.** A group of evergreen conifers with single needles and flowers of both sexes on the same tree. Topmost branches bear the solid cylindrical cones which break up when ripe, or are demolished by squirrels in search of the seeds, leaving the central spike on the tree.

European Silver Fir or Common Silver Fir

Abies alba Mill.
Native to central European mountains 800–1800m (2600–6000ft) altitude. Cultivated for timber but easily damaged by early frosts and greenfly attack. Grows slowly for first 6 years, then rapidly, gaining as much as 1m (3ft) in a year, to a height of 45m (150ft) and girth of 5m (18ft). Male flowers are grouped below previous years growth, shedding pollen in April. Females are green at first, developing into cones 12cm × 3cm (4½in × 1½in) red-brown when ripe with down curved toothed bracts (far left). Needles (p15) are white backed and notched at the tip. Bark (near left) is dark greyish and cracked into small square plates on old trees.

Red Silver Fir or Pacific Silver Fir

Abies amabilis Doug. ex Forbes
Native to mountains of S.E. Alaska to Vancouver Island, Oregon and Washington. Sometimes grown as an ornamental tree outside its native environment, but usually found only in collections. Height may reach 75m (250ft) in the north of its range but is usually more modest elsewhere. Numerous, globular male flowers grow on undersides of shoots, drying to shed pollen in April. Female flowers start red developing into deep purple cones, 10–15cm (4–6in) long and 5–6cm (2–2½in) wide (far left). When crushed, the foliage (p15) gives off a strong smell of tangerines. The bark (near left) is grey with white patches.

Santa Lucia Fir

Abies bracteata (D. Don) Nutt.
Native to the canyons and rocky mountain tops of the Santa Lucia Mountains, California at altitudes around 900m (3000ft). Grown as an ornamental tree elsewhere, notably N. Italy. Height to 45m (150ft). Male flowers are 2–3cm (1in) long clustered on undersides of leaves, shedding pollen at the end of May, females solitary 2–3cm (1in) long (far left) developing into unmistakable cones 10cm (4in) long (near left). The tree is also easily distinguished by its long, 5cm (2in), sharp pointed needles (p15) and chestnut brown pointed buds, which look similar to the buds of beech trees.

Greek Fir

Abies cephalonica Loud.
Native to mountains of southern Greece and planted for ornament in large gardens. Height to 49m (130ft). Male and female flowers (far left) open in April; males red, turning yellow, females green, about 2·5cm (1in) long. Cones (near left) may be 10cm (4in) long. Foliage (p15) is distinct since the needles radiate from all sides of the twigs. This, combined with the resinous buds and bracts on the cones, makes the Greek Fir unmistakable. Bark (p216) is dark brown, breaking into small plates.

Colorado Fir or White Fir

Abies concolor (Gord.) Hildebrand
Native to Colorado, Arizona, southern California, Utah and Mexico. Grown in collections and gardens but rare, the variety *lowiana* being more common (see below). Height to about 30m (100ft) in the wild. Flowers (far left) open in late April, males round and yellow, females yellow-green, about 2·5cm (1in) long. Cones (near left) are 7·5–12·5cm (3–5in) long, and may be dark purple or bright yellow-green. Leaves (p15) are rather long, and produce a strong lemon smell when crushed. (Drawing above left.)

A. concolor var. *lowiana* (Gord.) Lemm. **Low's Fir**
Generally taller than the type, and considered to come from coastal regions from Oregon to Sierra Nevada. Two forms have been described: the northern form, with needles flat in 2 rows each side of the shoot, and the southern form with leaves curved upwards in a U shape. Trees grade between these two extremes in its range. (Drawing above right.)

Abies delavayi Franch, **Delavay's Silver Fir**
Native to western China, and rare in cultivation. Flowers and cones are similar to those shown for var. *georgii* (below) but the deep purple cones have smaller spine-like bracts showing. Foliage is also similar with leaves bluntly rounded and usually notched.

Forrest's Silver Fir

A. delavayi var. *forrestii* (Rogers) Jacks
Native to Yunnan and Szechuan provinces of China, probably the most commonly cultivated variety. Similar to the var. *georgii* but leaves are longer and deeply notched, and cones have shorter narrower bracts. (Drawing above left.)
A. delavayi var. *georgii* (Orr) Melville
Flowers (far left) open in late April. The dark purple cones (near left) are about 6–10cm (2½–4in) long, with distinctively long bracts. Foliage is shown on p15; leaves are notched, with two white bands underneath, and usually bluish in first year. (Drawing above right.)

Momi Fir or Japanese Fir

Abies firma Sieb. & Zucc.
Native to south Japan, grown in collections and for ornament in large gardens. Height may reach 24–30m (80–100ft). Male flowers shed pollen at the end of April, females are 2·5cm (1in) long (far left), developing into 8cm (3½in) cones (near left). Foliage (p15) is bright green above, silvery below and has a distinct leathery feel to it. The needles are dark green and conspicuously tapering towards the base, with 2 sharp points at their tips. Bark is pinkish-grey.

Grand Fir or Giant Fir

Abies grandis Lindl.
Native to Vancouver Island, British Columbia south to California, now widely used as a forestry tree, due to its remarkably fast growth rate and tolerance to soil conditions. May reach 16m (55ft) in 20 years and trees of 90m (300ft) have been recorded in native environment. Male flowers (far left) are smaller than other silver firs and are produced only in upper part of the tree and shed pollen in April. The cones are 7–8cm (3in) ripening to dark brown in October (near left) from a lovely bright green. Foliage (p15) has a strong tangerine smell when crushed and needles have two bright white bands on undersides.

Nikko Fir

Abies homolepis Sieb. & Zucc.
Native to central Japan, cultivated for ornament in large gardens. Grows to 24–27m (80–90ft), tolerating pollution, so does better in or near cities and towns than most other silver firs. Male flowers are bright, light green, 2·5cm (1in) long, shedding pollen in late April. Females (far left) are 3·7cm (1½in) long, turning deep purple-blue through the summer and ripening dark purple brown (near left) in October, 8cm (3½in) long. Foliage (p15) is composed of needles 1·5–3·7cm (½–1½in) long, green above with two white bands below. Bark (p216) is pinkish grey or purplish grey eventually breaking up into small flakes.

Korean Fir

Abies koreana Wils.
Native to Korea, often grown in gardens since it is generally rather small and bushy and produces cones freely from a young age, making a very decorative small tree. Height to 9m (30ft) in cultivation. Both male and female flowers (far left) are produced in May, males on shoots all over the tree, and females 2–5cm (1–2in) on upper branches. Ripe cones (near left) are 5–7·5cm (2–3in) long and usually covered with white resin. Leaves are shorter than most silver firs, 1–2·5cm (½–1in) with blunt, notched tips and bright white undersides. Bark is dark, covered with lenticels or pores.

Alpine Fir

Abies lasiocarpa (Hook.) Nutt.
Found on mountain tops in Alaska, British Columbia and Alberta south to Washington and Oregon. Has never done well in cultivation but occasionally grown for ornament in northern parts of America and in collections elsewhere. May reach 40m (130ft) in native environment. Male flowers (far left) shed pollen in April, females develop into dark purple cones ripening to brown (near left) 15cm (6in) which break up in October. Foliage (p16) is waxy, blue-green with shorter needles on upper branches and when crushed gives off a strong balsam smell.

Red Fir

Abies magnifica Murr.
Native to Oregon and California at altitudes of 1500–1800m (5000–6000ft) but grown as an ornamental tree in other parts of America and in Europe, as it develops into a large, beautifully symmetrical tree. An old tree may reach 65m (220ft). Flowers (far left) are produced in May and cones (near left) are sparse but large; 20cm (8in) long. They are golden green or purplish when young, ripening to brown in the autumn. Foliage (p16) is made up of curved needles which become almost four-sided with age. Bark is grey and corky and on old trees in California turns red.

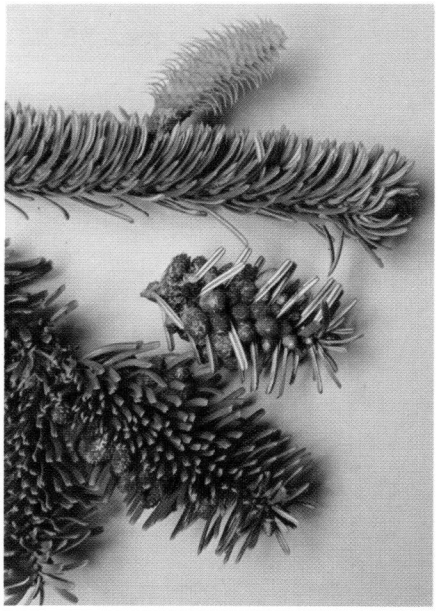

Caucasian Fir

Abies nordmanniana (Stev.) Spach.
Native to the Caucasus, grown in collections and gardens for ornament. Growth may be slow but the tree can reach 50–60m (165–195ft) in its native environment. Flowers (far left) are produced in late April, males on branches all over crown, females only at the top. Cones (near left) are 15cm (6in), green and resinous through the summer, ripening to brown in October. Needles (p16) form 2 rows, the upper ones being shorter, often producing dense, luxurious looking foliage. Bark is grey and smooth, eventually splitting into square plates.

Algerian Fir

Abies numidica De Lannoy ex Carr.
Native to mountains in a small part of Algeria, planted in gardens for ornament and grows better in cities and towns than most silver firs. Growth can be rapid once established reaching 25m (85ft). Flowers (far left) appear in April, the females developing narrow cones 13cm (5in) (near left) ripening brown and covered in resin. Foliage (p16) is distinct in having needles set all round the twigs and all pointing upwards, dark bluish green above sometimes with a triangular patch of grey near the rounded tip. Two white bands beneath. Bark is pale pink-grey to orange, splitting to form plates when older.

Noble Fir

Abies procera Rehd.
Native to Washington and Oregon at altitudes of 600–1500m (2000–5000ft) cultivated elsewhere for its timber which is close grained and useful in building. Also valuable as an ornamental tree. Growth is rapid after a few years, reaching 45–60m (150–200ft) in its native environment, though rather less in cultivation. Male flowers (far left) shed pollen in May and females form distinctive cones (near left), 20–25cm (9–10in) long, with toothed downward pointing bracts, which almost cover the cone. Cones may be produced on relatively small trees, 5m (15ft). Foliage (p16) is bluish and strongly parted on undersides of twigs, the needles sweeping upwards. Bark is pale grey or purplish and splits into long deep cracks with age.

Veitch's Silver Fir

Abies veitchii Lindl.
Native to central Japan, planted for ornament in gardens, tolerant to town conditions. Growth is quite fast, even in first few years, but trees tend to be short lived. Grows to 22m (75ft). Flowers (far left) appear in April. Females develop from 2–3cm (1in) into blue-purple cones (near left) 6–8cm (2½–3in) and which ripen to brown in October. Foliage (p16) is similar to *A. nordmanniana* but is much softer. Needles are notched at the tip, glossy green above with bands of silver beneath. Bark is dark grey with horizontal lines, and sometimes has white patches.

Mimosa or Silver Wattle

Acacia dealbata Link, family Leguminosae.
An evergreen, native to New South Wales and Tasmania, now widely grown in central and southern Europe for its fragrant yellow blossom which is sold in city florists in early spring. Distribution is limited by its sensitivity to frost, but in its native environment it may reach 24m (80ft) with a girth of 3m (10ft). Individual flowers are about 0·5cm (¼in) in diameter and appear in January through March (near right). Seed pods, not shown, are bluish white, 5–7cm (2–3in) long and 1cm (½in) wide. Leaves (p59) are made up of tiny leaflets 2cm (1–2in) long. Bark is bright green-grey on young trees (far right), but sadly, turns brown then almost black with age. Persian Acacia (*Albizia julibrissen*) has similar shaped leaves.

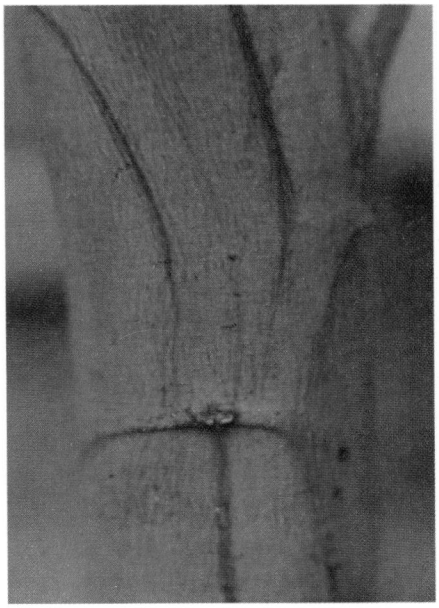

Acer family Aceraceae, **Maple**. Deciduous trees and shrubs, with opposite, usually lobed, leaves and unusual winged fruits, or 'keys', similar to ash fruits (*Fraxinus*) but in pairs.

Field Maple or Hedge Maple

Acer campestre L.
Native to Europe, including Britain. Often found in hedges and the timber is used for turning and carving since it is usually in short lengths. Height to 4·5–9m (15–30ft) sometimes much larger. Flowers are hermaphrodite (far left) clustered in upright heads of 10 or so, appearing in late April or early May and developing into the hanging fruits (near left). The leaves (p45) turn golden yellow to red in autumn (p76). Field Maple hybridizes with the Montpelier (*A. monspessulanum*) and Cretan (*A. sempervirens*) Maples in south Europe, where confusion may arise over identification. A milky sap exuded from the leaves distinguishes the Field Maple.

Red Snake-bark Maple

Acer capillipes Maxim.
Native to Japan, grown in large gardens and becoming popular in small gardens for its attractive appearance. Height may reach 9–14m (30–45ft). Flowers (far left) open in May, about 25 in a curved flowerhead. Fruits (near left) in the same long drooping bunches, have keys 1–2cm (½–¾in) long with wings spread at an angle of 120–180°. Leaves (p43) are similar to those of Moose-bark (*A. pensylvanicum*) and Grey-budded Snake-bark Maple (*A. rufinerve*) but do not have rusty hairs on undersides, and usually have bright red stems. They turn orange and red in autumn (near left) making a stunning display in a small garden. The green and silver striped bark (p216) gives the name Snake-bark.

Cappadocian Maple

Acer cappadocicum Gleditsch
Native tree of the Caucasus, the Himalayas and China, now grown in large gardens and collections, and as a street tree in Europe. Fast-growing, reaching a height of 25m (80ft) with a girth of 2·5m (8ft). Flowers (far left) open in May, are 5–8mm (¼–⅓in) with five pale yellow petals, 15 or so forming an upright cluster. Keys (near left) have widely spread wings about 7cm (2¾in) long. Leaves (p44) have tufts of hair in the axils underneath and turn bright golden yellow in autumn (p76).
A. cappadocicum cv. 'Aureum' has yellow unfolding leaves turning green in summer and back to yellow in autumn.
A. cappadocicum cv. 'Rubrum' is distinguished by having red unfolding leaves.

Hornbeam Maple

Acer carpinifolium Sieb. & Zucc.
Native to Japan, cultivated in some collections. Grows to 15m (50ft) in Japan but hardly ever reaches more than 10m (33ft) elsewhere. Flowers (far left) open in late April, early May in clusters 10–12cm (4–4¾in) long. Fruit (near left) have down curved wings about 1·5cm (⅝in) long. Leaves (p26) are unlike any other maple being more akin to a hornbeam leaf, though are opposite rather than alternate as on hornbeams. They turn rich shades of brown and yellow in autumn.

Vine Maple

Acer circinatum Pursh
Native to west N. America, growing on stream banks on British Columbia coasts southwards to Sacramento River, California. The wood is heavy and close-grained and was once used by the Indians of the northwest for making fishing net frames. The tree is now becoming popular in small gardens in Europe. It may grow to 10–12m (33–40ft) and has a stout trunk but in its native state is usually prostrate and bushy with branches rooting where they touch the ground. The flowers (far left) are unusually bright for a maple and have male and female parts in separate flowers in the same cluster. Keys (near left) have wings 3·7cm (1½in) long and are bright red when young. Leaves (p46) are bright red and orange in the autumn (p76).

Vine-leaved Maple

Acer cissifolium (Sieb. & Zucc.) K. Koch
Native of Japan, cultivated in large gardens and collections. Grows to 9m (30ft) with a girth of 1m (3ft). Male and female flowers (far left) are produced on the same tree in May, forming pairs of flowerheads 10–12cm (4–4¾in) long. Keys (near left) have red wings, 2–3cm (1in) long, diverging at an angle of 60° or less. Leaves (p50) have 3 leaflets. Compare with Box Elder (*A. negundo*) and Nikko Maple (*A. nikoense*). They turn pale yellow and red in autumn.

Hawthorn-leaved Maple

Acer crataegifolium Sieb. & Zucc.
Another snake-bark maple, native to Japan. Grown in large gardens and collections. Usually reaches about 9m (30ft). Flowers (far left) are produced in April in upright clusters, 3–5cm (1–2in) long. Keys (near left) have red wings 2–2·5cm (¾–1in) long, spread at 180°. Leaves (p38) are smaller than other snake-barks, have red stems and remain faintly pink throughout the summer. Bark is green with vertical white stripes most pronounced on young shoots.

Père David's Maple

Acer davidii Franch.
Named after the French missionary who discovered this tree in its native China. Now a rather confused species since it has several forms and has often been wrongly labelled and confounded with other snake-bark maples. It is thought that there are at least 4 types in cultivation, 2 of which are:
A. davidii 'George Forrest'. A narrow open tree, 14m (48ft) (drawing above left). Young shoots are purple or dark red, and leaves (p34) are flat, larger and broader than other types with little autumn colour.
A. davidii 'Ernest Wilson' is smaller, with a more rounded habit (drawing above right), narrower leaves (p34) which are folded along the middle. They colour orange in autumn.
Flowers (far left) open in May, in spikes about 7·5–10cm (3–4in) long. Those shown are from the Wilson type. Keys (near left) have wings 2·5–3·7cm (1–1½in) long. This specimen is of the Forrest type. Bark is green with white stripes.

Lime-leaved Maple

Acer distylum Sieb. & Zucc.
Native to Japan and found elsewhere only in larger collections. Has grown to 9m (30ft) in cultivation, though may reach 15m (50ft) in the wild. Flowers (far left) are produced in May in upright clusters 7·5–10cm (3–4in) long. Fruits (near left) form upright spikes (most maple fruit clusters droop). The keys have wings about 2·5cm (1in) long diverging at 100°. The leaves (p39) look rather like lime leaves, but are narrower, and the stem may be pink or red. Bark is green with orange stripes.

Forrest's Maple

Acer forrestii Diels.
Native to China, where it was discovered by George Forrest early this century. May grow to 12m (40ft) in its native environment. Flowers (far left) are open in May forming arched spikes up to 10cm (4in) long. The keys (near left) have wings 2·5cm (1in) long spread almost horizontally. Leaves (p43) have red stems, tufts of hair in axils beneath, and remain green in autumn. Bark is similar to other snake-barks, green with vertical white stripes.

Amur Maple

Acer ginnala Maxim.
Native to China, Japan and Manchuria, now becoming popular for small gardens. A rather small tree reaching 9m (30ft) often forming a bushy shrub. Flowers (far left) open in May in dense upright clusters, 3·7cm (1½in) across. Fruit clusters droop (near left) and have wings 2·5cm (1in) long, almost parallel with each other. Leaves (p43) have a red stalk, and usually have a red main vein. They turn bright crimson red early in the autumn.

Rock Maple or Dwarf Maple

Acer glabrum Torr.
Native to western N. America, where it is found by mountain streams at altitudes of 1500–1800m (5000–6000ft). Grows to 9–12m (30–40ft) but is often rather smaller and shrubby in cultivation. Flowers (far left) open in late April, male and female flowers usually on separate trees. Fruits (near left) have down curved wings 2·5cm (1in) long. Leaves (p44) are 3- or 5-lobed and may even by split into 3 leaflets.

Bigtooth Maple

Acer grandidentatum Nutt.
Native to western N. America, where it grows by mountain rivers. Closely related to Sugar Maple (*A. saccharum*) which it replaces on the western side of America. Height to 9–12m (30–40ft). Male and female parts are in separate flowers, though may be on the same drooping cluster, produced in May. Keys have wings 1–2cm (½–¾in) long, turning from pink to green at maturity. Leaves (p46) turn yellow and red in autumn. Bark is dark brown and scaly.

Paper-bark Maple

Acer griseum (Franch.) Pax
Native to China, often cultivated in gardens for its ornamental bark (p216). Grows to 14m (45ft). Flowers (far left) open in May in bunches of three or five. Fruits (near left) are unusually large, having wings 3·7cm (1½in) downcurved and almost parallel. Leaves (p50) have 3 leaflets, and turn bright clear red and orange in autumn. Bark (p216) is orange, peeling in papery strips.

Hers's Maple

Acer grosseri Pax var. *hersii* (Rehd.) Rehd.
Native to the Honan Province of China, now much planted in parks and gardens in England and N. America. Height to 14m (45ft). Flowers appear in May, 10–15 in a long spike (far left). Keys have large 5cm (2in) green wings which are almost horizontal (near left). Leaves (p43) turn yellow, orange and red in autumn (p189) and the bark is green with silver stripes as on other snake-bark maples.

Heldreich's Maple

Acer heldreichii Orph.
Native to the Balkans and Greece, cultivated in collections. Height to 19m (65ft) with a girth of 2m (7ft). Flowers are yellow and open in late May in erect clusters. Keys have downcurved wings 2·5–5cm (1–2in). Leaves (p45) are distinctly deeply cut and often likened to Virginia Creeper leaves. They have brown hairs on the veins underneath and turn yellow, sometimes red, in the autumn.

Balkan Maple

Acer hyrcanum Fisch. & Mey.
Native to south-east Europe, cultivated in some collections. Grows slowly to 6–15m (20–50ft) tall. Flowers (far left) are produced in April in bunches of 20 or so. Keys (near left) have wings 1·2cm (½in) long downcurved and almost parallel. Leaves (p45) are similar to Italian Maple (*A. opalus*) but are more deeply lobed and have long 10cm (4in) narrow yellow or pink stalks.

Downy Japanese Maple
or
Fullmoon Maple

Acer japonicum Thunb.
Native to Japan, grown in large gardens. Height to 9m (30ft). Flowers brightly coloured (far left) open in mid April. Keys (near left) are slightly downy at first, with widely spreading wings 2·5cm (1in) long, with red stems. Leaves (p46) are almost circular, with 7–11 lobes, more than most other maples, and remain green in autumn. *A. japonicum* cv. 'Aconitifolium', **Fernleaf Maple**, has deeply cut leaves with toothed lobes turning dark red in autumn (p76). Height reaches about 3m (10ft) though usually bushy. *A. japonicum* cv. 'Vitifolium' is similar to the species but is larger, to 13m (42ft) with larger leaves which turn glorious reds and orange in autumn (p76).

Chalk Maple

Acer leucoderme Small
Native to south-eastern United States, particularly Georgia and Alabama, and similar to the Sugar Maple (*A. saccharum*). Sometimes used as a street tree in some eastern American towns. Height to 6–7·5m (20–25ft). Flowers (far left) open at the end of April, male and female in the same bunch. Keys (near left) are slightly hairy when young and have spreading wings 1–2cm (½–¾in) long. Leaves (p44) are 3–5-lobed, often turning red in autumn.

Oregon Maple

Acer macrophyllum Pursh
Native to west coast of N. America from California to Alaska, sometimes grown in parks and in collections. Large tree to 30m (100ft). Flowers (far left) form a long spike 25cm (10in) opening in April. The keys have wings 5cm (2in) long joined at about 90°. Leaves (p45) are unusually large, 15–30cm (6–12in) across. A small specimen is shown. They display bright orange colours in autumn in their natural habitat, but are often less spectacular elsewhere.

Miyabe's Maple

Acer miyabei Maxim.
Native to Japan, but rather similar to the European Norway Maple (*A. platanoides*) though smaller, to 15m (50ft). Flowers (far left) open in May in spikes 5–7·5cm (2–3in) long. Fruits (near left) have downy nutlets and wide spreading wings 1–2cm (½–¾in) long. Leaves (p44) usually turn yellow with a red stalk in autumn.

Montpelier Maple

Acer monspessulanum L.
Native to south Europe and west Asia, where it grows on dry rocky ground. Cultivated in small gardens and parks, and often as a hedge in south Europe. May grow to about 15m (50ft) but is usually much less and often shrubby in form. Flowers (far left) open in June developing into a mass of usually red keys, with downcurved wings about 2·5cm (1in) long (near left). Leaves (p43) are similar to those of Cretan Maple (*A. sempervirens*), but fall earlier. Bark is dark, almost black with vertical cracks.

Box Elder or Ash-leaved Maple

Acer negundo L.
Native to a large area of east and central N. America, where it grows on swamp and streamsides. Box Elder has provided a source of sugar, or maple syrup, in the past but it is now more important as an ornamental tree both in Europe and in western N. America. Height to 12–15m (40–50ft). Male and female flowers (far left) are produced on different trees in April. Males are the dense red tassels, females the drooping green clusters. Keys (near left) have wings 3–3·7cm (1¼–1½in) long. Leaves (p53) have 5 leaflets, arranged like an ash leaf, but may have only 3 leaflets. Autumn colour is clear yellow (p77).
A. negundo cv. 'Variegatum'. A female clone, with white and green variegated leaves and fruit, making an attractive ornamental tree for streets and gardens.

Black Maple

Acer nigrum Michx. f.
Native to north-east N. America. A similar tree to the Sugar Maple (*A. saccharum*). Height to 24m (80ft). Tassels of pale green flowers are produced in April and keys are similar in shape to those of Sugar Maple (p78). Leaves (p44) are pale green and downy on the undersides and colour clear yellow in autumn.

Nikko Maple

Acer nikoense Maxim.
Native of Japan and central China where it may grow to about 15m (50ft) tall, with a trunk girth of 30–45cm (12–18in). In cultivation it is usually smaller and sometimes rather shrubby, making it useful in small gardens. Flowers (far left) are produced in May in bunches of three. Keys (near left) are downy, 3·7–5cm (1½–2in) long on hairy stalks. Leaves (p50) are also hairy, borne on hairy stalks, turning bright reds and yellows in autumn (p77).

Italian Maple

Acer opalus Mill.
Native to central and southern Europe, cultivated for ornament in large gardens. Grows to 9–19m (30–65ft) tall, though may sometimes be small and shrubby. Flowers (far left) are produced in April and make a spectacular display in their bright yellow hanging bunches with yellow opening leaves. Fruit (near left) have downcurved wings 2·5cm (1in) long, pinkish-green. Nuts turn red when ripe. Leaves (p44) are fairly similar to Sycamore (*A. pseudoplatanus*) but are smaller and have only three deeply-cut lobes. The base is usually more heart-shaped than is shown.

Japanese Maple

Acer palmatum Thunb.
A small maple, native to Japan, China and Korea, much grown in small and large gardens. Height to 6m (20ft) in cultivation but can grow much larger in its native environment. Flowers (far left) are small, 0·6–0·8cm (¼–⅓in) opening in early April in erect clusters. Fruits (near left) are also in erect bunches, though may be hanging in some of the many cultivated types. Leaves (p46) are 5–7-lobed, deeply cut, and turn red and purple in the autumn (p76). A huge number of cultivated varieties have been produced, the more common ones are briefly described below.

Acer palmatum cv. 'Atropurpureum' **Purple Japanese Maple**.
A cultivar of the Japanese Maple (above) popular in gardens of all sizes. Grows to 10m (33ft). Flowers (far left) open in April and fruits (near left) soon follow. The leaves are the most notable feature, being deep red purple throughout the year, similar in shape to Japanese Maple.
A. palmatum cv. 'Dissectum' has very deeply cut green leaves with 7–11 lobes, giving a fern-like appearance.
A. palmatum cv. 'Dissectum Atropurpureum' is similar to *A. palmatum* 'Dissectum' but has reddish purple leaves.
A. palmatum heptalobum cv. 'Osakazuki' has 7-lobed leaves, deeply cut, green through the summer turning brilliant red in October.
A. palmatum cv. 'Senkaki' **Coral-bark Maple** has deeply lobed yellowish green leaves, turning orange in October. Winter shoots are brilliant coral-red.

Moose-bark, Moosewood or Striped Maple

Acer pensylvanicum L.
A snake-bark native to north-east N. America, around New England, Quebec and Wisconsin, south to Georgia, often forming the undergrowth of forests. Cultivated for ornament in other northern states and also in Europe, as its striped bark and pretty fruits make it a most decorative tree. Height to 9–12m (30–40ft) though usually smaller in cultivation. Flowers (far left) are abundant, opening in May on long drooping spikes 15cm (6in) long. Fruit (near left) have wings 2·5cm (1in) long. Leaves p43) are large and variable but always with 3 forward-pointing lobes and bright green when young, turning red in autumn (near left). Leaf-stalks are usually pinkish, rather than red. Bark is green when young, reddish brown when mature, with vertical white stripes.

Norway Maple

Acer platanoides L.
Native to Europe from Norway southwards, but not to Britain. Cultivated in streets, parks, gardens and shelterbelts in Europe and N. America. Grows to about 18–21m (60–70ft). Flowers (far left) open in late March or early April. Fruits (near left) have wings almost horizontal, ripening from green to brown, often persisting on the tree through winter. Leaves (p45) have finely pointed, almost thread-like, lobes and the stems exude a milky sap when broken. They turn clear deep yellow in autumn (p189).
A. platanoides cv. 'Goldsworth Purple' has larger deep purple leaves (p45).
A. platanoides cv. 'Schwedleri' has unfolding leaves dark reddish purple, fading to green with a purple tinge in the summer (p45) and turning bright orange red and purple in the autumn.

Sycamore or Sycamore Maple

Acer pseudoplatanus L.
Native to central and southern Europe, cultivated as a shelter tree in town streets and parks, and for its timber which is used to make many small items from violins to wooden spoons, and as a veneer. Height to 30m (100ft). Flowers (far left) open in April in hanging spikes 6–12cm (2¼–4½in) long. Fruit (near left) have wings 2·5cm (1in) long which often turn bright red during the summer. Leaves (p45) may be only 3-lobed on some older fruiting trees. Leaf-stalks may be red or pinkish yellow.
A. pseudoplatanus cv. 'Atropurpureum' has leaves dark green above and dark purple beneath (p45).

Red Maple or Scarlet Maple

Acer rubrum L.
A large tree, native to eastern N. America, cultivated in Europe for its autumn colours, and used in America in furniture manufacture. Height to 36m (120ft) though often smaller in cultivation. Flowers (far left) open in late March or early April and often have male and female flowers on separate trees. The dense red clusters give the leafless tree a beautiful red glow. Fruit are also red on longer stalks than the flowers with wings 1cm (½in), spread at an angle of 60°. Leaves (p43) are similar to Silver Maple (*A. saccharinum*) but are less deeply lobed. They are most spectacular in autumn (near left).

Grey-budded Snake-bark Maple

Acer rufinerve Sieb. & Zucc.
A native of Japan, frequently cultivated for its ornamental bark and autumn colours. Distinguished from other snake-barks by its grey, downy young shoots. Height to about 13m (42ft) with a girth of 1m (3ft) and relatively short-lived. Flowers (far left) are 0·8cm (⅓in) produced in mid-April with the unfolding leaves in upright bunches 7·5cm (3in) long. Keys (near left) have red down on the nutlets at first and drop from June onwards. The leaves (p43) are about 10cm (4in) long, colouring orange to rich crimson in autumn (p77). The young bark is green with white stripes and as it matures loses the white becoming dull rough grey brown.

Silver Maple

Acer saccharinum L.
A handsome tree, native to eastern N. America from Quebec south to Florida, cultivated for ornament in Europe, particularly in Britain where it is often grown in parks, on roadsides and in gardens. Height to about 27–36m (90–120ft). Flowers (far left) open in March before the leaves unfold. Fruits have stalks 3·7–5cm (1½–2in) long and twisted wings spread widely. Since they form early, seed can germinate and produce several leaves before the end of the season, but in Britain seed is rarely set. Leaves (p46) have a silver underside and colour yellow and red in autumn (near left). Bark is smooth and grey and often covered with shoots and suckers.
A. saccharinum forma. *laciniatum* (Carr.) Rehd. has weeping branches and deeply cut narrowly lobed leaves.

Japanese Maple
Acer palmatum (p73)
Field Maple or
Hedge Maple
Acer campestre
(p65)
Acer japonicum
'Vitifolium' (p70)
Fernleaf Maple
Acer japonicum
'Aconitifolium' (p70)
Cappadocian Maple
Acer cappadocicum (p66)
Vine Maple
Acer circinatum (p67)

Paper Birch or
Canoe Birch
Betula papyrifera (p90)
Nikko Maple
Acer nikoense (p72)
Beech
Fagus sylvatica
(p116)
Box Elder or
Ash-leaved Maple
Acer negundo (p72)
Tupelo,
Black Gum or
Pepperidge
Nyssa sylvatica (p142)
Grey-budded
Snake-bark Maple
Acer rufinerve (p75)

Sugar Maple

Acer saccharum Marsh.
Native to eastern N. America. Cultivated as an ornamental or shade tree, but perhaps best known as the major source of maple sugar in N. America. Height to 30–36m (100–120ft). Flowers (far left) open in April on slender stalks 5cm (2in) long. Keys (near left) have wings about 2·5cm (1in) long. Leaves (p45) are similar to Norway Maple (*A. platanoides*) but the liquid in the stem is clear rather than milky. Leaf base is usually less heart-shaped than is shown. The autumn colours are considered the most spectacular of all American maples, turning crimson, orange and yellow in huge masses.

Acer sempervirens L. **Cretan Maple**
Native to the east Mediterranean, and grown in collections. Height to 9–10·5m (30–35ft) often shrubby. Flowers are yellow green in clusters 2·5cm (1in) long, opening in April. Keys have wings 1cm (½in) long at an angle of 60° or nearly parallel. Leaves (p43) may be unlobed and remain on the tree well into winter.

Mountain Maple

Acer spicatum Lam.
A small, sometimes bushy, maple native to east N. America, and sometimes cultivated in parks for ornament. Height to 7·5m (25ft). Flowers (far left) open in June in an erect spike, 7·5–15cm (3–6in) with male flowers at top and female lower down. The keys (near left) have wings about 1cm (½in) long, red and yellow, going brown in the autumn. Leaves (p45) are usually 3-, but sometimes 5-lobed, downy on the underside, and usually less heart-shaped at the base than is shown. They colour orange, yellow and red in autumn. Bark is smooth and reddish brown.

Tartar Maple

Acer tataricum L.
Native to south-east Europe and west Asia, cultivated in collections. Height to 9m (30ft) and may be bushy. Flowers (far left) open in erect bunches in late May developing into red keys (near left) with wings 2·5cm (1in) long. Leaves (p39) have 3 or 5 shallow lobes but often unlobed on mature trees, with down on the veins underneath. They colour yellow in autumn and fall early.

Van Volxem's Maple

Acer velutinum Boiss. var. *vanvolxemii* (Mast.) Rehd.
A native of the Caucasus, cultivated in collections. Height to 22m (75ft). Flowers (far left) open in late May in erect clusters 7·5–10cm (3–4in) long. Keys (near left) are downy. Leaves (p45) are similar to Sycamore (*A. pseudoplatanus*) but are larger, up to 20cm (8in) and have a longer stalk, which may be 27cm (11in) long. The veins have brown hairs underneath. Bark is smooth and grey, with rings formed by branch scars.

Zoeschen Maple

Acer × zoeschense Pax
A garden hybrid between Field Maple (*A. campestre*) and either Lobel's Maple (*A. lobelii*) or Cappadocian Maple (*A. cappadocicum*). Height to 15m (50ft). Flowers (far left) open in May in erect clusters about 5cm (2in) across. Keys (near left) have wings often tinged pink 2cm (¾in) long, a similar shape to Field Maple keys. Leaves (p45) are bright green and shiny with tufts of hair in the vein axils beneath and red stems.

Aesculus family Hippocastanaceae, **Horse Chestnut and Buckeye.** Deciduous trees with leaves made up of leaflets radiating from one point, and flowers in dense erect columns or 'candles'.

California Buckeye

Aesculus californica (Spach) Nutt.
Native to California and cultivated for ornament in western N. America and in parts of Europe. Height to 6–9m (20–30ft). Pale pink or white fragrant flowers (near right) open from June to August in clusters 15–20cm (6–8in) tall. The stamens protrude about 1cm (½in) from each flower giving a delicate shaggy appearance. The lopsided fruits 5–7·5cm (2–3in) (far right) ripen in October, splitting to release shiny brown nuts. Leaves (p51) usually have 5 leaflets on stalks 1–2·5cm (½–1in) long, but sometimes 7. They are smaller than other horse chestnuts and fall early, without autumn colour.

Red Horse Chestnut

Aesculus × carnea Hayne
A hybrid arising from the Common Horse Chestnut (*A. hippocastanum*) and Red Buckeye. (*A. pavia*) Cultivated all over Europe as a shade tree, in avenues, parks and gardens. Height to 18–25m (60–80ft) in continental Europe but frequently much less. The red flowers (near right) open in May in clusters 12–20cm (5–8in) long developing into the fruit (far right) smaller than Common Horse Chestnut and less spiny, if at all. They split in October to release 2 or 3 brown nuts. The leaves (p51) are dark green and often crinkly, with 5 or sometimes 7 almost sessile leaflets.
Aesculus × carnea cv. 'Briottii' is a cultivar of the Red Horse Chestnut (*A. × carnea*) above. It has brighter heads of flowers (near right below) 15cm (6in) long. Leaves are darker glossy green.

Yellow Buckeye or Sweet Buckeye

Aesculus flava Soland., synonym *A. octandra* Marsh.
Native to south-east United States where it grows on river banks and mountainsides. Height to 15–27m (50–90ft). Its wood has been put to use as paper pulp and in manufacture of artificial limbs. Grown in parks and gardens in Europe and eastern states of America. Flowers (far right) are produced in May and June, usually yellow, but sometimes pink, in narrow clusters 10–15cm (4–6in) tall. Fruit is spherical and smooth, 5–6cm (2–2½in) usually containing 2 brown nuts. Leaves (p51) have 5 or 7 leaflets and colour yellow in autumn (p188).

Ohio Buckeye

Aesculus glabra Willd.
Native to south-east and central United States, grown in collections and gardens in eastern N. America and in Europe. May grow to 21m (70ft) but usually half this size. Flowers open in April and May and are comparatively drab, spikes 10–18cm (4–7in) long. These are not illustrated but similar to *A. glabra* var. *sargentii* flowers (near right). Fruits are 2·5–5cm (1–2in) long with prickles on outside, usually containing 2 brown seeds. Leaves (p51) have short stalks on the 5 leaflets. Bark (far right) is rough, dark grey and scaly. It is the only American horse chestnut with prickly fruit.
A. glabra var. *sargentii* Rehd. is found in Missouri, Kansas, Ohio and Mississippi. It differs from the type in having more leaflets which are narrower and more tapering, with more jagged edges (see flower photograph near right).

Common Horse Chestnut

Aesculus hippocastanum L.
Native to north Greece and Albania and long cultivated in other parts of Europe in parks, gardens, streets and greens, where children gather the nuts, or conkers, to play their game of 'conqueror'. May grow to more than 30m (100ft). Flowers are white with a yellow turning to red patch on the petal bases and form clusters up to 30cm (12in) tall (near right). Fruits (far right) have hard spines, are about 6cm (2¼in) across, and split in October to release one or two of the familiar shiny brown conkers. Leaves (p52) usually have 7, sometimes 5, broad stalkless leaflets. Bark (p216) is dark reddish or greyish brown and splits into large plates.
A. hippocastanum cv. 'Baumannii' is a cultivar having double, longer-lasting flowers which do not produce nuts. A popular horse chestnut for gardens.

Indian Horse Chestnut

Aesculus indica (Camb.) Hook.
Native to north-west Himalaya, cultivated in parks and gardens since it is a highly decorative tree. Grows to 30m (100ft). Flowers (near right) open in June and July in panicles about 10–15cm (4–6in) tall, though may be two or three times as large. Stamens protrude from the flowers which may be pink or with upper pair of petals flushed yellow or red. Fruit (far right) has thin smooth skin enclosing 2 or 3 wrinkled brown seeds. Leaves (p52) have 7, sometimes 5 or 9, stalked leaflets. Bark is smooth reddish grey on old trees, greenish grey on young trees.
A. indica cv. 'Sydney Pearce' has darker green leaves and larger flowers 2·5cm (1in) across and flowerheads 30cm (12in) tall. Each flower is pale pink or white dotted with yellow and red.

Red Buckeye

Aesculus pavia L.
A small horse chestnut, native to south-east United States, best known as a parent of the Red Horse Chestnut (*A.* × *carnea*). May often be shrubby but as a tree reaches 6m (20ft). Flowers (near right) open in June on spikes 15cm (6in) tall. Fruit is smooth and egg-shaped, containing one–two seeds which ripen in August. The leaves (p52) are composed of 5–7 short-stalked leaflets and colour red in autumn (far right).

Japanese Horse Chestnut

Aesculus turbinata Blume
A large tree, native to Japan and similar in appearance to the Common Horse Chestnut (*A. hippocastanum*) but more slow growing, has larger leaves and rough, but not spiny, egg- or pear-shaped fruit (far right). Flowers (near right) open 2–3 weeks after the Common Horse Chestnut in late May or early June. Leaves (p52) have 7 unstalked leaflets with tufts of orange down in vein axils underneath. They colour bright orange, then brown, and drop early in autumn. Bark is smooth with some wide cracks. On young trees it has white fissures.

Tree of Heaven

Ailanthus altissima (Mill.) Swingle, family Simaroubaceae.
Native to China, now widely planted in Europe and Central America as an ornamental, especially useful in cities. It produces many suckers and seedlings and is often considered something of a weed. Height to 30m (100ft). Male and female flowers open in late July on separate trees and look similar from a distance. Male flowers are shown far left. Female trees produce large bunches of fruits (near left) which ripen during August and September. Each winged seed is about 3·7cm (1½in) wide and the bunches often 30cm (12in) across. Leaves (p58) can be enormous, up to 1m (3ft) on young vigorous trees. Each leaflet usually has only 1–3 teeth on each side.

Persian Acacia, Silk Tree or Pink Siris

Albizia julibrissin (Willd.) Durazz., family Leguminosae.
A native to western Asia now commonly planted as a shade tree in Europe and China, in areas where it can be unaffected by severe frost. In Britain it is most commonly planted as an annual bedding plant, being destroyed or taken into a greenhouse in winter. Height may reach 12m (40ft). The brightly coloured flowers (shown right) open in July and August, their long pink stamens giving the appearance of a soft brush. The seed pod is 7·5–15cm (3–6in) long constricted between each seed.

Alnus family Betulaceae, **Alder.** Deciduous trees and shrubs. Male and female parts are separate on the same tree. Males are in long hanging catkins produced in early winter, expanding the following spring to release pollen. Females are tiny erect catkins produced in spring at shoot tips and ripen to form green then woody 'cones'.

Italian Alder

Alnus cordata Desf.
Native to south Italy and Corsica, cultivated in parks and gardens. Height to 15m (50ft). Male catkins extend to about 7·5–10cm (3–4in) and shed their pollen between February and April (far left) when tiny red females are produced. Fruit (near left) is 2·5cm (1in) long, much longer than other alders. The ripened cone, after shedding its seed, is shown with the flowers. The leaves have 5–6 pairs of veins, are shallowly toothed and dark glossy green with tufts of down in vein axils beneath (p39). Bark is smooth, grey, covered with lenticels and some short vertical cracks.

Common Alder or Black Alder

Alnus glutinosa (L.) Gaertn.
Native to Europe (including Britain), west Asia and north Africa. Grows wild in damp boggy ground and riversides, and its timber was used to make clogs in north England and Normandy. Little cultivated but sometimes planted as an ornamental in N. America. Height may reach 19m (65ft) or more. Male catkins (far left) shed pollen in early March, when they are 5–10cm (2–4in) long. Females (also far left) are about 0·5cm (¼in) long. Fruit (near left) is 1–2cm (½–¾in). They turn woody through winter as shown with flowers. Leaves (p39) are rounded with an indented tip and 7 pairs of veins, each with long tufts of hair in axils underneath. Bark (p216) is dark brown, soon splitting into thick plates.
A. glutinosa cv. 'Imperialis' is one of the many cut-leaved forms, having deeply and narrowly lobed leaves. Grown in gardens where it never attains a large size.

Grey Alder or European Alder

Alnus incana (L.) Moench
Native to Europe and the Caucasus, easily distinguished from the Common Alder (*A. glutinosa*) by its grey pointed leaves. Flowers (far left) are open in late February, the males 5–10cm (2–4in) long, females much smaller, developing into green fruits (near left) 1cm (½in) long. Ripe woody fruit is shown with flowers. Leaves (p34) have 9–12 pairs of downy veins, and are rather grey on underside. Bark is dark grey covered with pores and a few long cracks.

Red Alder or Oregon Alder

Alnus rubra Bong.
Native to western N. America, from Alaska south to California and Idaho. Alaskan Indians hollowed out trunks to make canoes and the timber is used in furniture and paper manufacture. Height to about 12–15m (40–50ft). Male catkins are 10–15cm (4–6in) long when they shed pollen in April (far left). Females develop into fruits 1–2cm (½–¾in) long (near left). Leaves (p34) have 10–15 pairs of veins which are often covered by orange down on underside. Bark is silver-grey in its home environment, but usually dark grey in cultivation.

Snowy Mespilus or Allegheny Serviceberry

Amelanchier laevis Wieg., family Rosaceae.
A small deciduous tree, native to eastern N. America. Grows to 12m (40ft), producing delicate white fragrant blossom in late April, early May (near right) among pink unfolding leaves. Fruits (far right) ripen in July and August, through red to dark purple, 0·5cm (¼in) in diameter. Leaves (p37) colour bright red in autumn.

Devil's Walkingstick, Hercules Club or Angelica Tree

Aralia spinosa L., family Araliaceae.
An unusual tree, native to south-east United States, rarely cultivated. Height may reach 9m (30ft). Flowers are small, white, and open in August in round clusters grouped into a huge panicle, sometimes about 1–1·2m (3–4ft) long. Fruit are small, round, black and fleshy, ripening in October. Leaf (p59) is unlike any other, 1–1·2m (3–4ft) long, 0·7m (2½ft) wide. Each leaflet has a tiny stalk, but other *Aralia* species have sessile leaflets. The twigs bear stout prickles (see left). The berries and bark of roots contain a stimulant which has been used in medicine.

Monkey Puzzle or Chile Pine

Araucaria araucana (Mol.) K. Koch, family Araucariaceae.
Evergreen conifer, native to Chile and Argentina, grown as an ornamental in Europe and N. America. Height to 30m (100ft). Male and female flowers (near right) are produced on separate trees, and only on topmost branches. Males are about 10cm (4in) long and shed pollen in July; females are solitary, erect and green. They develop into cones about 10–17cm (4–7in) long, ripening from green to brown in their second autumn. The seeds used to be eaten as dessert nuts in South America, and Archibald Menzies first brought the Monkey Puzzle into cultivation by slipping some nuts from a Chilean banquet into his pocket. Foliage (p13) is composed of large thick dark green prickly leaf-like scales. Bark (p216) is grey and wrinkled, and marked with rings formed by old branch scars.

Arbutus family Ericaceae, **Strawberry Tree**.
Evergreen trees, bearing dark green shiny leaves and clusters of bell-shaped flowers.

Cyprus Strawberry Tree or Eastern Strawberry Tree

Arbutus andrachne L.
Native to eastern Mediterranean. Height to about 9–12m (30–40ft). Flowers (far left) open in late March or April, in a bunch 5–10cm (2–4in) wide, each flower about 0·5cm (¼in) long. Fruits are round 1cm (½in) diameter, smooth and orange red. Leaves are shown on p27, mature ones untoothed, but young ones on vigorous shoots are toothed. Bark (near left) is red-brown, peeling.

Hybrid Strawberry Tree

Arbutus × *andrachnoides* Link.
A hybrid arising from a naturally occurring cross between Cyprus Strawberry Tree (*A. andrachne*) and Strawberry Tree (*A. unedo*). Grows wild in Greece. Height to 6–9m (20–30ft). The white flowers (far left) are produced in late autumn or in March in spiked clusters 7cm (2¾in) long, developing into the fruit. Leaves (p26) are toothed and have dark red stalks. Bark (near left) can be quite spectacular, dark red, brown peeling off in thin scales leaving paler areas underneath.

Madrona

Arbutus menziesii Pursh.
Native to western N. America from British Columbia south to California and named after its first discoverer Archibald Menzies who described it in 1792. Grown in gardens in western and southern Europe. Height may reach 30m (100ft) in native environment, but usually 6–9m (20–30ft) in cultivation. Flowers (far left) open in May in an upright cluster from 7·5–23cm (3–9in) long, each flower about 0·5cm (¼in). Fruits are about 1cm (½in) across, orange-red and produced in bunches of 12–15. Leaves are toothed on young vigorous growth, but leaves from mature growth (p27) are untoothed. Bark (near left) peels to expose smooth clean pink-orange wood and has been used in tanning leather.

Strawberry Tree

Arbutus unedo L.
Native to south-west Ireland, and to south and south-west Europe. May grow to about 4·5–9m (15–30ft) high. Flowers (far left) and fruit (near left) from previous years flowers are both produced in the autumn, the fruit ripening and falling in October. These round strawberry-like fruits give the tree its English name. Flowers are 0·5cm (¼in) long and may be pinkish, forming hanging clusters 5cm (2in) long. Fruit are 2cm (¾in) across. Leaves are toothed (p26). Bark is less attractive than other species, becoming covered with muddy brown scales.

Papaw

Asimina triloba (L.) Dun., family Annonaceae. A deciduous small tree, sometimes shrubby, native to eastern United States. Although the name Papaw has long been used for this tree it is not the one which bears the fruit named Pawpaw (*Carica papaya*). Height to 10·5–12m (35–40ft). Flowers (right) are produced before leaves in early June, and are 2·5–3·7cm (1–1½in) across when fully open. Fruit, rarely produced in Britain, is cylindrical, 7·5–15cm (3–6in) long, unevenly shaped, ripening in September and October to dark brown, and containing a sweet, orange edible flesh. Leaves are shown on p28.

Athrotaxis family Taxodiaceae, **Tasmanian Cedar**. Primitive, evergreen conifers with scale-like leaves. Male and female parts in separate flowers on the same tree, fruit are small cones.

Smooth Tasmanian Cedar

Athrotaxis cupressoides D. Don
Native to western Tasmania at altitudes of 900–1200m (30000–4000ft), cultivated in botanical collections and large gardens. Height to 6–15m (20–50ft). Male and female flowers appear in March (far left), males shedding pollen, females developing into green cones (near left) about 1cm (½in) across, turning orange-brown in October and November. Foliage (p11) is made up of smooth scale-like leaves closely pressed to the stems, diamond shaped, about 0·3cm (⅛in) across. Compare with the cypresses (*Cupressus*).

Summit Cedar

Athrotaxis laxifolia Hook.
Native to western Tasmania, with foliage intermediate in appearance to the other 2 Tasmanian Cedars, and grows better in cultivation. Height to 12–21m (40–70ft), though smaller in the wild. Flowers (far left) open in March, the tiny males clustered at tips of branches, females clustered or solitary developing into bright yellow green spiky cones (near left) which ripen orange brown in October, 2cm (¾in) across. Foliage (p11) is composed of leaves 0·4–0·6cm (1/6–¼in) spreading slightly from the stem, which are sharp pointed. Bark is dark orange brown, split and peeling into flakes.

King William Pine

Athrotaxis selaginoides D. Don
The largest of the Tasmanian Cedars, also native to western Tasmania, where it is of great importance as a forestry tree, producing a strong dark timber similar to redwood. Height to 27m (90ft). Flowers (far left) open in March, males shedding pollen. The tiny female flowers develop into pairs of orange brown cones, 2·5cm (1in) across (near left). Foliage (p11) consists of sharply pointed leaves 1·2cm (½in) long, bright green with two bands of white on inner surface. Bark is dark orange red, splitting and peeling, often soft and fibrous like the Wellingtonia (*Sequoiadendron giganteum*).

Chilean Incense Cedar

Austrocedrus chilensis (D. Don) Florin & Boutelje, synonym *Libocedrus chilensis* (D. Don) Endl., family Cupressaceae
An evergreen, native to Chile and Argentina, grown in botanical collections. Height to 24m (80ft). Male and female flowers are produced on the same tree, males (near right) 0·3cm (⅛in) shedding pollen in March. Females develop into green ripening to brown cones (far right), 0·8cm (⅓in) long, consisting of 4 scales. Foliage (p11) is very distinct, flattened pairs of leaves or scales with bright white bands beneath. Bark is dark brown splitting into curled plates.

Betula family Betulaceae, **Birch**. Deciduous trees and shrubs, with male and female catkins on same tree, males being produced in late autumn and expanding the following spring to release their pollen, forming 'lambs' tails'. Female catkins are smaller and more slender, produced in a cluster above the males.

Blue Birch

Betula coerulea-grandis Blanch.
Native to eastern N. America from Nova Scotia south to Vermont. In native environment it often forms a shrub, but may grow to 9m (30ft) or twice that in cultivation. Flowers (far left) are open in May, male catkins 3–5cm (1¼–2in) long, females about 0·8cm (⅓in). Fruit are clustered into a cylinder (near left) about 2·5cm (1in) long which looks similar to a catkin but which breaks up in September, releasing the winged nuts. Leaves (p38) are bluish green, hence English name. Bark (p216) is pinkish white and does not peel.

Cherry Birch, Sweet Birch or Black Birch

Betula lenta L.
A large birch, native to eastern N. America, where it is used in forestry, yielding a strong timber used for flooring, furniture and sometimes boatbuilding. A sweet oil similar to Oil of Wintergreen is distilled from the bark and timber. This gives twigs and bark a sweet aromatic smell when crushed. Height to 21–24m (70–80ft). Flowers (far left) are open in May, males 5–7·5cm (2–3in) long when shedding pollen, females about 0·8cm (⅓in), expanding to ripe unstalked, erect fruiting catkins (near left) about 2·5cm (1in) long and 1·2cm (½in) wide. These break up in September and October. Bark is very dark and flaky but does not peel. Leaves (p38) have tufts of hairs in vein axils underneath.

Yellow Birch

Betula lutea Michx.
A large tree, native to north-eastern N. America, where the timber is used for flooring, furniture and boxes. Twigs have a smell and taste of wintergreen. Height to 30m (100ft) in the wild. Flowers (far left) open in May, the male catkins 7 5–10cm (3–4in) long, females 1·2–2cm (½–¾in) long, developing into unstalked, erect fruiting catkins (near left) 2·5–3·7cm (1–1½in) long which differ from those of *B. lenta* by being fatter and downy. Leaves (p38) have tufts of hairs in vein axils underneath and turn clear yellow in autumn. Bark is light golden brown, outer layers peeling back.

River Birch or Red Birch

Betula nigra L., synonym *B. rubra* Michx.
Native to the eastern United States, where it grows in wet ground near rivers. Cultivated as an ornamental in northern states. Height to 24–27m (80–90ft), usually with the trunk split low down into 2 or 3 stems. Flowers open in late April, male catkins 5–7·5cm (2–3in) long, females 0·8cm (⅓in). Fruiting catkins are downy, 2·5–3·7cm (1–1½in) long, erect and have short stems. They ripen and break up early in the year in June. This allows seeds to germinate on river banks, when the water level is at its lowest. Leaves (p38) are doubly toothed, almost lobed and downy on veins underneath. Bark (near left) is distinctly dark and flaking.

Western Birch

Betula occidentalis Hook.
Native to western N. America, where it tends to be rather shrubby forming dense thickets along streamsides. Height to 6–7·5m (20–25ft) but may be shrubby in cultivation. Flowers (far left) open in April, male catkins 5cm (2in) long, females about 0·8cm (⅓in), ripening to erect, stalkless fruiting catkins 2·5–3·7cm (1–1½in) long, only slightly downy. These shed seeds in September. Leaves (p38) are dark green with only 3–5 pairs of veins and no hairs underneath with rounded or slightly heart-shaped bases. Young leaves and twigs are rather sticky. Bark (near left) is shiny dark brown, almost black, and does not peel into layers.

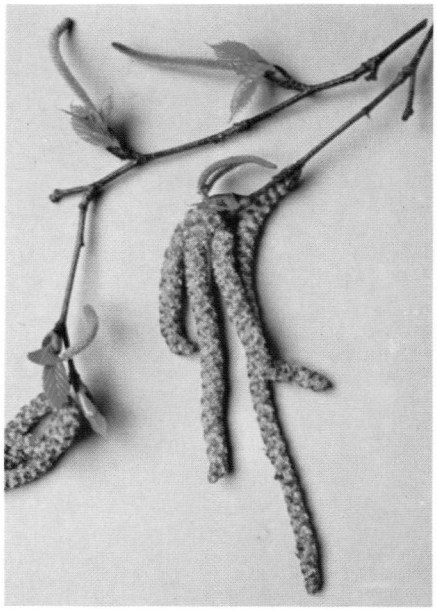

Paper Birch or Canoe Birch

Betula papyrifera Marsh.
Native across northern part of N. America, where its waterproof bark was used in making canoes by Indians. Its wood was used in turnery, and as fuel. A decorative tree, often planted for ornament. Height to 18–21m (60–70ft). Flowers (far left) open in March and April, the male catkins 10cm (4in) long, females 2·5–3cm (1–1¼in). Fruiting catkins are about 3·7cm (1½in) long hanging on slender stalks. Bark (near left) is shiny creamy white, peeling off in thin papery layers exposing pale orangey young bark underneath. On old trees it becomes much darker, cracked and scaley. Leaves (p38) are hairy, with black gladular dots on veins underneath, and colour yellow in autumn (p77).

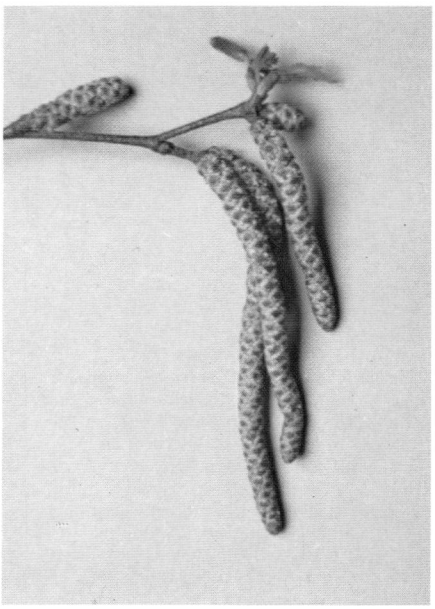

Silver Birch or European White Birch

Betula pendula Roth
Native to Europe, including Britain, and Asia Minor, planted in gardens in Europe and N. America for its graceful, pendulous form. Its timber is used in making plywood, and the tree is often planted to protect other young trees in forestry plantations. Height to 12–18m (40–60ft), but sometimes much larger. Catkins (far left) open in late March and April, males 3cm (1¼in) long, females 1·2–2cm (½–¾in) long, ripening to hanging fruiting catkins (near left) 2·5–3cm (1–1¼in) long, breaking up in late autumn and winter. Leaves (p38) are not downy and have wedge-shaped bases. Bark is white with thin horizontal lines and large dark diamond-shaped cracks and on older trees dark ridges and cracks at the base. Young twigs have no down, which distinguishes this from other birches.

Grey Birch or White Birch

Betula populifolia Marsh.
Native to eastern N. America, often used for reseeding abandoned farmland and areas devastated by fire, providing protection to other species arriving later. Height to 6–12cm (20–40ft). Catkins (far left) open in early April, males 6–10cm (2½–4in), females about 1·2cm (½in) on short stalk. Fruiting catkins (near left) are downy and hanging, about 2cm (¾in) long. Leaves (p38) turn pale yellow in autumn. Bark is creamy white, similar to Paper Birch (*B. papyrifera*), but does not peel so readily. Dark triangular marks and cracks cover the stem.

Downy Birch

Betula pubescens Ehrh.
Native to Europe, including Britain, and north Asia, this was once classed with Silver Birch (*B. pendula*) by Linnaeus, but differs in lacking the pendulous branches, having darker bark and downy young shoots. Often planted to protect other young trees. Timber is used for wood pulp and plywood; bark has been used as roofing in Scandinavia, and an aromatic oil from the stem and bark is used in leather making. Height to 21m (70ft). Catkins (far left) open in April, males 3cm (1¼in) long, females 1·2–2cm (½–¾in) long, ripening to 2·5–3cm (1–1¼in) long fruiting catkins (near left). Leaves (p38) have down on veins underneath and often have rough upper surface when young. Bark is white, peeling into papery layers and with horizontal lines and dark branch scars, but no diamond-shaped cracks (p217).

Himalayan Birch

Betula utilis D. Don
Native to the Himalayas and China, cultivated in botanical collections and other gardens. Height to 18m (60ft) but may be almost twice as large. Catkins (far left) are open in late April, males about 5cm (2in) long, females 1·2cm (½in) on stalks the same length, ripening to fruiting catkins 3·7cm (1½in) long. Leaves (p38) have downy stems and usually 9–12 pairs of downy veins. Bark may be white with grey patches or orange brown and peeling (near left).

Paper Mulberry

Broussonetia papyrifera L.) Vent., family Moraceae.
A native of China and Japan, now widely cultivated in the east where its bark is used in papermaking. A fibre is also yielded and woven into a fine cloth, which Captain Cook saw being worn by the principal inhabitants of Otaheite. It is planted as an ornamental tree in east Asia, Europe and in eastern N. America, where it can also be found growing wild. Height to 15m (50ft), often a rounded shrub. Flowers (near right) open in June, male and female on separate trees. Male catkins are 3·7–7·5cm (1½–3in) long, furry and often curled. Females are spherical, about 1·2cm (½in) across. Fruit (far right) about 2·5cm (1in) across, falls in October. Leaves (p39) are rough and woolly. Compare with the true mulberries (*Morus*).

Buxus family Buxaceae, **Box.** Evergreen trees and shrubs with opposite leathery leaves. Male and female flowers on same plant, clustered in small bunches.

Balearic Box

Buxus balearica Lam.
Native to the Balearic Islands and south-west Spain, grown in gardens in south Europe, occasionally elsewhere. Height to 10m (30ft) in the wild but often small and shrubby. Flowers (far left) open in May about 1·2cm (½in), males clustered around females, which are therefore difficult to see. Fruits (near left) have 3 two-horned cells and are about 1·2cm (½in), green to start with, becoming brown and woody. They fall from the trees in August/September and split open from the centre to release their seeds. Leaves (p32) larger and brighter green and more even than Common Box (*B. sempervirens*).

Common Box

Buxus sempervirens L.
Native to Europe, N. Africa and west Asia. Often planted in gardens, its many cultivars providing ideal plants for hedges, winter cover and topiary. The wood is good for engraving, carving and marquetry, since it is extremely hard and can be highly polished. An extract used medicinally as a blood purifier. Height to 4·5–6m (15–20ft), occasionally larger, but most commonly rather bushy. Flowers (far left) open in April, males clustered around the females. Fruit capsules (near left) are about 0·8cm (⅓in) long, with 3 double horns. They split open and fall from the tree in September. Leaves (p32) are darker green than Balearic Box, notched at the tip. The many garden cultivated varieties differ from the type in their leaf shapes and sizes, as well as growth habits.

Incense Cedar

Calocedrus decurrens (Torr.) Florin, synonym *Libocedrus decurrens Torr.*, family Cupressaceae.
Native to California and Oregon, planted for ornament in Europe and middle and eastern United States. Height may reach 30m (100ft) in home range with spreading branches but may reach 45m (150ft) or more in cultivation in Britain where the shape is usually columnar. Flowers (near right) appear in January, the males 0·6cm (¼in), colouring the top half of the tree golden yellow. Females are less conspicuous, looking much like extensions of the foliage. They develop into bright golden yellow fruits (far right) about 2–2·5cm (¾–1in) long, splitting to release seed in September/October. Foliage (p10) is composed of tiny scale-like leaves closely pressed to stems. Bark is red brown, ridged and covered with scales.

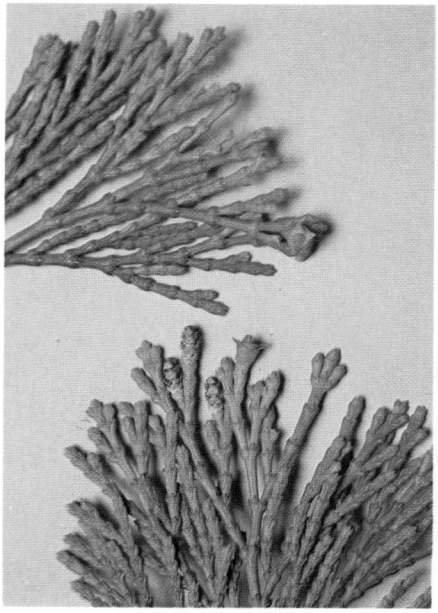

Carpinus family Carpinaceae, **Hornbeam**. Deciduous trees, with male and female flowers in separate catkins on same tree. Unlike *Betula* and *Alnus*, the male catkins remain in bud through the winter, emerging in the spring. The fruits are small nuts with large conspicuous bracts.

European Hornbeam or Common Hornbeam

Carpinus betulus L.
Native to Asia Minor and Europe, including south-east England. Cultivated in Europe and N. America as a hedge, park or street tree and for its hard, fine-grained timber which is used to make, among other things, mallets, skittles and some of the moving parts inside pianos. Height to 19m (65ft). Flowers (far left) open in March, the male catkins 3·7cm (1½in) long, the females smaller emerging from the tips of growing shoots. Fruiting catkins (near left) may be 7·5cm (3in) long and turn brown in November. Leaves (p33) colour bright yellow in the autumn. Bark (p217) is grey striped brown and vertically ridged or fluted.

American Hornbeam or Blue Beech

Carpinus caroliniana Walt.
Native to western N. America and Central America. Its wood is used for small items, such as tool handles. Height to 12m (40ft). Flowers (far left) emerge in April, male catkins 2·5–3·7cm (1–1½in) long, females 1·2–2cm (½–¾in) at growing tips. Fruiting catkins (near left) may be 12·5cm (5in) long, composed of nutlets 0·8cm (⅓in) surrounded by bracts which turn papery brown and fall from the tree in the autumn. Leaves (p33) are more tapered at the tip than European Hornbeam (*C. betulus*) and turn orange and red in the autumn. Bark is smooth grey and fluted.

Japanese Hornbeam

Carpinus japonica Blume
Native to Japan, cultivated as an ornamental and in botanical collections. Height to 12–15m (40–50ft). Flowers (far left) open in April, male catkins 2·5–5cm (1–2in) long, females at tips of shoots 1·2cm (½in) long. Fruiting catkins (near left), 5–6cm (2–2½in) long with toothed inward-curving bracts, colour from green to pink-tinged, then crimson in autumn. The leaves (p33) have numerous strong veins, and are longer and darker than European Hornbeam (*C. betulus*). Bark is smooth pinkish grey or dark with lighter stripes.

Carya family Juglandaceae, **Hickory**.
Large deciduous trees, with male and female flowers on same tree, males in three-branched catkins, females in few flowered clusters. Fruit is a nut enclosed by a husk, hardening as it ripens. Leaves have leaflets arranged in pairs, the lowest pair being shorter than the others.

Bitternut or Swamp Hickory

Carya cordiformis (Wangenh.) K. Koch
Native to eastern N. America, cultivated in Europe in botanical collections and large gardens. Distinguished from other hickories by its yellow winter buds. Height to 30m (100ft). Male catkins (near right) expand to 6–7·5cm (2½–3in), shedding pollen in late May or early June. The female flowers are also shown, but are inconspicuous between leaves at tips of growing shoots. Fruit (far right) has 4 ridges on the top half. Leaves (p54) have 7 or 9 leaflets.

Pignut Hickory

Carya glabra (Mill.) Sweet
Native to eastern N. America, from Ontario south to Alabama. Cultivated in botanical collections. Height to 18–27m (60–90ft). Male catkins (near right) expand to 7·5–12·5cm (3–5in), shedding their pollen in late May when the females appear at the tips of growing shoots (just visible in the photograph). Fruit (far right) may be pear-shaped or rounded, about 2·5cm (1in) long. The husk is thin, sometimes splitting in autumn to expose an unridged nut. Leaves (p53) usually have 5 leaflets, and turn yellow and orange in the autumn.

Big Shellbark Hickory, Bottom Shellbark Hickory or King-nut

Carya laciniosa (Michx. f.) Loud.
Native to eastern United States where its sweet nuts are harvested and sold. Cultivated in Europe in gardens and botanical collections. Height to 36m (120ft). Male catkins (near right) expand to as much as 12·5cm (5in) and shed pollen in June. Female flowers open at the same time, at the tips of shoots (also shown near right). Fruit (far right) may be spherical or oval, 4·5–6·5cm (1¾–2½in). The husk has 4 or 6 ridges and is orange tinted, ripening to brown. Leaves (p54) usually have 7, sometimes 5 or 9 leaflets, downy underneath on a slightly downy stalk. The end leaflet has a short stalk of its own. Bark is grey and splits into long 1–1·2m (3–4ft) plates, which remain hanging on the trunk.

Shagbark Hickory or Little Shellbark Hickory

Carya ovata (Mill.) K. Koch
Native to eastern United States where its edible nuts, hickory nuts, are a valuable crop. Cultivated for ornament in gardens and botanical collections in Europe. Grows to 21–27m (70–90ft) tall, occasionally larger. Male flowers (near right) expand to 7·5–12·5cm (3–5in) and shed their pollen in June. Females are single or in pairs in tip of growing shoot (also shown near right). Fruit (far right) is 2·5–5cm (1–2in) long, ripening to dark brown, when it splits to release the 4-angled nut, white when first exposed. Leaves (p53) are made up of 5 leaflets, the end one on a short stalk of its own. A rather large specimen is shown. The bark is grey and shaggy, splitting from the trunk in 30cm (1ft) or more long flakes.

Mockernut, Big Bud Hickory or White Heart Hickory

Carya tomentosa (Poir.) Nutt.
Native to eastern N. America, cultivated in Europe in botanical collections. Height to 30m (100ft). Male catkins (near right) expand to shed pollen in June, when the female flowers also appear at the tip of growing shoot (not shown but looks similar to other hickories). Fruit (far right) is 3·7–5cm (1½–2in) long and splits along its grooves to release an extremely hard shelled nut, which contains an edible kernel. Leaves (p54) are aromatic when touched, and the winter buds are larger 1·2–2cm (½–¾in) than on any other hickory. Young shoots are covered with woolly down. Bark is dark grey, ridged and covered with small scales.

Sweet Chestnut or Spanish Chestnut

Castanea sativa Mill., family Fagaceae.
Native to south Europe, north Africa and Asia Minor. Cultivated in Europe for its edible nuts and for ornament in parks and gardens, and in N. America as an ornamental. Height to 30m (100ft) with broad trunk, as much as 9–12m (30–40ft) in girth. Flowers (far left) are open in late June and July when the male catkins, about 15–25cm (6–10in) long shed their pollen. Female flowers (centre of photograph far left) are in clusters of 5–6 at the base of a short unopened male catkin. Fruit (near left) ripens in one season, some trees producing 1–2 round nuts, some producing 3–4 flat nuts which are not good enough to eat. Leaves (p26) turn yellow then dark brown in October. Bark (p217) is dark brown and ridged, often spirally.

Catalpa family Bignoniaceae.
Deciduous trees and shrubs with large, opposite heart-shaped leaves and large loose groups of flowers. Fruit are long thin pods. *Catalpa* is a name used by the Cherokee Indians for the Indian Bean (see below).

Indian Bean or Southern Catalpa

Catalpa bignonioides Walt.
Native to south-eastern United States, cultivated in parks and gardens in eastern States and in west, central and south Europe, including Britain. Height to 7·5–15m (25–50ft). Flowers (near right) open in June and July, each about 5cm (2in) across in a bunch about 15–20cm (6–8in) tall. Fruit (far right) are 15–37cm (6–15in) long, hanging, and turn brown in the autumn splitting the following spring to release white papery seeds about 2·5cm (1in) long. Leaves (p42) are downy underneath and may be shallowly lobed. They do not unfurl till late June and turn black before falling in autumn. Bark is pinkish brown or grey and flaky or ridged.

Hybrid Catalpa

Catalpa × *erubescens* Carr., synonym *C. hybrida* Spaeth
A group of cultivated hybrids arising from the Indian Bean (*C. bignonioides*) and the Yellow Catalpa (*C. ovata*). *C.* × *erubescens* 'J. C. Teas' first raised in Indiana is the best known form of this hybrid. Height to about 14m (45ft), occasionally taller. Fragrant flowers (near right) open in July and August, similar to but smaller than *C. bignonioides*, though the bunch may contain more flowers. Fruit (far right) are pods to 40cm (16in) long, but contain no seed. Leaves (p42) unfold purple, soon turning bright green, with 5 points or shallow lobes. They are slightly downy above and have hairs along veins underneath. Bark is dark grey covered with ridges and cracks.

Yellow Catalpa

Catalpa ovata G. Don
Native to China, cultivated in botanical collections. Height to 6–9m (20–30ft). Flowers (near right) are distinctively coloured. They open in July and August in bunches 10–25cm (4–10in) high, each flower about 2·5cm (1in) across. Fruit (far right) is a pod about 30cm (12in). Leaves (p42) are darker green and more definitely 3-lobed than the American *Catalpa* species.

Western Catalpa

Catalpa speciosa Engelm.
Native to central United States, cultivated in Mississippi for timber and for ornament in eastern States and Europe. Height to 36m (120ft). Flowers (near right) open in June and July, each 6cm (2¼in) across 7–10 in a bunch 12·5–15cm (5–6in) tall. Fruits (far right) are 20–50cm (8–20in) long and split in early spring to release 2·5cm (1in) long brown seeds. Leaves (p42) are dark green with down underneath, and often have 3 shallow lobes. Bark is light reddish brown covered with thin scales.

Cedrela sinensis Juss., **Chinese Cedar** family Meliaceae.
Deciduous, native of China. Height to 21m (70ft). Flowers in June, white, in clusters 30cm (1ft) long. Fruit about 2·5cm (1in) long, with winged seeds. Leaves (p58) have 5–12 pairs of leaflets.

Cedrus family Pineaceae, **Cedar**. Evergreen conifers, with needles in bunches. Male flowers in dense clusters appearing in early summer shedding pollen in the autumn. Females, small and solitary, appear on the same tree, as males shed pollen. Cones take at least 2 years to ripen and remain on the tree after releasing the winged seed.

Atlas Cedar

Cedrus atlantica Manetti
Native to Atlas Mountains of Algeria and Morocco. Most commonly cultivated as the blue form. Foliage is green (p23).
Cedrus atlantica Manetti forma *glauca* Beissn. **Blue Cedar**.
Blue form of the Atlas Cedar. Cultivated for ornament in parks and gardens in Europe and N. America. Height to 36m (120ft). Male flowers (far left) shed pollen in late September, 2·5–5cm (1–2in) long, females (also far left) develop into a green cylindrical, flat-topped cones about 8cm (3¼in) long, 3·7–5cm (1½–2in) wide, ripening to dark woody brown (near left). Foliage (p23) is blue green. Bark is paler grey than Atlas Cedar.

Deodar

Cedrus deodara (Roxb.) G. Don
Native to Himalaya, planted for ornament in parks, gardens and churchyards in Europe and N. America, also occasionally for timber in southern Europe. Height to 75m (250ft). Male flowers are pale green, 2–3cm (¾–1¼in) appearing during the summer, and expanding to about 8cm (3¼in) to shed pollen (far left) in early November. Females (also far left) are not always produced and are often rather high in the crown. Cone (near left) is about 10cm (4in) tall, remains green for 2 years when it turns brown and woody, releasing seed. Foliage (p23) consists of needles rather longer 2·5–5cm (1–2in) than on other cedars. Small branches hang down distinctively and young twigs are downy.

Cedar of Lebanon

Cedrus libani A. Richard
Native to Near East, including Lebanon, planted as an ornamental in Europe and N. America. Height to 24–36m (80–120ft). Male flowers are abundant 1cm (½in) and pale green through the summer, expanding to 5cm (2in) to shed pollen in November (far left). Females (also far left) appear in November and develop into large purplish green cones (near left) 9–15cm (3½–6in) which taper to the top. Foliage (p23) is made up of dark green needles up to 2cm (¾in) long. Young twigs are almost hairless.

Cyprus Cedar

Cedrus libani var. *brevifolia* Hook f.
Native to mountains of Cyprus where height is about 12m (40ft). May grow larger in cultivation. Flowers (far left) similar to other cedars, males expanding to about 6cm (2¼in) and shedding pollen in early November, females appearing at that time. Cones (near left) are smaller than of Cedar of Lebanon (*C. libani*), about 12·5cm (5in). Foliage (p23) is the most distinctive feature, being very short, about 1·2cm (½in).

Southern Nettle-tree

Celtis australis L., family Ulmaceae.
Native to south Europe and south-west Asia. Planted for shade at roadsides in south Europe and occasionally for ornament elsewhere, though may be damaged by frost. The wood has been used to make small items, for joinery and charcoal, and the bark yields a yellow dye. Height to 15–21m (50–70ft). Flowers (near right) open in May, male and female on same tree, females developing into the fruit (far right) which are about 1·2cm (½in) across and ripen to reddish brown in September. These are edible but rather tiny. Leaves (p25) are rough to the touch above, downy beneath. Bark is smooth and grey, not unlike a beech tree.

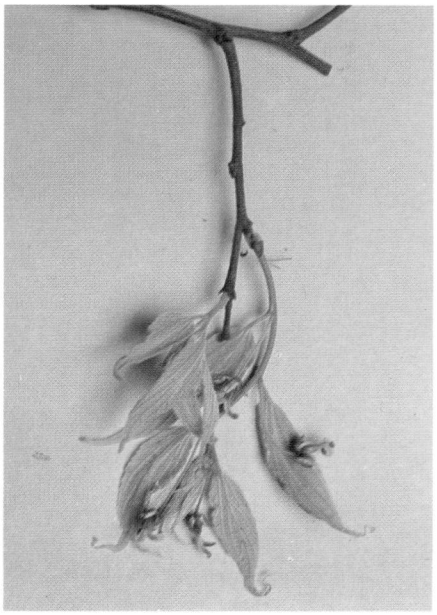

Sugarberry or Mississippi Hackberry

Celtis laevigata Willd.
Native to south-east United States, where it is often planted as a shade tree. Height to 18–24m (60–80ft). Flowers (near right) open in May, male and female separate on the same tree. Fruit is 0·6cm (¼in) and ripens from orange or yellow to dark purple. Leaves (p27) are distinctively untoothed. Bark (far right) often covered with projecting growths.

Hackberry or Nettle Tree

Celtis occidentalis L.
Native to eastern N. America, planted as a shade or ornamental tree in Mississippi, eastern States and Europe. Height to 9–12m (30–40ft). Flowers (near right) open in May, the females developing into fruit (far right) which is about 0·8cm (⅓in) across similar to fruit of *C. laevigata*, orange red ripening to dark purple. Leaves (p29) are downy on the main vein beneath. Bark is grey brown with distinctive warty growths.

Cephalotaxus family Cephalotaxaceae, **Plum Yew.** Evergreen shrubs and small trees. Male and female flowers occur on separate plants. Fruits are oval and fleshy, containing one seed. Foliage is similar to *Torreya* but much softer.

Chinese Plum Yew

Cephalotaxus fortunei Hook
Native to central China, cultivated in collections and gardens in Europe. Height to 6m (20ft) in cultivation and often low and bushy. Male flowers (far left) are produced in heads 0·6cm (¼in) across along the underside of young shoots and shed pollen in April and May. Females (also far left) are in pairs, stalked and also open at the same time. Fruit (near left) ripens the same year, about 3cm (1¼in) long, colouring brown. Foliage (p13) has long slender needles, about 5cm (2in).

Cephalotaxus harringtonia (Forbes) K. Koch
Thought to have been a Japanese garden plant originating from central China. Height to 2·7–5m (9–18ft) as a small tree but usually shrubby. Flowers open in May and look similar to those of *C. harringtonia* var. *drupacea* but male heads have longer stalks, about 2cm (¾in). Fruit (near left) is 2·5cm (1in) long, ripening from green to brown. Foliage (p13) has needles shorter than *C. fortunei*.
C. harringtonia var. *drupacea* (Sieb. & Zucc.) Koidzumi **Cow's Tail Pine or Japanese Plum Yew.** The wild type native to Japan and Korea. Flowers (far left) open in May, males in larger clusters with stalks only 0·6cm (¼in) long. Fruits look similar to those of *C. harringtonia*, but leaves (p13) are more regular, set in two almost vertical rows.

Katsura Tree

Cercidiphyllum japonicum Sieb. & Zucc., family Cercidiphyllaceae.
A deciduous tree, native to Japan and China, where it yields a valuable light timber. Grown for ornament throughout Europe but is sensitive to late spring frost. Height to 30m (100ft) in the wild often with several stems. Male and female flowers (far right) are on separate trees and open in April before the leaves unfold. Males have bunches of 15–20 red stamens about 0·8cm (⅓in) long, females have bunches of 3–5 twisted red styles about 0·6cm (¼in) long, elongating during the summer to form fruit pods (near right) 1·5–5cm (½–2in). Leaves (p39) are bright red at first, green through summer, then yellow, orange, red and purple in October.

Judas-tree

Cercis siliquastrum L., family Leguminosae.
Deciduous tree, native to east Mediterranean and south Europe, planted for ornament in gardens of all sizes in other parts of Europe. Height up to 12m (40ft) but usually lower with more than one stem. Flowers (far left) open in May and appear from old joints on branches including the trunk. Fruit (near left) may be about 10cm (4in) long and are often bright rosy purple in the summer. Leaves (p39) are similar in shape to those of Katsura Tree (*Cercidiphyllum japonicum*) but are arranged alternately along the shoots.

Chamaecyparis family Cupressaceae, **False Cypress.** Evergreen coniferous trees, with scale-like leaves on flattened twigs. Male and female flowers are on same tree, and cones are smaller than on true cypresses (*Cupressus*).

Lawson Cypress or Port Orford Cedar

Chamaecyparis lawsoniana (A. Murr.) Parl. Native to California and Oregon, planted with its many cultivated forms in gardens and parks in Europe and N. America. Also grown for timber in N. America and occasionally in Europe. Height may reach 60m (200ft) in the wild though usually half this in cultivation. Male flowers (near right) are produced all over the tree and shed pollen in March. Females (also near right) are tiny and green and open at the same time. Cones (far right) are about 0·8cm (⅓in) with 8 scales turning brown when ripe. Foliage (p10) usually has scale leaves closely pressed to twigs as in flower photograph. The cultivated varieties have distinctive tree shapes and foliage colours.

Nootka Cypress or Stinking Cypress

Chamaecyparis nootkatensis (D. Don) Spach A native to western N. America, from Alaska to Oregon, yielding a valuable fragrant timber. Cultivated for ornament in western States and western and central Europe. Height to 36m (120ft). Male flowers (near right) shed pollen in March and are yellow rather than red as on *C. lawsoniana*. Female flowers (also near right) which open at the same time are produced on upper branches. Cones (far right) are about 1·2cm (½in) across, with 4 or 6 spiked scales ripening in the autumn of their second year to red brown and opening to release seeds. Foliage (p10) does not have white marks on underside and has a rough texture since the leaf tips are usually not pressed against the twigs as seen in cone photograph. When crushed the leaves have a pungent catty smell.

Hinoki Cypress

Chamaecyparis obtusa (Seib. & Zucc.) Endl. Native of Japan where its timber is of great value. Cultivated for ornament in Europe and N. America. Height to about 36m (120ft) in its native environment, but slow growing in cultivation and often smaller. Male flowers (near right) shed pollen in April, when the bluish females (also near right) are produced on shoot tips. Cones (far right) are about 0·8cm (⅓in) across, with 8 scales bearing small points. Foliage (p10) has distinctively blunt ended leaves, with a thin line of blue around edges underneath. There are many cultivated varieties of differing shapes and colours.

Sawara Cypress

Chamaecyparis pisifera (Seib. & Zucc.) Endl.
Native of Japan, cultivated as an ornamental in N. America and Europe. Height up to 45m (150ft), usually less. Male flowers (near right) shed pollen in April, females (also near right) being produced at the same time. Cones (far right) are about 1·2cm (½in) with 10 pointed scales. Foliage (p10) has leaves with fine points and bluish patches at their bases underneath. Again, there are many garden varieties cultivated for their colours and shapes.

White Cypress

Chamaecyparis thyoides (L.) Britt., Sterns & Pogg.
Native to eastern N. America, where it grows in swamps near the coast. Cultivated for ornament in eastern United States and in Europe. Grows to 25m (80ft) in the wild but usually about 6–15m (20–50ft) in cultivation. Male flowers (near right) shed pollen in March, when females (also near right) are produced. Cones (far right) are about 0·6cm (¼in) across with 6 scales. Leaves (p10) have pointed tips.

Golden Chestnut

Chrysolepis chrysophylla (Hook.) Hjelmqvist, family Fagaceae.
An evergreen, native to California and Oregon, where it may grow to as much as 30m (100ft). When cultivated in Europe it is usually lower and sometimes bushy. Male and female flowers are produced on the same catkins, about 2·5–3·7cm (1–1½in) long, males for most of their length with a few females clustered at the base. These open in July (far left). Fruit (near left) is formed in clusters similar to those of Sweet Chestnut (*Castanea sativa*) about 2·5–4cm (1–1½in) across, ripening in the second autumn to release 1 or 2 golden brown nuts, which contain sweet, edible kernels. Leaves (p24) last for 2 or 3 years, when they colour yellow and fall from the tree.

Yellow Wood

Cladrastis lutea (Michx.) K. Koch, family Leguminosae.
Deciduous tree, native to south-eastern United States, grown for ornament in eastern States and Europe. The wood is bright yellow when first cut and yields a yellow dye. Height to about 12m (40ft) but may be taller in forest conditions. Blossom is white and fragrant and opens in June in bunches 20–35cm (8–14in) long, though not always produced in Europe. Each flower is about 2·5cm (1in) long on a hairy stalk. Seed pods are 7·5–10cm (3–4in) long, 1·2cm (½in) wide containing 4–6 seeds and ripening in September. Leaves (p53) are the best feature in Europe, turning bright yellow in autumn (near right). Bark is shown far right.

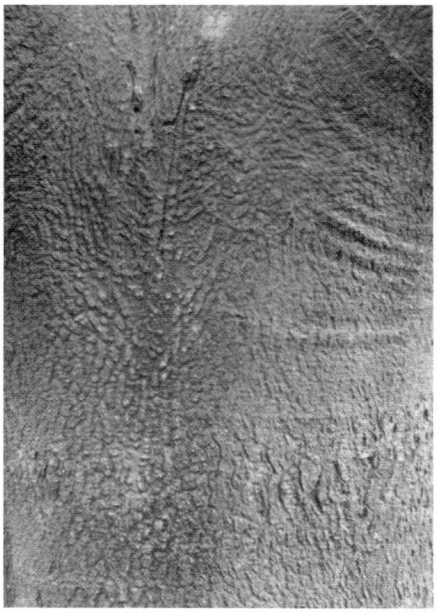

Chinese Yellow Wood

Cladrastis sinensis Hemsl.
Deciduous tree, native of China, cultivated in gardens and botanical collections. Height to 15m (50ft) or more in the wild. Fragrant flowers (near right) open in July in bunches as much as 30cm (12in) long. Seed pods (far right) are about 5–7·5cm (2–3in) long when ripe, falling in late September. Leaves (see near right) have 11–13 leaflets, arranged alternately on a central stalk.

Cornus alternifolia L. f. **Alternate-leaf Dogwood**, family Cornaceae.
Deciduous, native to eastern N. America. Height to 6m (20ft). Flowers in flat heads 5cm (2in) open in June. Fruit round, black 0·6cm (¼in). Leaves (p35) are alternate.

Table Dogwood

Cornus controversa Hensl.
Deciduous, native to Japan. Height to 9–15m (30–50ft). Flowers (near left) open in late June in heads 5–10cm (2–4in) across. Fruit is round, black 0·6cm (¼in) wide. Leaves (p35) are alternate. (Drawing above left.)
Cornus florida L. **Flowering Dogwood** (drawing above right)
Deciduous, native to eastern N. America. Height to 3–6m (10–20ft) or more. Flower clusters surrounded by large bracts (far left) which unfold in May. Fruit in tight clusters, oval red berries 1·2cm (½in) long, ripen in October. Leaves (p35) may colour red, yellow and orange in autumn.

Cornelian Cherry

Cornus mas L.
Native to central and south-east Europe, planted in gardens of all sizes for its winter blossom and attractive fruits. Wood, though in short pieces, has been of value for small domestic items, and the berries may be made into a syrup or jam. Height to as much as 14m (45ft) but often low and shrub-like. Flowers (far left) open in February and March, before the leaves unfold. Each is about 0·4cm (1/6in) across. Fruit (near left) is large, about 2cm (¾in) long, ripening in September. Leaves (p35) are almost round with 3–5 pairs of veins.

Nuttall's Dogwood or Pacific Dogwood

Cornus nuttallii Audubon
Native of western N. America, where it may reach a height of 12–18m (40–60ft). Flowers are in a tight head, about 2cm (¾in) across surrounded by 4–8 large bracts (far left), which make this tree a stunning sight in flower. The flower buds are visible all winter, finally opening in May. Fruit is a tight cluster of red berries. Leaves (p35) colour red, orange and yellow in autumn (near left).

Corylus family Corylaceae, **Hazel**.
Deciduous trees or shrubs with alternate, toothed leaves. Male and female flowers are separate, but on same tree: males in bunches of hanging catkins, females a tassel of tiny styles. Fruit is a nut surrounded by a leafy bract.

Hazel or Cobnut

Corylus avellana L.
Native to west Asia, north Africa and Europe, including Britain. Often grown for its edible nuts, and as hedging. Coppicing produces thin flexible rods useful for woven fencing and diviners' rods. In the wild it forms bushy thickets 4–6m (13–20ft) high and sometimes forms a small tree. Male catkins expand to 3·7–6cm (1½–2½in) and shed their pollen in February and March; females are tiny red tassels (both near right). Fruit (far right) ripen in October and make good eating. Leaves (p39) are coarse and hairy.

Turkish Hazel

Corylus colurna L.
Native to south-east Europe and west Asia, cultivated for ornament in large gardens and botanical collections. Height to 21–24m (70–80ft). Male catkins expand to 5–7·5cm (2–3in), shedding pollen in February; females are tiny red tassels (both shown near right). Nuts (far right) are 1·2cm (½in) wide surrounded by 4cm (1½in) wide bract, easily distinguished from other hazel fruits. Leaves (p39) are larger than Cobnut (*C. avellana*) and are often almost lobed.

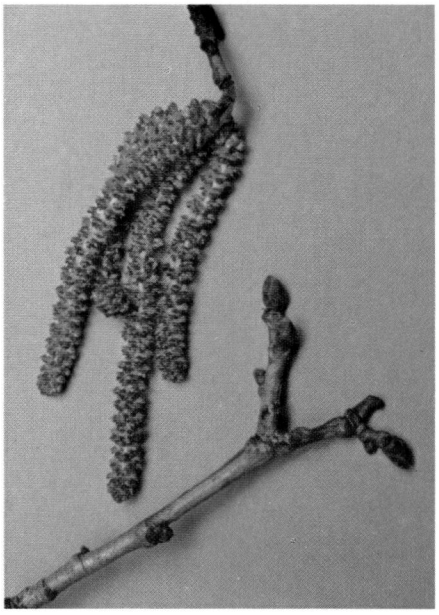

American Smoketree

Cotinus obovatus Raf., synonym *C. americanus* Nutt., family Anacardiceae
Native to south-eastern United States, apparently becoming rare due to exploitation for an orange-red dye extracted from its wood. Cultivated as an ornamental in eastern States and Europe. Height to 9m (30ft) in the wild but often bushy in cultivation. Male and female flowers open in June on separate plants. Male flowers are shown far left. Female flowerheads look similar but have fewer flowers, leaving a mass of empty threadlike stalks which give a cloudy appearance to the tree, hence the name Smoketree. Fruit is likewise sparse, about 0·3cm (⅛in) long. Leaves (p32) are bronze when they first unfold and colour beautiful clear reds in autumn (near left).

Himalayan Tree-cotoneaster

Cotoneaster frigidus Wall., family Rosaceae.
A small deciduous tree or shrub, native to Himalaya, grown for ornament in gardens and parks. Height to 4·5–6m (15–20ft). Flowers (near right) open in June and are about 0·8cm (⅓in) across in flat clusters which can be as much as 5cm (2in) wide. Perhaps the most striking feature are the fruits (far right) which clothe all branches. They ripen in September and remain on the tree through winter. Leaves (p32) are downy when young but become hairless through the summer.

Crataegus family Rosaceae, **Hawthorn**.
A large group of deciduous shrubs and trees, usually bearing sharp spines. Leaves are toothed, may also be lobed and usually have two leafy bracts, or stipules, where their stalks meet the twig. Flowers contain both sexes and are usually produced in clusters. Fruit is fleshy, containing hard nutlets, like a tiny apple.

Azarole or Mediterranean Medlar

Crataegus azarolus L.
Native of south Europe, north Africa and west Asia, grown for its apple-flavoured fruits which are used in jams and liqueurs. Height to about 9m (30ft). Flowers (far left) open in June, each about 1·2cm (½in) across in bunches about 5–7·5cm (2–3in) wide. Fruit (near left) is 2–2·5cm (¾–1in) in diameter, ripening in September, usually orange-yellow, but varies and may be red or white. Leaves are deeply cut and downy underneath.

Cockspur Thorn

Crataegus crus-galli L.
Native to central and eastern N. America, often grown for ornament or hedging in eastern States and also in northern Europe. It bears long thorns, usually 3·7–7·5cm (1½–3in) long but old ones may be 10–15cm (4–6in) long and branched. Height to 7·5m (25ft). Flowers (far left) are about 1·2cm (½in) across, produced in June in clusters 5–7·5cm (2–3in) across. Fruit (near left) is about 1·2cm (½in) across, ripens in October and persists on the tree through winter. Leaves (p37) colour scarlet in autumn.

Black Hawthorn

Crataegus douglasii Lindl.
Native to eastern and central N. America, cultivated for ornament in gardens and botanical collections in Europe. Height to 9m (30ft). Flowers (far left) open in May, 1·2cm (½in) wide in clusters about 5cm (2in) wide. Fruit (near left) is about 0·8cm (⅓in) across, ripens to glossy black and falls from the tree in August and September. Leaves are shown on p38. Thorns are thick, about 2–2·5cm (¾–1in) long, but may often be absent.

Oriental Thorn

Crataegus laciniata Ucria
Native of China, planted in Europe as an ornamental. Height to 4·5–6m (15–20ft). Flowers (far left) open in June, each about 2cm (¾in) across, developing to fruit (near left) of about 2cm (¾in) diameter, which ripen in October. Leaves (p47) are deeply cut, and downy on both sides but particularly underneath. Oriental Thorn bears few spines.

Midland Hawthorn, May or English Hawthorn

Crataegus laevigata (Poir.) DC, synonym *C. oxyacantha* L. emend Jacq.
Native of Europe, including Britain, smaller than Common Hawthorn (*C. monogyna*), reaching 4·5–6cm (15–20ft), with fewer thorns. Flowers (far left) open in May, about 1·2cm (½in) across with two, sometimes three styles. Fruits (near left) are oval, about 0·6–2cm (¼–¾in) long, containing two or sometimes three stones. Leaves (p47) are less lobed than on *C. monogyna*.

Crataegus laevigata cv. 'Paul's Scarlet'
Originated in England around 1858 from a tree of the pink double flowered variety (below). Commonly grown in parks and gardens of all sizes. Flowers (far left) open in late May or June, double and strongly coloured. Fruit is rarely formed. Leaves are similar to those of the wild type.

Crataegus laevigata cv. 'Punicea Flore Pleno'
A cultivated variety of Midland Hawthorn (*C. laevigata*) thought to have originated somewhere on the continent of Europe. Grown for ornament in parks and gardens but is less common than 'Paul's Scarlet' (above). Flowers (near left) open in late May or June and are double and pink.

Hybrid Cockspur Thorn

Crataegus × lavallei Herincq ex Lav.
A hybrid thought to have originated in France, now planted as an ornamental in gardens and collections. Height to 4·5–6m (15–20ft). Flowers (far left) open in June, each about 2·5cm (1in) across in bunches about 7·5cm (3in) wide. Fruit (near left) persists on the trees through winter. Each is about 2cm (¾in) wide, often speckled brown. Leaves (p37) are darker glossy green than on most hawthorns. Thorns are few, about 2·5cm (1in) long.

Downy Hawthorn

Crataegus mollis (Torr. & Gr.) Scheele
Native to central United States, planted as an ornamental in Europe. Height to 9–12m (30–40ft). Flowers open in June, white with red disk in the centre, about 2·5cm (1in) across. Fruit ripens in September; red, downy and spherical, 2–2·5cm (¾–1in) across. Leaves (p38) are downy, particularly on the undersides. Thorns are about 5cm (2in) long.

Common Hawthorn

Crataegus monogyna Jacq.
Native to Europe, including Britain and has ancient associations with May-day festivities and superstitions. Height to 10·5m (35ft). Fragrant flowers (far left) open in mid-May (around May 1st on the Old Style calendar). Fruit (near left) ripen in September, each containing only one stone. This is one of the main differences between this and the Midland Hawthorn (*C. laevigata*). Leaves (p47) are 5- to 7-lobed. Bark (p217) is dark brown and cracked into thin rectangular plates.

C. monogyna cv. 'Biflora' **Glastonbury Thorn**
Legend has it that this variety arose at Glastonbury from the staff of Joseph of Arimathea. He drove it into the ground and it burst into flower although it was then Christmas Day. It produces flowers and leaves through mild winters.

Crataegus oxycantha L. see *Crataegus laevigata* p107

Scarlet Hawthorn

Crataegus pedicellata Sarg.
Native to eastern N. America, where it may reach 6m (20ft) in height. Flowers (far left) open in May and June with a distinctive red disk in the centre of each. Fruit (near left) about 2cm (¾in) long, which ripen in September. Leaves (p38) are rough on upper surface, but not downy or hairy. They usually have about 5 shallow lobes on each side and are coarsely toothed. Thorns are shiny, brown and 5cm (2in) long.

Broad-leaved Cockspur Thorn or Frosted Thorn

Crataegus prunifolia (Lam.) Pers.
Origins of this thorn are uncertain, but it is certainly similar to the Cockspur Thorn (*C. crus-galli*). Height to 6m (20ft). Flowers (far left) open in June 1·8cm (¾in) across. Fruit (near left) is about 1·2cm (½in) across, ripening in September, soon falling from the tree. Leaves (p37) turn red in the autumn. Thorns are hard 3·7–7·5cm (1½–3in) long and sharply pointed.

Japanese Cedar

Cryptomeria japonica (L. f.) D. Don, family Taxodiaceae
An evergreen conifer, native to China and Japan. It is an important forestry tree in Japan, where it yields valuable timber. Cultivated as an ornamental in Europe and N. America. Grows to 30–55m (100–180ft) in Japan, usually smaller in cultivation. Male and female flowers (near right) are separate, but on the same tree. Male catkins are present throughout winter, then turn yellow, then shed pollen in late February or early March. Females are the tiny green rosettes at tips of shoots. They develop into green cones (far right) about 1·5cm (⅗in) across by autumn. These dry out, turn brown (also far right) and release their seed the following autumn. Foliage is shown on p12. Bark is reddish-brown and peels away in thin vertical strips.

Chinese Fir

Cunninghamia lanceolata (Lamb.) Hook., family Taxodiaceae
An evergreen conifer, native to China, where it plays a major role in forestry. Named after James Cunningham, who discovered it in 1701 and was the first European plant-hunter to visit China. Grown in large gardens and botanical collections. Height to 45m (150ft) in home environment, but usually about 30m (100ft) in cultivation. Male and female flowers (far left) are separate on the same tree. Males are in large bunches at tips of shoots, and shed pollen in April. Females are also at shoot tips, about 1·2cm (½in) across. Cones (near left) are up to 4·5cm (1¾in) across. Foliage (p13) consists of hard, pointed needles. Bark is brown and scaly.

Leyland Cypress

×*Cupressocyparis leylandii* (Dallim. & Jacks.) Dallim., family Cupressaceae
A hybrid between Nootka Cypress (*Chamaecyparis nootkatensis*) and Monterey Cypress (*Cupressus macrocarpa*). Mainly planted as ornamentals in gardens, or as hedging. Height to about 30m (100ft) so far. Male and female flowers (near right) are on the same tree. Males appear in the autumn and open to shed pollen the following March. Females, small and green, develop into shiny cones (far right) about 1–2cm (½–¾in) across. A large number of clones now exist. The two most important are:
×*C. leylandii* cv. 'Haggerston Grey' (clone 2) has blue grey foliage, and the branchlets are set at all angles round the brown woody twigs. Flowers and fruit are shown right and foliage on p10.
×*C. leylandii* cv. 'Leighton Green' (clone 11) has stouter green shoots, and branchlets from woody twigs in one plane. Silhouette above is of this clone.

Cupressus family Cupressaceae, **Cypress**
Evergreen coniferous trees, with tiny scale-like leaves pressed against the branches and twigs. Male and female flowers are separate on the same plants. Wood is resinous and fragrant.

Rough-barked Arizona Cypress

Cupressus arizonica Greene
Native to south-west United States and north Mexico. Planted as an ornamental in large gardens and botanical collections. Height to 23m (75ft) in native environment. Flowers (far left) are on separate branches; males shed pollen in February, and the tiny rose-like females develop into cones (near left) about 1·8cm (¾in) with 6–8 scales bearing stout bosses. Foliage is shown on p11. Bark of young trees is brown and stringy, breaking into thin plates, and turns grey with age.

Smooth Arizona Cypress

Cupressus glabra Sudw.
Native to Arizona, to the west of *C. arizonica* with which it has often been confused. Height to 14–18m (45–60ft). Male flowers (far left) shed pollen in February: females develop into cones (near left) about 1·5cm (⅗in). Foliage (p11) is blue-grey with depressions on leaf backs. Bark is smooth and reddish brown, breaking into scales which are shed.

Monterey Cypress

Cupressus macrocarpa Gord.
Native of California, cultivated in western N. America in gardens and as hedging and shelterbelts. Also planted in Europe, S. America and Australia. Height to 18m (60ft) in the wild but may be twice as tall in cultivation (silhouettes of both shown). Flowers (far left) open in March, the males turning yellow and shedding pollen. Females develop into cones (near left) which are about 2·5–3·7cm (1–1½in) across, made up of 4–6 scales. Foliage is shown p11. Bark is red brown, ridged and broken into scales.

Italian Cypress

Cupressus sempervirens L.
Native to Mediterranean Europe, cultivated in much of Europe and in N. America. It yields a strong, long-lasting wood, used in the Middle Ages to build chests, its pleasant odour making them particularly suitable for storing clothing. Height to 25–45m (80–150ft) and may be either narrow with upright branches as shown above or wider with horizontal branches. Flowers (far left) open in March, the yellow males shedding pollen. Female flowers develop into cones (near left) which are about 1·8–3cm (¾–1¼in) with 8–14 spiked scales. Foliage is shown p11. Bark is reddish brown, thin and shallowly ridged.

Quince

Cydonia oblonga Mill., family Rosaceae
Deciduous tree, probably native to Central Asia, though long cultivated in Mediterranean Europe for its fruit, now naturalised in many parts. Height to 4·5–6m (15–20ft). Flowers (near right) open in May each about 5cm (2in) across. Fruit (far right) is pear-shaped, about 7·5–10cm (3–4in) long, usually covered with a thick, white felt. Despite its wonderful mouth-watering fragrance, the unprepared quince fruit is most unpalatable, being hard and acid. The main use, in Britain, is for flavouring cooked apple and pear dishes and for making jams and jellies. A candy, 'Contignac', is made in France from quinces and sugar. Leaves (p32) are covered with felty down when young.

Dove Tree or Handkerchief Tree

Davidia involucrata Baill., family Davidiaceae. Deciduous tree, native to China where it was discovered by the French Jesuit, the Abbé David in 1869. Height to 12–19m (40–65ft). Flowers open in May in a tiny round head about 2cm (¾in) across, almost hidden by the large, up to 20cm (8in), showy white bracts (far left). Male and female parts are produced in separate flowerheads. Fruit (near left) is solitary, about 3·7cm (1½in) long, ripening to reddish brown in October and containing 3–5 seeds. Leaves (p41) are bright, light green, the lower surface downy and the upper with fine white hairs. They are fragrant when they first unfold.
D. involucrata var. *vilmoriniana* (Dode) Wanger has similar flowers and fruit but the leaves lack down on the undersides.

Date Plum

Diospyros lotus L., family Ebenaceae. A deciduous tree, native to China, cultivated for its fruit in the Far East and Italy and for ornament in gardens and collections in the north of Europe. Height to 12m (40ft) but may be twice as tall in warm climates. Flowers open in July: males (near right) are in clusters in leaf axils, females look similar but single and on a separate tree. Each flower is about 0·6cm (¼in) across. Fruit (far right) is 1·2–2cm (½–¾in) wide, ripening yellow to purple. Leaves (p27) are dark shiny green.

Common Persimmon

Diospyros virginiana L.
Deciduous tree, native to eastern and central United States. In some parts, particularly the southern States, the astringent fruit is gathered in abundance from wild trees. Height to 12–20m (40–65ft), occasionally much taller. Flowers open in July. Female flowers (near right) are solitary, about 2cm (¾in) long; males are clustered and slightly smaller. Fruit is similar to that of Date Plum (*D. lotus*), about 2·5–5cm (1–2in) across, coloured pale orange and often with a reddish flush on one side. Leaves are shown on p27. Bark (far right) is very dark, thick, and deeply cut into small rectangular blocks.

Dipteronia sinensis Oliver, family Aceraceae. Deciduous tree, native to central China. Height to 9m (30ft) though may sometimes be bushy. Flowers (far left) contain both sexes. They open in June in clusters 15–30cm (6–12in) long. Fruits (near left) have wings 2–2·5cm (¾–1in) long and are completely distinctive. Leaves (p57) usually have 7–11 leaflets, with small tufts of hair in the vein axils beneath.

Winter's Bark

Drimys winteri J. R. & G. Forst., family Winteraceae.
An evergreen tree, or sometimes shrub, native to South and Central America. This form is sometimes known in gardens as var. *latifolia*. It was first discovered by Captain William Winter, on a voyage with Sir Francis Drake. He brought back pieces of its bark which he found to be useful in spicing meat and preventing scurvy. Fragrant flowers (near right) open in June, about 3·7cm (1½in) across. Fruit (far right) ripen in October when they fall from the tree. Several black fleshy fruit, containing 15 or so seeds, cluster together at the ends of long stalks, 5–7·5cm (2–3in) long. These are also clustered. The photograph (far right) shows only one stalk bearing two fruits. Leaves (p24) vary from long and narrow to oval. Bark (p217) is aromatic and smooth grey-brown or orange-brown.

Oleaster

Elaeagnus angustifolia L., family Elaeagnaceae. Deciduous tree, or sometimes shrub, native to west Asia and naturalised in south Europe. Cultivated in parks and gardens, particularly in central Europe. In the Far East a sweet sherbet is made from its fruit. Height to 12m (40ft). Flowers (far left) open in June, and are about 0·6cm (¼in) wide with an unusual heavy fragrance. Fruits are oval, about 1·2cm (½in) long silvery yellow and sweet. Leaves (p24) are distinct for their silver scales on undersides. Bark is shown near left.

Chilean Fire Bush

Embothrium coccineum J. R. & G. Forst, family Proteaceae.
Evergreen tree, or shrub, native to Chile, cultivated in gardens for ornament. Height to 12m (40ft). The distinctive scarlet flowers (near right) open in June, each about 3·7–5cm (1½–2in) long. The woody fruits (far right) are 5–7·5cm (2–3in) long, splitting to release winged seeds. Leaves (p24) are rather variable in size and shape, usually long, up to 15cm (6in), but often much shorter and rounder.

Eucalyptus family Myrtaceae, **Gum Tree**
A large group of evergreen trees, almost entirely native to Australasia. Leaves come in two types: juvenile and adult, the former usually stemless and rounded, the latter long and stalked. Flowers look like tassels of stamens, opening a year after the buds are formed.

Cider Gum

Eucalyptus gunnii Hook f.
Native to Tasmania, cultivated for ornament in European gardens, young foliage often being used in flower arranging. Height to about 30m (100ft). Flowers (far left) open in July and August, usually in bunches of 3. Fruits (near left) are about 0·6cm (¼in) long (leaves in this photograph are covered with spots caused by scale insects). Leaves are shown p24: juvenile leaves are almost round, clasping the stem in pairs; adult leaves are alternate, long and thin on a yellow stalk about 2·5cm (1in) long. Bark (p217) is smooth, peeling off to expose almost white wood which ages to dark brownish grey.

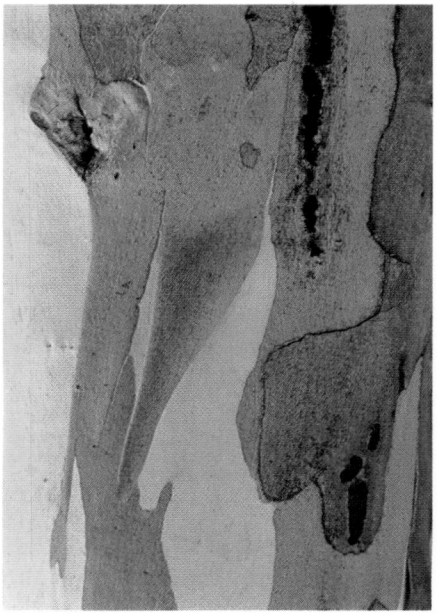

Snow Gum

Eucalyptus niphophila Maiden & Blakely
Native to mountains of New South Wales and Victoria at high altitudes to 2000m (6,500ft). Cultivated in gardens in Europe and quite resistant to frost. Height to 6m (20ft) in the wild but may grow larger in cultivation. Flowers (far left) open in August in bunches of 9–11. Fruit (also far left) is about 0·6cm (¼in) long. Leaves (p24) are adult from very early, about one year, unfolding orange brown, soon becoming grey-green with stalks red on one side, yellow underneath. They may be either short and rounded but typically long, thin and curved. Bark (near left) is grey, peeling in large plates, to expose clear white new bark.

Spinning Gum

Eucalyptus perriniana Rodway
Native to Tasmania, Victoria and New South Wales where it grows at altitudes of 300–600m (1,000–2,000ft). Grown in Europe and often coppiced to encourage juvenile foliage for flower arranging and decoration. Height to 6m (20ft) in the wild. Flowers (far left) open in August in bunches of 3. Fruit (also far left) are about 0·5cm (1/5in). Foliage (p24) consists of distinctive juvenile leaves which are actually pairs joined together to form a circular leaf surrounding the stem. These eventually break off and spin around the stem in the wind. Adult leaves are long, thin and may be curved. Bark (near left) is dark and distinctively ringed by old leaf scars.

Eucommia ulmoides Oliver, family Eucommiaceae
A deciduous tree, native to China, where it was found by western botanists in cultivation rather than in the wild. Also cultivated in European gardens and botanical collections. A type of rubber is produced and may be detected as thin strands by carefully breaking a leaf. Height to 9–20m (30–65ft). Male and female flowers are produced on separate plants and open in February before the leaves unfold. Males (near right) are clusters of anthers: females are single green pistils and very inconspicuous. Fruit (far right) is rather like an elm fruit, each about 3·7cm (1½in) long containing one seed. Leaves are shown p33.

Nyman's Hybrid Eucryphia

Eucryphia × nymansensis Bausch, family Eucryphiaceae
An evergreen hybrid between *E. glutinosa* and *E. cordifolia*, 2 species from Chile, first grown at Nymans in Sussex early this century. Often shrubby but as a small tree may reach 12–15m (40–50ft) tall. Flowers (far left) open in August, each about 6cm (2½in) across. They cover the plant, giving a wonderful display of blossom. Fruits (near left) are rather small, about 0·6cm (¼in) long and do produce some fertile seed. Leaves (p50) are mostly with 3 leaflets but many are single: they reflect the leaves of parent trees.

Korean Euodia

Euodia daniellii (Benn.) Hemsl., family Rutaceae
Deciduous tree, native to Korea and north China cultivated for ornament in large gardens, parks and collections in Europe. Height to 15m (50ft). Flowers (near right) are strong-smelling and open in August and September and are usually of separate sexes: the flowerheads may be as much as 10–15cm (4–6in) across, when fully open. Fruits are reddish-black capsules with a hooked point. Leaves (p53) colour clear yellow in October (far right).

Fagus family Fagaceae, **Beech**
Deciduous trees, all from N. hemisphere. Leaves are alternate, each with prominent pairs of parallel veins. Male and female flowers are in separate clusters but on the same tree. Fruit is 1 or 2 edible nuts, enclosed by a woody, prickly husk.

Oriental Beech

Fagus orientalis Lipsky
Native to Asia Minor, the Caucasus and Balkans, growing in lower more sheltered places than the Common Beech, (*F. sylvatica*). Height to 30m (100ft) in the wild. Flowers (far left) open in May, drooping male clusters on stalks 2·5–5cm (1–2in) long, the female produced at the tip of the shoot. Fruit (near left) have husks about 2·5cm (1in) long on stems 5–7·5cm (2–3in) long and which split and fall in October to release the triangular nuts. Leaves (p33) are longer than Common Beech, with 7–12 pairs of veins. Bark is smooth, dark grey and furrowed.

Common Beech or European Beech

Fagus sylvatica L.
Native to Europe, including south England, much cultivated throughout Europe for timber, ornament and shade. Also planted widely in N. America. The edible nuts are a source of oil, which was extracted on a large scale in Germany during the World Wars, and may be made into a kind of margarine. Height to 30m (100ft) with a large thick trunk sometimes 2–2·5m (6–8ft) across. Flowers (far left) open in May, numerous drooping clusters of males and one or two female clusters at the tip of the shoot. Fruit (near left) is ripe in September or October, releasing triangular nuts, about 1·5cm (⅝in) long. Leaves (p33) have 5–9 pairs of veins. Bark (p117 top right) is smooth and grey.

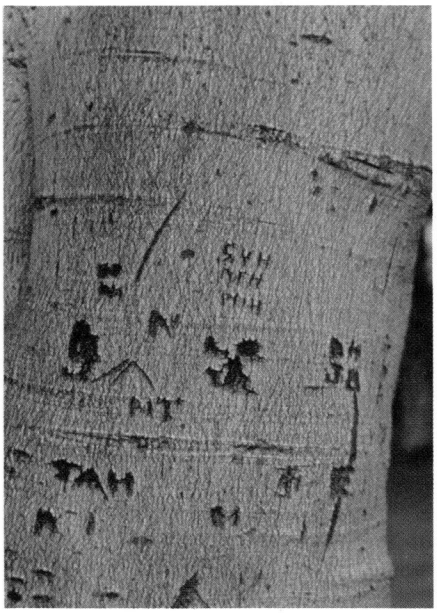

Fern-leaved Beech

Fagus sylcatica cv. 'Asplenifolia'
Often called 'Heterophylla' the leaves (p47 and far left) are deeply cut, though may occasionally revert to simple entire leaves. Flowers (far left) are similar to Common Beech (*F. sylcatica*). Bark is as *F. sylcatica* (near left).

Dawyck Beech

F. sylcatica cv. 'Dawyck' was first grown in Dawyck, Peeblesshire, and has an unusual columnar shape. Leaves and flowers are similar to the type *F. sylcatica*.

Weeping Beech

F. sylcatica forma *pendula* (Loud.) Schelle
Usually smaller than Common Beech (*F. sylcatica*) and has masses of drooping, pendulous branches. Flowers and leaves are similar to those of the type.

Purple Beech

F. sylcatica forma *purpurea* (Ait.) Schneid
Much planted in gardens and parks, Purple Beech has dark purple leaves (p33). Flowers (far left) and fruit (near left) also have a pinkish brown tint.

Fig

Ficus carica L., family Moraceae
Deciduous tree, native to west Asia and eastern Mediterranean, cultivated through south Europe and in California for its sweet fruits which are eaten raw, tinned, dried or sugared. They have a mild laxative effect. Height to 9m (30ft), but often low and bushy. Male and female flowers are produced on separate trees and are unusual in that they are borne inside a fleshy receptacle (near right) which develops into the fruit. They are pollinated by fig wasps, which crawl through a tiny hole at the tip. Fruit (far right) is fleshy and may be green, purple or brown. Varieties cultivated for fruit may often produce several crops in one year, but in cool climates flowers form in May and ripen in October. Leaves (p44) may have 3 or 5 lobes.

Patagonian Cypress

Fitzroya cupressoides (Mol.)
I. M. Johnston, family Cupressaceae
An evergreen, coniferous tree, native to Chile and Argentina where it yields a valuable timber. Named after Robert Fitzroy who commanded the famous 5-year surveying voyage of the *Beagle* which carried the young Charles Darwin as its naturalist. Cultivated in botanical collections and large gardens. Height to 50m (160ft) and slender in the wild, but in cultivation (see silhouette above) it may be very low and shrubby. Female flowers (far left) open in April and are about 0·5cm (1/5in) across. Males are yellow about 0·2cm (1/12in) long. Cones (near left) are about 0·8cm (⅓in) across and ripen from green to brown, splitting to release seed, but remaining on the tree through winter. Foliage (p11) has blunt leaves in rings of 3, each with 2 white bands on either side. Bark is deep reddish brown, peeling off to expose smooth grey trunk.

Fraxinus family Oleaceae, **Ash**
Deciduous trees. Flowers usually have no petals, and may be one sex only, or both together. One sexed flowers may sometimes be on separate trees, sometimes together. Leaves have 2 rows of leaflets either side of a central stem. Fruit have single wings.

White Ash

Fraxinus americana L.
Native of eastern N. America, where it yields a valuable timber useful in house interiors, furniture etc. Also grown for ornament and shade in eastern states and west and north Europe. Height to 35m (120ft) in the wild. Male and female flowers are borne on separate trees, opening in May. Male flowers shown near right; females are also petalless, in looser clusters. Fruit is about 2·5–6·2cm (1–2½in) long, about 0·6cm (¼in) wide with slightly pointed tips in clusters about 15cm (6in) long. Leaves (p53) have 7–9 leaflets and turn clear yellow in the autumn. Bark (far right) is thick and grey, and older trees have diamond-shaped ridges.

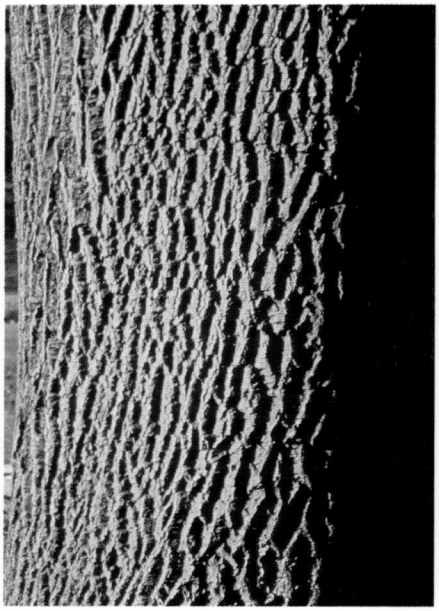

Narrow-leaved Ash

Fraxinus angustifolia Vahl
Native to west Mediterranean and north Africa, cultivated in collections and large gardens. Height to 18–25m (60–80ft). Flowers open in May; females are shown near right; males are in tighter clusters at the same time of year. Fruit is 2·5–3cm (1–1¼in) long, ripening in September. Leaves (p55) have 7–13 narrow hairless leaflets. Bark (far right) is dark grey, more deeply ridged and knobbly than Common Ash (*F. excelsior*). Easily distinguished from narrow leaved forms of Common Ash by its brown rather than black winter buds.

Common Ash or European Ash

Fraxinus excelsior L.
Native to Europe, including Britain, Common Ash is an important timber tree, its light coloured wood being strong and hard-wearing, and useful for furniture, house interiors and many wooden implements. Height to 30–42m (100–140ft). Flowers open in April with male and female in separate clusters on the same tree, on different trees or in the same flower. Male clusters (near right) are purple turning yellow when pollen is shed. Female clusters are pale green and looser in appearance. Fruit (far right) has wings about 4cm (1½in) long with slightly notched tip and a tiny spike. They turn brown in October and remain on the tree for some time after leaves have fallen. Leaves (p55) usually have 9–11 leaflets and turn clear yellow in autumn. Winter buds (see near right) are black.

Single-leaved Ash

F. excelsior forma *diversifolia* (Ait.) Lingelsh
Has simple leaves i.e. one leaflet only (p33), though may have 3 leaflets, but otherwise similar to Common Ash.

Weeping Ash

F. excelsior cv. 'Pendula'
Has drooping branches, forming a dome-shaped tree. Leaves and flowers similar to Common Ash.

Oregon Ash

Fraxinus latifolia Benth.
Native to western N. America, where a valuable timber is produced. Height to 23m (75ft). Male and female flowers (both near right) open in April on separate trees. Fruit (far right) are about 2·5–5cm (1–2in) long in dense clusters. Leaves (p53) have 5–9 rather broad leaflets, the side ones with no stalks. Bark is dark grey, or tinged red with broad scaly ridges.

Manna Ash or Flowering Ash

Fraxinus ornus L.
Native to south Europe and Asia Minor, cultivated as an ornamental in other parts of Europe. The stems exude a sweet sap, manna, which is used medicinally as a mild laxative. Height to 15–20m (50–65ft). Flowers (near right) unlike most ashes, bear showy petals. They open in May in dense clusters about 7·5–10cm (3–4in) long. Fruit (far right) is narrow, about 2·5cm (1in) long. Leaves (p53) have 5–9 toothed leaflets, and are rather variable in size and form.

Red Ash or Green Ash

Fraxinus pennsylvanica Marsh.
Native to east and central N. America, also grown for timber in central and southern Europe. Height to 12–18m (40–60ft). Male and female flowers (near right) are produced on separate trees, in April, just as the leaves are beginning to emerge. Fruit is about 2·5–6·2cm (1–2½in) long and may be pointed at the tip. Leaves (p53) have 7–9 leaflets and may be similar to those of Oregon Ash (*F. latifolia*) but side leaves have short stems. Bark (far right) has scaly ridges and may be red tinged.

Velvet Ash or Arizona Ash

Fraxinus velutina Torr.
Native to south-west United States and Mexico. The wood is not strong but was used in Arizona to make wagons. Height to 7·5–12m (25–40ft). Male and female flowers (near right) are produced on separate trees in April. Fruits (far right) are about 1·2–1·8cm (½–¾in) long, the wing having a notch at the tip and only about half the length of whole fruit. Leaves (p53) have only 5 leaflets, sometimes 7 or 3, covered with soft down. Bark is dark grey with broad ridges breaking into scales. Young shoots are velvety.

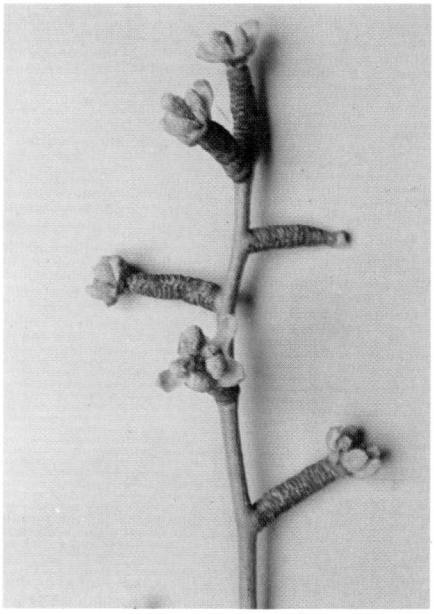

Maidenhair Tree

Ginkgo biloba L.,
family Ginkgoaceae
The only representative of a type of plant which was widespread in prehistoric times. Native to China but cultivated in gardens, streets and parks in all temperate countries. Deciduous tree to 30m (100ft). Flowers are produced on separate trees: males (far left) about 2·5–3·7cm (1–1½in) long shedding pollen in March; females tiny on a stalk about 5cm (2in) developing into the fruit (near left) which contains an edible nut. As the flesh decays it becomes foul-smelling and slimy and can be a hazard to traffic in busy town streets. Leaves (p43) may be 2-lobed as shown, but often fan-shaped with only shallow lobing. They colour yellow in autumn before falling. Bark is brown and corky, becoming ridged with wide cracks on mature trees (p217) and often fluted.

Honey Locust

Gleditsia triacanthos L., family Leguminosae
A deciduous tree bearing stout branched thorns, native to central N. America, planted as an ornamental in Europe, particularly in the south. Height to 42m (140ft) in the wild. Male and female flowers open in June in separate clusters on the same tree. Male catkins (near right) expand to about 5cm (2in), each flower about 0·5cm (1/5in) wide with equal petals. Female clusters have few flowers. Fruit pod (far right) is 25–45cm (10–18in) long. They dry out around October and fall during winter. Leaves (p56) have 7–16 pairs of leaflets and turn yellow in autumn. The bark is dark brown, ridged and scaled, but the stem is most easily recognised by the masses of thick branched spines which grow from it (p217).

Gymnocladus dioica (L.) K. Koch, family Leguminosae **Kentucky Coffee Tree**
Native to eastern and central United States, where the seeds were supposed to have been roasted and ground to make a coffee-like beverage. Height to 33m (110ft). Male and female flowers open in June on separate trees: males are in bunches about 7·5–10cm (3–4in) long, females in bunches 3 times that size, each flower about 1·8–2·5cm (¾–1in) long. Leaves (p59) are branched, or bipinnate.

Mountain Snowdrop Tree or Silver Bell

Halesia monticola (Rehd.) Sarg., family Styracaceae
Native to south-eastern United States, grown as an ornamental in eastern states and in Europe, as it grows quickly and flowers profusely when still rather young. Height to 25–30m (80–100ft) in the wild. Flowers (far left) open in May as the leaves emerge, each about 2·5cm (1in) long. Fruit (near left) are about 3·7–5cm (1½–2in) long. Leaves (p26) are downy when they first appear.

Ilex family Aquifoliaceae, **Holly**
Deciduous and evergreen trees and shrubs. Male and female flowers on separate trees; fruit is one or more seeds, with a fleshy covering, and is poisonous.

Highclere Holly

Ilex × *altaclarensis* (Loud.) Dallim.
A group of evergreen hybrids between Common Holly (*I. aquifolium*) and another called Canary Holly (*I. perado*). Many cultivars have been produced, and most differ from Common Holly in having larger, less prickly leaves, and larger flowers and fruit. Height to 15m (50ft).
I. × *altaclarensis* cv. 'Camelliifolia'
A female clone, flowers (near right) open in May and develop into fruit (far right) about 1·2cm (½in) across, which are ripe by November. Young shoots, leaf stems and petal bases are tinged purple. Leaves (p36) may be up to 12·5cm (5in) long and may sometimes have a few short spines.

Ilex × altaclarensis cv. 'Golden King'
Despite its name this is a female clone. Flowers are similar to other Highclere Hollies and open in May. Fruit (near right) about 1cm (2/5in) across, ripening in November. Leaves (p36) are the main feature, having an almost smooth edge and yellow margins. Some may be completely yellow (near right).

Ilex × altaclarensis cv. 'Hendersonii'
A female clone with flowers opening in May and sparse large fruits (far right) about 1·2cm (½in) ripening in December. Leaves (p36) are broad, dull green with few spines. Young shoots are usually green.

Ilex × altaclarensis cv. 'Hodginsii'
A male clone, so does not produce berries. Flowers (near right) are tinged purple, about 1·2cm (½in) across and open in May. Leaves (p36) are similar to 'Hendersonii' but are shiny rather than dull. Young shoots are tinged with purple. This cultivar is very resistant to atmospheric pollution so is commonly planted in industrial areas.

Ilex × altaclarensis cv. 'Wilsonii'
A female with flowers opening in May and berries (far right) about 1cm (2/5in) across ripening in November. The leaves (p36) are shiny green and have more spines, about 4–10 on each side, than other Highclere Hollies. Leaf edges and spines are clear yellow.

Common Holly or English Holly

Ilex aquifolium L.
Evergreen tree, native to west Asia and Europe, including Britain, much planted throughout Europe and parts of N. America for shelter and ornament. The wood is hard and fine-grained, so used in detailed work such as turnery, marquetry, engraving and making printing blocks. The bright red berries are well known in Europe as traditional Christmas decorations. Height to 25m (80ft). Flowers (near right, males on upper twig, females below) are about 08cm (⅓in) across, ripening to 4-seeded berry (far right) also 0·8cm (⅓in) in November. Leaves (p36) are distinctive: glossy, wavy and sharply spiney, though may be almost spineless on old trees. Bark (p217) is smooth grey with some dark marks. People often carve names and initials on old holly trunks. Naturally variable and many cultivated varieties have also been produced, some of which are shown below.

Ilex aquifolium cv. 'Argentea Marginata'
A female, with flowers similar to Common Holly, berries about 0·8cm (⅓in) ripening in November. Leaves (p36) are green with whitish cream edges.

Ilex aquifolium cv. 'Aurea Marginata'
Similar to 'Argentea Marginata' but with narrow yellow, rather than cream leaf edges. This difference is clearer on leaf photograph (p36). Berries (far right) are about 0·8cm (⅓in) ripening in November.

Ilex aquifolium bacciflava (West.) Rehd.
Leaves and flowers (near right) are similar to Common Holly but the fruit is bright yellow (far right).

Hedgehog Holly

Ilex aquifolium cv. 'Ferox'
This is a male clone so does not bear berries, but this is more than made up for by its unusual leaves (near right with flowers and p36) with upper surfaces covered with prickles. Leaves are smaller than Common Holly, about 3·7cm (1½in).

Ilex aquifolium cv. 'Recurva'
Also male, flowers shown far right. Leaves (p36) are small, about 3·7–5cm (1½–2in) and curved backwards.

Himalayan Holly

Ilex dipyrena Wall.
Evergreen tree, native to Himalaya and further east. Grown as an ornamental in large gardens and botanical collections. Height to 12m (40ft). Flowers (males shown right) are in tight clusters in leaf axils. Fruit (far right) is about 1·2cm (½in) long, widely spaced along the twigs. Leaves (p36) are dull green, usually with no or very few spines on mature trees, but may have several on each side.

American Holly

Ilex opaca Ait.
Evergreen tree, native to central and eastern United States, where many cultivated varieties and hybrids have been produced. Wood has similar uses to the European Common Holly and berry-bearing branches are also used in N. America for Christmas decoration. Height to 12–15m (40–50ft) in the wild. Flowers open in June, males and females (near right) on separate trees. Berries (far right) are about 0·6cm (¼in) across, ripen in November and persist on the tree through winter. Leaves (p36) dull with sharp spines, though leaves in upper parts of old trees may have entire margins.

Perny's Holly

Ilex pernyi Franch.
Evergreen tree, native to central and west China, and named after the French missionary, Paul Perny, who discovered it. Now cultivated as an ornamental in gardens and collections. Height to 6–9m (20–30ft). Flowers (near right) are yellowish and open in June, each about 0·3–0·6cm (⅛–¼in). Fruit (far right) is about 0·6cm (¼in) wide with no stalk. It ripens in November. Leaves (p36) are small, about 1·2–5cm (½–2in) long and of distinctive shape.

Juglans ailantifolia Carr. **Japanese Walnut**
Native to Japan. Height to 15m (50ft). Male catkins up to 30cm (12in), fruit about 5cm (2in) long. Leaves (p57) have 11–17 pointed leaflets, downy underneath. Bark (p218) is light grey with dark vertical cracks.

Juglans cinerea L. **Butternut or White Walnut**
Native to eastern N. America. Height to 15–18m (50–60ft). Male catkins about 5–10cm (2–4in) long; fruit about 3·7–6·2cm (1½–2½in) long. Leaves (p58) have 7–19 leaflets, hairy at first on upper surface.

Black Walnut

Juglans nigra L.
Native to eastern and central United States, grown in eastern States and in Europe as an ornamental. Height to 25–30m (80–100ft), sometimes more. Male and female flowers (far left) open in late May or early June, male catkins about 5–10cm (2–4in) long. Fruit (near left) ripens in October, and is usually round but may be tapered, about 3·7–5cm (1½–2in) across. Leaves (p58) have 11–23 leaflets with the end one often absent. Bark (p218) is dark brown, broken into a network of narrow ridges.

English Walnut or Persian Walnut

Juglans regia L.
Native distribution is uncertain, since it has long been cultivated throughout Europe, including Britain, and parts of Asia. The timber is highly prized for veneers and furniture and the fruit is harvested for pickling or for eating raw. Height to 30m (100ft). Flowers (far left) open in June, male catkins about 5–10cm (2–4in) long; fruit (near left) is smooth and about 3·7–5cm (1½–2in) across. Leaves (p54) usually have 5–7 leaflets, sometimes more. Young shoots have no down. Bark is smooth and grey with wide, deep cracks.

Juniperus family Cupressaceae, **Juniper**
Evergreen coniferous trees and shrubs. Foliage comes in 2 types: juvenile, which has needle-like leaves in pairs or rings of 3; adult, which has scale-like leaves, closely pressed to the stem. Both types are found on adult trees of some species, others lose the juvenile type. Male and female flowers usually occur on separate plants. Fruit is berry-like, but really a cone with 3–8 scales merged together. Crushed foliage usually has a distinctive aroma.

Chinese Juniper

Juniperus chinensis L.
Native to Japan, China and Mongolia. Height to 18m (60ft), often shrubby. Male flowers (near right) shed pollen in March, females usually on separate trees develop into cones (far right) which are about 0·6cm (¼in) across. Both adult and juvenile foliage (p12) are found on adult trees, juvenile needles usually in 3s. There are many cultivated varieties for growing in gardens.

Common Juniper

Juniperus communis L.
Native to northern Europe, N. America and south-west Asia. The fruit are best known as a flavouring for gin, and in various dishes, but have also been used as a source of oil, as a diuretic in medicine, and in Norway to make a beer. Commonly a sprawling shrub, but may form a tree about 2–4m (6–12ft) tall. Flowers (near right) open in March, fruit (far right) are about 0·6cm (¼in) across and ripen to black in their second or third year. Foliage (p12) is of needle-type only, in whorls of 3 with a broad white band on upper surface and grey undersurface. Many garden varieties have been raised.

Syrian Juniper

Juniperus drupacea Labill.
Native to mountains of Syria, Greece and Asia Minor. Height to 9–15m (30–60ft). Male flowers (near right) are in small clusters, yellow when fully open in March. Fruit are large, about 2·5cm (1in) across, dark brown or blue-black. Foliage (p12) is easily distinguished since needles are 1·2–2·5cm (½–1in) long and sharp with 2 bands of white on upper surface. No adult, scale-type leaves are produced.

Mexican Juniper

Juniperus flaccida Schlecht.
Native to Mexico and Texas, cultivated in gardens and collections in Europe, particularly the south. Height to 9m (30ft) with long drooping branches. Male flowers (far right) open in March; fruits are reddish-brown, about 1·2cm (½in) wide. Foliage (p12) shows both types of leaves.

One-seed Juniper or Cherrystone Juniper

Juniperus monosperma Sarg.
Native to south-west United States and occasionally grown for ornament. Height to 9–15m (30–50ft). Flowers (females near right) open in March. Fruit (far right) ripens to grey blue, about 0·6cm (¼in) containing only one seed. Foliage (p12) shows both adult and juvenile types, the prickly juvenile eventually being lost by old trees.

Drooping Juniper or Himalayan Juniper

Juniperus recurva D. Don
An unusual juniper native to China, Himalaya and Burma, grown in gardens and collections. Height to 9–12m (30–40ft). Male and female flowers (both near right) open in March on the same tree. Fruit (far right) are oval, ripening to dark purple in their second year. Foliage (p12) is all of the juvenile needle type but closely pressed to the stem and dull blue green, changing to brown before falling. They give the tree a rather straggly almost unhealthy appearance.

Temple Juniper or Needle Juniper

Juniperus rigida Sieb. & Zucc
Native to Japan, occasionally grown in western gardens where it often forms a shrub. Height to 6m (20ft) but may be twice as tall. Male and female flowers (both near right) open in March on separate trees, males in round yellow clusters about 0·3cm (⅛in) across, females half the size, green. Fruit (far right) ripen through brown to dark blue-black in second year. Foliage (p12) is always needle-like, in spreading rings of 3. Each has a band of white on upper surface.

Pencil Cedar or Eastern Redcedar

Juniperus virginiana L.
Native to eastern and central N. America, often cultivated in these areas as an ornamental, and also in west and central Europe. The wood has been used to line chests and cupboards for storing clothes as it has a pleasant smell and repels moths. One common name refers to its use in making lead pencils. Height to about 15m (50ft), occasionally twice this size, and the tallest of junipers grown in gardens. Male and female flowers (near right) open in March, sometimes on the same tree, but usually separate. Males are round, yellow; females smaller and green. Fruit is smaller than other junipers 0·3–0·6cm (⅛–¼in) long, blue. Foliage (p12) has both types; the needle-like leaves are usually in pairs and the scale-like leaves are pointed. There are several cultivated varieties: cv. 'Glauca', shown with berries far right has blue-green foliage.

Prickly Castor-oil Tree

Kalopanax pictus (Thunb.) Nakai, family Araliaceae
Native to Japan, east Russia, Korea and China, a tree which resembles a maple, but has alternate leaves and stout yellow prickles on its branches and suckers. Height to 25–28m (80–90ft) in the wild, usually much smaller in cultivation. Small white flowers open in August and September in round clusters, grouped into a large head sometimes as much as 60cm (2ft) across. Fruit (far left) is tiny, about 0·5cm (1/5in) ripening black and falling in December. Leaves are up to 18–25cm (7–10in) wide with 5 or 7 lobes, generally cut about ⅓ into the leaf, dark green above, and downy below when young (see photograph left). Bark (near left) is dark grey and ridged, often knobbly with spines.
K. pictus var. *maximowiczii* (Van Houtte) Li comes from Japan and has often been confused in gardens and collections with the type species. It has more deeply lobed leaves (p44).

Pride of India or Goldenrain Tree

Koelreuteria paniculata Laxm., family Sapindaceae
A deciduous tree, native to China, Korea and Japan, cultivated for ornament in large gardens and collections. Height to 9–18m (30–60ft). Flowers (near right) open in August in a cluster which may reach 30cm (1ft) long, each flower about 1·2cm (½in). Fruit (far right) is even more spectacular, each red pod about 3·7–5cm (1½–2in) long containing 3 black seeds. Leaves (p57) have 9–15 leaflets and turn yellow in the autumn, a fine complement to the red fruits.

Adam's Laburnum

+*Laburnocytisus adamii* (Poiteau) Schneid., family Leguminosae
A fascinating tree, originally produced by grafting Dwarf Purple Broom (*Cytisus purpureus*), onto the Common Laburnum (*Laburnum anagyroides*) forming a hybrid, or chimaera, at the graft junction. Flowers of a hybrid, yellow-purple type are produced along with flowers of both parent trees (left). The purple broom flowers occur on sprouts of broom type foliage. Height to about 7·5m (25ft), grown for its curiosity value in collections and gardens, but a rather unattractive straggly tree when not in flower. Leaves are shown p50.

Laburnum family Leguminosae
Small group of deciduous trees. Leaves have 3 leaflets and pea-type flowers are in large bunches. Fruit is a pod containing poisonous seeds, which have been known to prove fatal. The wood can be used as a substitute for ebony in furniture making.

Scotch Laburnum

Laburnum alpinum (Mill.) Bercht. & Presl
A small tree, originally from the Alps, Yugoslavia and Czechoslovakia, long cultivated in Europe, including Britain. Height to about 6m (20ft). Flowers (near right) open in June and are in larger, denser flowerheads than Common Laburnum (*L. anagyroides*). Each flower is about 1·8cm (¾in) long with hairless stalks. Seed pods are about 5–7·5cm (2–3in) long. Leaves (p50) are less downy than Common Laburnum.

Common Laburnum or Golden Chain

Laburnum anagyroides Med.
Native to central and southern Europe, widely cultivated for ornament throughout Europe, and naturalised in some places. Height to 6–9m (20–30ft). Flowers (above right) open in May, each about 2·5cm (1in). Seed pods (near right) are 5–7·5cm (2–3in) and similar to those of Scotch Laburnum (*L. alpinum*) but with a thickened edge. Leaves (p50) are rather downy on undersides.

Voss's Laburnum

Laburnum × *watereri* (Wettst.) Dipp. cv. 'Vossii'
A hybrid between Common and Scotch Laburnum, (*L. anagyroides* and *L. alpinum*). Blossom (far right) has large flowers 2·5cm (1in) in long dense heads and open in June. Foliage (p50) is thicker than Common Laburnum. Fruit is sparsely produced, only a few in each cluster.

Larix family Pinaceae, **Larch**
Deciduous conifers, with needle-like leaves in bunches. Male and female flowers separate on same tree. Fruit a woody cone, remaining on tree after seeds have been shed.

Common Larch or European Larch

Larix decidua Mill.
Native to mountains of central and southern Europe, cultivated in plantations and shelterbelts or as an ornamental in Europe and N. America. Height to 30–42m (100–140ft). Male and female flowers (far left) open in late March, early April; males turning yellow when pollen is shed; females about 1cm (2/5in) long curve round to sit pointing vertical and may be pale or nearly white. Cones (near left), ripen from green to brown in autumn: they may be long, about 4·5cm (1¾in) or short and oval, 1·5–3cm (3/5–1 1/5in) long, each scale slightly wavy. Foliage (p23) turns golden yellow in November before falling. Bark (p218) is grey or pinkish grey with vertical cracks and scaly ridges.

Dunkeld Larch

Larix × eurolepis A. Henry
A hybrid between European Larch (*L. decidua*) and Japanese Larch (*L. kaempferi*) first raised in Dunkeld, Scotland, at the end of the last century and now used as a forestry tree in plantations and shelterbelts. Characters may be variable, but always intermediate to the 2 parents. Height to about 30m (100ft). Flowers (far left) open in March; females about 1cm (2/5in) vary in colour from purple to cream tinged with red. Cones (near left) are long, about 3–4cm (1 1/5–1½in), like European Larch (*L. decidua*) and usually have scales turning outwards, though less dramatically than on Japanese Larch (*L. kaempferi*). Foliage (p23) consists of needles, dark green above with 2 grey bands beneath. Bark is dark blackish brown split into scales.

Dahurian Larch

Larix gmelinii (Rupr.) Kuzeneva
Native to Siberia, cultivated in botanical collections. Height to 30m (100ft) in the wild. Flowers (far left) open in early March; males greenish yellow becoming yellow when pollen is shed; females red and green, about 0·5–1cm (1/5–2/5in), ripening through the summer to a purple cone, which finally turns brown (near left) in October or November, opening to release seed. Cones are about 2·5cm (1in) long with glossy rounded scales turned slightly outwards. Foliage (p23) has needles flat on upper surface and slightly keeled underneath. Bark is dark reddish brown, broken into long scales.

Japanese Larch

Larix kaempferi (Lamb.) Carr.
Native to Japan, widely used as a forestry tree in western Britain. Height to 25–30m (80–100ft). Flowers (far left) open in March; males yellow when shedding pollen, females about 1cm (2/5in) red and greenish cream each scale showing both colours. Cones (near left) are distinctive, usually rather round, about 2·5cm (1in) across. The back-turned bracts give the appearance of a small rose. Foliage (p23) has leaves with dark green upper surface and 2 bands of grey on underside. Bark is dark reddish brown, cracked or broken into scales.

Tamarack, Hackmatack or American Larch

Larix laricina (Du Roi) K. Koch
Native to Alaska and Canada south to Pennsylvania, where its timber has been used for telegraph poles and railway sleepers. Cultivated in north-east N. America and occasionally in Europe as an ornamental tree. Height to 18–25m (60–80ft). Flowers (far left) open in March smaller than other larches; females dark red usually less than 1cm (2/5in), males yellow. Cones (near left) are also small, about 1·5cm (3/5in) long with smooth scales. Foliage (p23) turns golden in September and October. Bark is reddish brown and scaly.

Western Larch or West American Larch

Larix occidentalis Nutt.
Native to western N. America from British Columbia to northern Montana. Cultivated in eastern states of N. America and in Europe. An important forestry tree in British Columbia, producing a timber useful for construction, mine timbers and railway sleepers. It has an attractive figure when used for flooring and interior finish. Height to 30–60m (100–200ft). Flowers (far left) open in March, males yellow and females red and green, about 1·2cm (½in) long. Cones (near left) are about 2·5–3·7cm (1–1½in) long, with long thin bracts sticking out from scales before they open (top cone). After seed has been shed the scales turn backwards on themselves and the bracts fall away (2 lower cones). Foliage (p23) is made up of 3-sided pointed needles. They colour golden in September and October. Bark is dark grey-brown and scaly, reddish brown on old trees.

Tibetan Larch

Larix potaninii Batal.
Native to western China and Tibet, cultivated in botanical collections. Height to 18–21m (60–70ft). Flowers (far left) open in March, males emerging green (as in photograph) and turning yellow when pollen is shed; females are about 1·5cm (3/5in) long, pink and green. Cones (near left) are about 5cm (2in) long with shiny brown scales and long bracts pointing about 0·5cm (1/5in) out above them. Foliage (p23) is on rather stout shoots and needles are almost 4-sided with 2 bands of white on lower side. They have a strong distinctive smell when crushed. Bark is dark pinkish grey with scaly cracks.

Bay or Laurel

Laurus nobilis L., family Lauraceae
Evergreen tree or shrub, native to the Mediterranean. Long cultivated, its aromatic leaves being used as a herb in cooking all sorts of dishes. The ancient Romans made the leaves into wreaths to crown heroes and poets. Also makes a decorative tree for gardens and patios, commonly grown in tubs and placed at entrances to hotels, restaurants and houses. Height to 12–18m (40–60ft), though often low and bushy and trimmed like a hedge. Flowers are on separate trees, opening in June. Males and females are both about 0·5cm (1/5in) long, females shown near right, males with clusters of pollen shedding anthers. Fruit (far right) is about 1·2cm (½in) long and ripens to black. Leaves (p32) are dark green, almost leathery, and have a strong aroma when broken.

Liquidambar orientalis Mill., family Hamamelidaceae **Oriental Sweet Gum**
Deciduous tree, native to Asia Minor. Height to 30m (100ft) in the wild. Leaves (p44) are hairless and more rounded at lobe tips, and with deeper rounded teeth on main lobes than on *L. styraciflua*.

Sweet Gum

Liquidambar styraciflua L.
Deciduous tree, native to eastern United States and Central America. The timber is sometimes known as 'satin walnut'. Height to 45m (150ft) in the wild. Flowers (near right) open in May: males in round heads on a spike 5–7·5cm (2–3in) long; females solitary or in pairs about 1·2cm (½in) across. Fruits (far right) are about 2·5–3·7cm (1–1½in) across. Leaves (p44) are 5, sometimes 7 lobed, with fine toothed edges. The vein axils on the underside bear rust coloured tufts. Autumn colours are purple, deep red and orange (p188).

Libocedrus chilensis (D. Don) Endl.
see *Austrocedrus chilensis* (p88).

Libocedrus decurrens Torr.
see *Calocedrus decurrens* (p92).

Tree Privet or Glossy Privet

Ligustrum lucidum Ait. f., family Oleaceae
An evergreen tree, or shrub, native to China and making a fine ornamental or shade tree in Europe especially in cities. Height to about 15m (50ft) as a tree, less than half that as a shrub. Flowers (far left) open in late August and September, when few other trees are flowering. Fruit ripens to black oval berries about 1·2cm (½in) long. Leaves (p32) are also noteworthy, being dark green and very glossy on upper surface. Bark (near left) is dark grey and smooth with light streaks.

Liriodendron chinense (Hemsl.) Sarg., family Magnoliaceae **Chinese Tulip Tree**
Deciduous tree, native to China. Similar to *L. tulipifera*, but generally smaller, with leaves (p43) narrower in the middle. Pale orange flowers open in July about 6cm (2¼in) across.

Tulip Tree or Whitewood

Liriodendron tulipifera L.
Deciduous tree, native to eastern N. America, cultivated as an ornamental in eastern states and west and north Europe. The timber, called 'white wood' is used in N. America for house interiors, and a heart stimulant has been extracted from the bark. Height to 45–58m (150–190ft) in the wild. Flowers (far left) open in June and July, each petal about 3·7cm (1½in) long. Fruit (near left) is about 5cm (2in) long, ripening from green to brown in September. Leaves (p43) have 4 lobes and turn orange and yellow in autumn (near left and p188).

Tanbark Oak

Lithocarpus densiflorus (Hook. & Arn.) Rehd., family Fagaceae
Evergreen tree, native to California and Oregon, where its bark is used in tanning leather. Height to 21m (70ft), sometimes twice as much. Flowering is irregular, occurring in April or May and again in September. Male flowers (near right) are in catkins 7·5–10cm (3–4in) long. A few females are usually produced below the male catkins and develop into acorns about 1·5–2·5cm (3/5–1in) in 2 years (far right). One year old acorns are shown with flowers near right. Leaves (p26) have 12–14 pairs of parallel veins and are covered with thick pale orange wool when young, becoming smooth and glossy with age. Young shoots are also covered with this down. Bark is thick, broken into scaly ridges.

Osage Orange

Maclura pomifera (Raf.) Schneid., family Moraceae
Deciduous tree, native to south and central United States, Arkansas and Oklahoma south to Texas. The bark has been used in tanning leather, but also yields a yellow dye, and the Osage Indians used the wood to make weapons. Cultivated as hedging around the Mississippi, and as an ornamental in eastern states and sometimes in Europe. Height to 12m (40ft). Male and female flowers are on separate trees. They open in June, males (far left) about 1·5–2·5cm (3/5–1in) across, females with shorter stalk but about the same size and green. Fruit (near left) is large, about 7·5–12·5cm (3–5in) across and very heavy, ripening yellow and falling in November. When broken it exudes a white milky sap. Leaves are shown on p35.

Magnolia family Magnoliaceae
Deciduous and evergreen trees and shrubs, with large showy flowers containing both male and female parts. Leaves are simple, untoothed and alternate. Most have strongly aromatic barks. Named in honour of Pierre Magnol, a professor of botany and medicine at Montpelier in late 17th century.

Cucumber Tree

Magnolia acuminata L.
Deciduous forest tree, native to eastern N. America. Cultivated in eastern states and in Europe as an ornamental. Height to 18–27m (60–90ft). Flowers open in May (near right, not fully open) with erect petals about 5–7·5cm (2–3in) long. Fruits (far right) are usually about 7·5cm (3in) long, and when young and green look something like a cucumber, giving this tree its common name. Leaves are shown p28.

Campbell's Magnolia

Magnolia campbellii Hook. f. & Thoms.
Deciduous tree, native to Himalaya, much cultivated for its wonderful flowers. Height to about 18m (60ft) though may be twice as much in the wild; often with several trunks. Flowers (near right) open in February and March, may be 25cm (10in), varying from deep to pale pink or white. Fruits are about 20cm (8in) long. Leaves shown p28.

Yellow Cucumber Tree

Magnolia cordata Michx.
Small deciduous tree or shrub, native to south-east United States. Height to about 6m (20ft). Flowers (far right) are also smaller, petals about 3·7cm (1½in) long. Fruit is about 2·5–3·7cm (1–1½in) long, red and often curved. Leaves (p32) are rounder than most magnolias and slightly heart-shaped at the base.

Yulan

Magnolia denudata Desrouss.
Deciduous tree, native to China, long cultivated there as an ornamental, especially near temples. Height to 9–14cm (30–45ft). Hairy winter buds open in March to produce clear white flowers (near right) which usually have 9 petals about 6cm (3in) long. Fruit is tapered, about 11cm (5in) long, leaves about 8–15cm (3–6in) long narrowing sharply to a point at the tip.

Fraser Magnolia or Ear-leaved Umbrella Tree

Magnolia fraseri Walt.
Deciduous tree, native to south-east United States. Height to 9–12m (30–40ft). Strong-smelling flowers (far right) open in May and June, petals about 7·5–10cm (3–4in) long. Fruit is red, about 10–12·5cm (4–5in) releasing scarlet seeds. Leaves (p28) are a distinctive shape.

Evergreen Magnolia, Southern Magnolia or Bull Bay

Magnolia grandiflora L.
Evergreen, native to southern United States. Height to 18–30m (60–100ft) in the wild. Fragrant flowers (near right), open in July through to September in northern Europe, but usually earlier in N. America. They are about 20–25cm (8–10in) across when fully open. Fruit is orange-green, cylindrical 5cm (2in) long. Leaves (p27) are glossy green above, with thick orange down on underside.

Japanese Big-leaved Magnolia

Magnolia hypoleuca Sieb. & Zucc., synonym *M. obovata* Thunb.
Deciduous tree, native to Japan. Height to 15–25m (50–80ft) or more. Strong-smelling flowers (far right) open in June, 20cm (8in) across. Fruit is red, 12·5–20cm (5–8in) long. Leaves (p28) are rather wider than most magnolias and tend to be clustered at tips of shoots.

Northern Japanese Magnolia

Magnolia kobus DC.
Deciduous tree, native to Japan. Height 9–12m (30–40ft). Flowers (near right) are about 10cm (4in) across and have a downy covering when in bud. They open in April. Fruits are pink, about 5cm (2in) long, splitting all over to release bright red seeds which dangle by threads before dropping. Leaves are shown p27.

Magnolia × loebneri Kache cv. 'Leonard Messel'
A cultivated hybrid believed to be between *M. kobus* and a pink form of the shrubby *M. stellata*. Flowers (far right) are produced in great profusion in April, 12 narrow petals about 5cm (2in) long, pale pink on outside. Leaves are shown p32.

Willow-leaved Magnolia

Magnolia salicifolia (Sieb. & Zucc.) Maxim.
Deciduous tree, native to Japan. Height to 6–12m (20–40ft). Flowers (near right) open in March, about 7·5–10cm (3–4in) across. The flower bud is hairy. Fruits are 5–7·5cm (2–3in) long, pink, with scarlet seeds. Leaves are shown p24. Bark has a sweet lemony scent when bruised.

Magnolia × soulangiana Soulange-Bodin
A hybrid between Yulan (*M. denudata*) and a shrubby magnolia (*M. liliflora*). Popular in all sizes of garden in Europe. May eventually form a small tree, to about 7·5m (25ft) tall. Flowers (far right) open late April, each petal about 7·5–10cm (3–4in) long. Many cultivars have been produced and all have white petals stained purple-pink, deepest at the base on outer side. A leaf is shown on p27.

Umbrella Tree

Magnolia tripetala L.
Deciduous tree, native to eastern N. America. Cultivated as an ornamental in northern states and in Europe. Height to 9–12m (30–40ft). Flowers (near right) have a strong scent and open in May and June, outer petals about 10–12·5cm (4–5in) long. Fruit (far right) is about 10cm (4in) long. Seeds are scarlet. Leaves (p28) are large and distinguished by their tapering bases. They grow in umbrella-like clusters, giving the tree its common name.

Magnolia × veitchii Bean
A deciduous hybrid between *M. campbellii* and the Yulan (*M. denudata*), first raised early this century by Peter Veitch of the Royal Nurseries, Exeter. It has so far attained a height of around 28m (85ft). Flowers open in April, about 15cm (6in) long and are pale pink, although white flowered clones have also been raised. Leaves (p28) are purplish when young becoming dark green in the summer.

Sweet Bay

Magnolia virginiana L.
Native to eastern United States, evergreen in the southern part of its range, deciduous in the north. In Britain it may retain some leaves in the winter or be deciduous. Height to 9m (30ft). Fragrant flowers (near right) are produced from June to September, about 5–7·5cm (2–3in) wide. Fruits are red about 5cm (2in) long, with scarlet seeds. Leaves (p35) are smaller than most magnolias.

Wilson's Magnolia

Magnolia wilsonii
(Fin. & Gagnep.) Rehd.
Deciduous tree, or shrub, native to China. Height to 7·5m (25ft). Flowers (far right) are fragrant, about 7·5–10cm (3–4in) across. They open in May and June from the underside of branches and so point downwards. Fruit is pink, about 5–7·5cm (2–3in) long, ripening to release shiny red seeds in September. Leaf (p27) has a velvety underside.

Malus family Rosaceae, **Apple** or **Crab**
Deciduous trees, with simple toothed leaves. Flowers are in clusters, varying from white to deep rose pink. Fruit is fleshy and may be round or oval. Many cultivated forms grown for either blossom or fruit.

Siberian Crab

Malus baccata (L.) Borkh.
Native to a large area from east Siberia to Manchuria and north China. Height to 6–15m (20–50ft). Flowers (far left) open in April, each about 3·7cm (1½in) across. They are easily distinguished by rather narrow widely spaced petals. Fruits (near left) are about 1–2cm (2/5–4/5in) across, may be yellow, and persist on the tree during winter. Leaves (p37) are rather slender.

Sweet Crab Apple or Garland Tree

Malus coronaria (L.) Mill.
Small tree, native to eastern N. America, often grown in gardens as it makes a charming ornamental. Height to 6–9m (20–30ft). Flowers (far left) open in May and June, with a beautiful sweet fragrance, each about 2·5–5cm (1–2in) across in clusters of 4–6. Fruits (near left) are about 2·5–3·7cm (1–1½in) across ripening in October, but not palatable, being rather acid. Leaves (p37) may be almost 3-lobed and turn yellow in the autumn.
M. coronaria cv. 'Charlottae' is a cultivated variety with double, pink tinted flowers and leaves colouring well in autumn.

Hawthorn-leaved Crab Apple

Malus florentina (Zucc.) Schneid.
Small tree or bush, native to north Italy, bearing some resemblance to a common hawthorn (*Crataegus monogyna*). Flowers (far left) are about 1·8cm (¾in) across, 5–7 in a cluster and open in June. Fruit (near left) are oval, about 1·2cm (½in) long, ripening from yellow to red in October. Leaves (p47) are dark green above, and covered with white down underneath.

Japanese Crab

Malus floribunda Sieb. ex Van Houtte
A Japanese tree, probably a hybrid rather than wild, now widely planted in Europe in gardens, parks and streets, as it flowers profusely every year. Height to about 6–9m (20–30ft). Flowers (far left) open in late April and early May, each about 2·5–3cm (1–1¼in) wide in clusters of 4–7. Fruits (near left) are about 2cm (¾in) in diameter, ripening yellow in October. Leaves are usually more toothed than is shown on p37, and may occasionally be lobed.

Oregon Crab

Malus fusca (Raf.) Schneid.
Native to western N. America, sometimes cultivated in eastern states and in Europe. The wood has been used in western America for making tools, tool handles and suchlike, as it is hard and heavy. Height to about 6–12m (20–40ft). Flowers (far left) are about 1·8cm (¾in) across and open in clusters of 6–12 in May. Fruits (near left) are oval, 1·2–2cm (½–¾in) and may be red or yellow. They have a pleasant sharp flavour. Leaves (p37) colour bright red and orange in the autumn.

Hupeh Crab

Malus hupehensis (Pampan.) Rehd.
Native from Himalaya to central and western China, where a tisane called red tea is made from the leaves. Cultivated in European gardens for its spring blossom. Height to as much as 12m (40ft) which is tall for a crab. Fragrant flowers (far left) open in April, each about 2·5–3·7cm (1–1½in) wide in clusters of 3–7. Fruits (near left) are about 0·8cm (⅓in) across, ripening to red from yellow and orange in September. Leaves are oval, and pointed, about 5–10cm (2–4in), usually rounded at the base, dark green above, and downy beneath. They may be purple tinged when young. Bark is dark grey-brown and breaks into flakes when older.

Prairie Crab Apple

Malus ioensis (Wood) Britt.
Native to central United States, similar to Sweet Crab Apple (*M. coronaria*). Height to 9m (30ft). Flowers (far left) are 3·7–5cm (1½–2in) across, 4–6 in a cluster and open in June. Fruits are yellow, green and round, about 3·7cm (1½in) across: similar to *M. coronaria* fruit but with duller surface. Leaves (p37) and branchlets are more downy.
M. ioensis cv. 'Plena', **Bechtel Crab**, has large double flowers about 5–6·2cm (2–2½in) and is much planted in American gardens.

Magdeburg Crab

Malus 'Magdeburgensis'
A hybrid between Chinese Crab (*M. spectabilis*) and the French Paradise Apple (*M. pumila*). Flowers (near left) open in late April and May, about 2·5cm (1in) across. Leaves are shown on p37.

Purple Crab

Malus × purpurea (Barbier) Rehd.
A cultivated hybrid, first raised in France, taking its bright red colours from one of the parents which itself does not grow well in cultivation nor flowers reliably. Height to 7·5m (25ft). Flowers (far left) are about 4cm (1 3/5in) across, in clusters of 6–11, opening in April. Fruits (near left) are about 2cm (4/5in) ripening from red to purple. Leaves (p37) are purple-red through summer, fading to purple tinted green at fruiting time (see photographs left). There are many other purple hybrids, one being *Malus* 'Profusion' which is considered by many to be a better tree in Europe than Purple Crab. Flowers are abundant and dark crimson, but turn pale pink quickly. Leaves are larger, about 7·5cm (3in) long.

Chinese Crab

Malus spectabilis (Ait.) Borkh.
A decorative tree from China where it was found in cultivation, but not in the wild. Height to 9m (30ft). Flowers (far left) are usually profuse, opening in late April and May; each is about 5cm (2in) across when fully open, 6–8 in a cluster. Fruit is round, yellow, about 2·5cm (1in) across. Leaves are oval or almost round, about 5–7·5cm (2–3in) long, round at base, and pointed at the tip. Bark (near left) is dark brown with fine ridges, often spiralled, and breaking into scales.

Crab Apple or Wild Crab

Malus sylvestris (L.) Mill.
Native of Europe, including Britain, found in hedgerows and thickets. Rarely cultivated but undoubtedly a parent of orchard apples. Height to 9m (30ft). Flowers (far left) are about 2·5–3·7cm (1–1½in) wide opening in late May. Fruits (near left) are about 2·5cm (1in) across and ripen in September or October when they may be flushed orange red. They are rather sour and bitter but make delicious conserves, especially mixed with other fruits. Leaves (p37) usually have a partly red stalk, and some branches may bear thorns. Bark is brown and broken into square flakes.

Medlar

Mespilus germanica L., family Rosaceae
A deciduous tree or shrub, native to south-east Europe and west Asia, cultivated throughout Europe for its fruits which are made into a conserve, but are edible raw only when left to turn half rotten. It has become naturalised in parts of Britain and north Europe. Height to about 6m (20ft). Flowers (near right) are similar to a hawthorn (*Crataegus*) flower but are solitary and larger, about 2·5–3·7cm (1–1½in) across. They open in late May and early June. Fruits (far right) are also distinctive, about 2·5cm (1in) across, with a large 'open' end. Leaves (p26) are downy, and old trees may bear hard thorns, about 1·2–2·5cm (½–1in) long.

Dawn Redwood

Metasequoia glyptostroboides
Hu & Cheng, family Taxodiaceae
A deciduous conifer, native to China, of great interest to botanists as it is the only living member of a genus, which before 1944 was only described from fossils. It was discovered by Chinese scientists in 1941 and seeds were sent a few years later to the Arnold Arboretum from where it was distributed through N. America and Europe. Grows to about 35m (115ft) in the wild. Male flowers have not yet been seen in Britain, females (far left) are about 0·6cm (⅓in) long, produced when leaves first emerge. Cones (near left) are about 1·8–2·5cm (¾–1in) long, ripening in their first year to dark brown. Leaves (p13) are similar to *Taxodium distichum* but branchlets and leaves are in opposite pairs. They turn beautiful reddish brown in autumn before falling. Bark is dark grey, cracked and peeling.

White Mulberry

Morus alba L., family Moraceae
Deciduous tree, native to China but long cultivated in other eastern countries and south Europe as the food plant of the silkworm. Height to about 9m (30ft). Flowers (near right) are in separate catkins, males in longer spikes than females, which are about 1·2cm (½in) long. Fruits (far right) are about 1·2–2·5cm (½–1in) long, usually white or pink, sometimes dark purple. Leaves (p39) are shinier and less downy than the common mulberry.

Common Mulberry or Black Mulberry

Morus nigra L.
A deciduous tree, probably native to the Far East, but has been cultivated in Europe and Asia for so long that its origins are obscure. The fruit has an unusual flavour, and some people love to eat it raw, but often used in jam and wine making. Often a crooked tree, to about 9m (30ft), occasionally low and domed. Male and female flowers are in separate catkins, females (near right) are about 1·2cm (½in) long, males about twice that length. Fruit (far right) grow to as much as 2·5cm (1in) long. Leaves (p39) may be unevenly lobed or simple but always heart-shaped at the base. They are covered with short rough hairs above and downy below.

Nothofagus family Fagaceae, **Southern Beech**
Evergreen and deciduous trees which represent the beech family in the southern hemisphere. Male and female flowers are in separate clusters, males 1–3 together, females usually in 3s. Fruits are like miniature beech nuts.

Antarctic Beech or Nirre

Nothofagus antarctica (Forst. f.) Oerst.
Deciduous tree, native to southern Chile, where it may reach 15m (50ft) in height, but often low and straggly on exposed mountain sites. Flowers (far left) open in April and May; males in profusion about 0·4cm (1/6 in) long, the females just visible in the photograph as a tiny nut shape with a red tassel. Fruit (near left) with 3 nutlets, about 0·6cm (¼in) long. Leaves are shown p29. Bark is dark brown with deep cracks forming thick flaking plates.

Dombey's Southern Beech or Coigüe

Nothofagus dombeyi (Mirbel) Blume
Evergreen tree, native to Chile and Argentina. Height to 25m (80ft), or more in the wild. Flowers open in late May, males (far left) have red anthers and are about 0·4cm (1/6in) long. Females are tiny, similar to those of Antarctic Beech. Fruit (near left) is about 0·6cm (¼in) long, splitting to release seed in October. Leaves (p29) are glossy green and covered with minute dark spots (see fruit photograph). Bark is dark greyish brown with broad shallow cracks, and eventually peels in strips to expose orange underneath.

Roblé Beech

Nothofagus obliqua (Mirbel) Blume
Deciduous tree, native to Chile and western Argentina, where it once formed extensive natural forests and is still an important timber tree. Its wood being similar to that of oak, the Spanish gave it their name for oak, Roblé. Height to 30m (100ft) in the wild. Flowers (far left) open in May; males are single with as many as 30–40 stamens; females are tiny green and nut-shaped. Fruits (near left) are about 1cm (2/5in) long, opening in September to release the nutlets. Leaves (p29) usually have 8 or 9 pairs of veins. Bark (p218) on mature trees is brown and broken into small rectangular curved flakes.

Raoul or Rauli

Nothofagus procera (Poepp. & Endl.) Oerst.
Deciduous tree, native to the Andes in Chile, and in Argentina near the Chilean border, where it is one of the most important timber trees. Its use in forestry is being extended to Britain where it apparently has great potential. Its wood is superior to the Roblé Beech (*N. obliqua*) and it has a fast growth rate. Height to 25m (80ft) and more. Flowers (far left) open in May; males about 0·6cm (¼in) long, females tiny green and nut-shaped in leaf axils towards the ends of shoots. Fruits (near left) are about 1cm (2/5in) long, breaking open in September to release seeds. Leaves (p29) have more pairs of veins than *N. obliqua*, usually 14–18 pairs. Bark is smooth, greyish-brown with vertical wide dark cracks.

Tupelo, Black Gum or Pepperidge

Nyssa sylvatica Marsh., family Nyssaceae
A deciduous tree, native to eastern N. America where it grows in swamps or damp ground. Cultivated as an ornamental in eastern states and in Europe. Height to 30m (100ft) in the wild, with a tapering trunk. Male and female flowers (near right) are produced in June on separate trees: both in round heads about 1·2cm (½in) across, but females have only a few flowers to the cluster. Fruits (far right) are about 1·2cm (½in) long, and ripen to dark bluish-black in October. Leaves (p35) are usually long and tapered at both ends. They colour brilliant orange and red in the autumn (p77). In the United States it is one of the earliest trees to display autumn foliage.

Ostrya family Carpinaceae, **Hop Hornbeam**
A small group of deciduous trees, similar in many ways to the hornbeams (*Carpinus*), but distinguished mostly by the fruits: each nutlet is completely enclosed by a bladder-like, thin papery husk.

European Hop Hornbeam

Ostrya carpinifolia Scop.
Native to southern Europe, Asia Minor and the Caucasus. Grows to 15–18m (50–60ft) tall, the crown becoming rounded with age. Flowers (far left) open in April, male catkins about 3·7–7·5cm (1½–3in) long, the females rather small and green, opening among the emerging leaves. Fruit clusters (near left) are about 3·7–5cm (1½–2in) long, turning light brown in September and October. They look very much like hops, hence the English name. Leaves (p33) have 12–15 pairs of veins and are rather hairy on the upper surface, less so underneath.

Eastern Hop Hornbeam or Ironwood

Ostrya virginiana (Mill.) K. Koch
Native to eastern N. America, where it yields a very hard timber used for making mallets and fence posts amongst other things. Sometimes cultivated for ornament in European gardens and collections. Height 9–18m (30–60ft). Flowers (far left) open in April, male catkins about 5cm (2in) long, females often red among the emerging leaves. Fruit clusters (near left) are about 3·7–5cm (1½–2in) long on hairy and longer stalks than *O. carpinifolia*. They turn light brown in autumn. Leaves (p33) are hairy on upper surface and more downy beneath with hairy stalks.

Sorrel Tree or Sour Wood

Oxydendrum arboreum (L.) DC., family Ericaceae
Deciduous tree, native to eastern N. America. Cultivated in parks and gardens, in eastern states, and in western Europe. The leaves are rather acid and have been used medicinally as a tonic and diuretic. Height to about 18m (60ft) in the wild, but often half this height or even shrubby in cultivation. Flowers (near right) open in August and September, each about 0·6cm (¼in) long in clusters which may be as much as 25cm (10in) long. The fruits are hard, woody bell-shaped capsules about 1·2cm (½in) long. Leaves (p27) are alternate, tapered and sometimes hairy on the mid vein and stalk. They colour bright red in the autumn (far right).

Persian Ironwood or Iron Tree

Parrotia persica (DC.) C. A. Mey., family Hamamelidaceae
Deciduous tree or shrub, native to the area to the south and south-west of the Caspian Sea, from north Persia to the Caucasus. Both in the wild and in gardens it can be very shrubby, forming dense thickets, but may be found as a tree to about 12m (40ft) tall. Flowers (far left) open in February and March before the leaves emerge; the clusters are about 1·2cm (½in) across, with bright red anthers. Fruit is like a small brown nut about 1·2cm (½in) in a cluster of 3–5. Leaves (p32) colour brilliant reds, orange and yellow (near left). Bark (p218) is smooth and grey, breaking off in flakes, to expose light green patches.

Foxglove-tree

Paulownia tomentosa (Thunb.) Steud., family Scrophulariaceae
Deciduous tree, native to China, cultivated in Japan, roadsides in south Europe, and in gardens throughout Europe, but does not do well in colder parts as the flowerbuds are produced in autumn and lie waiting through the winter. Height to 12m (40ft). Flowers (near right) open in May, each about 5cm (2in) long, in large upright clusters. Fruit (far right) is up to about 5cm (2in) long, drying up, and splitting to release lots of winged seeds. Leaves (p42) are variable, smaller ones unlobed, and larger ones with 3 or 5 shallow lobes. They have silky hairs on top surface and grey down on lower surface.

Amur Cork-tree

Phellodendron amurense Rupr., family Rutaceae
Deciduous tree, native to China, including the Amur region. Height to about 15m (50ft). Flowers open in July, male and female on separate trees, similar to *P. japonicum* flowers, about 0·6cm (¼in) long, in erect clusters about 7·5cm (3in) tall. Fruits (far left) are about 1·2cm (½in) across. Leaves (p55) have 5–11 leaflets, which are hairless except around the edge and at the base of the main vein.

Phellodendron japonicum Maxim.
Deciduous tree, native to Japan and growing to about 9m (30ft). Flowers open in July, male clusters (near left) about 10cm (4in) long. Females, on separate tree, are in a more slender cluster. Fruits are black, about 1·2cm (½in) across. Leaves have broader leaflets which are very downy on the underside.

Picea family Pinaceae, **Spruce**
Evergreen coniferous trees, with needle-like leaves arranged singly and spirally around the shoot. Bare shoots bear tiny peg-like projections where the leaves were once attached. Male and female flowers are on the same tree. Fruit are hanging woody cones.

Norway Spruce

Picea abies (L.) Karsten
Native to mountains from Scandinavia to north-west Russia and in central Europe, grown throughout northern and central Europe and in eastern United States. The timber, known as white wood, or deal, has many uses, including roofing, house interiors and paper pulp. Turpentine is extracted from the stem and the bark is still used for tanning in Germany, but Norway Spruce is perhaps best known in Britain as the Christmas tree. Height to about 36m (120ft) but may be larger. Flowers (near right) open in May, males are about 1cm (2/5in) long, clustered at shoot tips. They turn yellow when shedding pollen. Females are erect, pink turning green at the end of May, turning downwards as the cone ripens. Cone (far right) ripens from green to shiny brown in the autumn, 12·5–15cm (5–6in) long. Foliage (p17) has hard pointed needles and dark brown round buds. Bark is reddish brown flaking into thin scales, but on very old trees is darker and broken into plates.

Dragon Spruce

Picea asperata Mast.
Native to western China, cultivated in collections and large gardens. Height to about 30m (100ft) in the wild, but rather less has been attained in cultivation. Flowers (near right) open in April, each about 2cm (5in) long, males pink turning yellow when shedding pollen, females dark crimson. Cones (far right) are about 7·5–12·5cm (3–5in) long, with round scales. Foliage (p17) is rather blue, needles more dense on upper part of the shoot, with lower needles bending round to point upwards. Bark is dark brown, flaking into lighter brown papery scales.

Sargent Spruce

Picea brachytyla (Franch.) Pritz.
Native to central and western China, cultivated in botanical collections and large gardens. Height up to about 25m (80ft), though often much less. Flowers (near right) open in late May, males about 1·5cm (3/5in) long, turning yellow, females slightly larger at shoot tip. Cones (far right) are about 6·2–7·5cm (2½–5in) long. Foliage (p17) is dinstinctive since needles are flattened, rather than 4-sided as in most spruces, and are arranged only on sides and upper parts of the twigs. They are bright glossy green above and white beneath. Bark is smooth, grey and covered with white spots of resin.

Brewer's Weeping Spruce

Picea breweriana S. Wats.
Native to a small part of California and Oregon at altitudes up to 2,000m (7,000ft). Its decorative curtains of hanging branchlets make this a graceful ornamental for gardens. Height to 36m (120ft) in the wild, but usually much less. Flowers (near right) open in May; males rather round, about 1·5cm (3/5in) long, females erect about 2·5cm (1in) long, usually dark pink (but shown pinkish green) developing into a purple cone, about 7·5cm (3in) long, with round scales, ripening to brown in autumn (far right). Foliage (p17) is made up of needles pointing forwards all round the twigs. Bark is dark pinkish grey, with round peeling plates.

Blue Engelmann Spruce

Picea engelmannii (Parry) Englem.
forma *glauca* Beissn.
The blue form of the Engelmann Spruce, native to the mountains of western N. America. Height to about 30m (100ft). Flowers open in May, males are dark purple (not shown) and females (near right) are reddish purple, about 3cm (1 1/5in) long. Cones (far right) are about 5–7·5cm (2–3in) long and differ from the White Spruce (*P. glauca*) in having slightly toothed scales. Foliage (p17) is also distinctive, as the needles point forwards and are soft to the touch with spiney tips, and have a smell of camphor when crushed. Bark is orange, and flakes into papery scales.

White Spruce

Picea glauca (Moench) Voss
Native across the northern regions of N. America, often planted in Canada, New England and northern Europe as an ornamental. Height to about 21m (70ft). Flowers (near right) open in April, males about 2·5cm (1in) long when shedding pollen, females about the same, developing into a cone (far right) about 3·7–5cm (1½–2in) long with rounded scales. Foliage (p17) is made up of rather blue 4-sided needles which are denser on top of the shoot and point forwards. They are hard but do not have a spined tip, and when crushed produce a strong unpleasant smell. Bark is purplish-grey, and breaks into rounded flakes.

Hondo Spruce

Picea jezoensis (Seib. & Zucc.) Carr. var. *hondoensis* (Mayr) Rehd.
Native to Japan, grown in collections and large gardens. A variety of a species which is widely distributed through north-east Asia. Height to 28m (90ft) in the wild. Flowers (near right) open in May, males are about 2·5cm (1in) long when shedding pollen, females a bit larger (shown right on leading shoot). Cones (far right) are about 5cm (2in) long with toothed, inward-curved scales. Needles (p17) are spine tipped, with 2 white bands underneath and point upwards and forwards, attached on top and sides of shoots. Bark is smooth brown, or paler and greyish, cracked and plated.

Koyama's Spruce

Picea koyamai Shirasawa
Native to central Japan at altitudes between 1,500–1,800m (5,000–6,000ft) and also Korea. Height to about 18m (60ft). Flowers (near right) open in May, males about 2·5cm (1in) long, females dark purple and slightly longer. Cones (far right) are about 10cm (4in) long with scales rounded and slightly wavy. When dry, they expand to half their length. Needles (p17) are very sharp at the tip, 4-sided and rather blue. They radiate all round the twig but lower ones curve and point upwards, upper ones point forward. Bark may be dark brown or light purplish grey, with grey flakes breaking away.

Likiang Spruce

Picea likiangensis (Franch.) Pritz.
Native to a large area of western China and Tibet, first discovered in the Lichiang mountains in Yunnan province. Grown as an ornamental in botanical collections and gardens. Height to 45m (150ft) in the wild. Flowers (near right) open all over the tree in April. Cones (far right) are usually about 5cm (2in) long, with round but wavy scales. Foliage (p17) may be rather variable in colour, from green to blue-green; needles are 4-sided and upper ones point forwards. Bark is light grey and rough, with some long dark cracks.

Black Spruce

Picea mariana (Mill.) Britt., Sterns and Pogg.
Native across northern regions of N. America south to Wisconsin and Virginia. Sometimes cultivated but short-lived. Its timber has been used locally in Canada, but is of no great value, and spruce-beer is made from its leaves. Height to about 9m (30ft) but may be found three times as high. It takes a columnar form in Canada but rather pyramidal when cultivated (both silhouettes are shown). Flowers (near right) open in May in great profusion, male and female both about 2cm (4/5in) long. Cones (far right) are 2·5–5cm (1–2in) long with rounded or slightly toothed scales, and may persist on the tree for many years. Foliage (p17) consists of needles pointed at the tip, but not sharply. They are 4-sided, with a blue-grey band on each face. Bark is pinkish or purplish-grey and flaky.

Siberian Spruce

Picea obovata Ledeb.
A spruce similar to Norway Spruce (*P. abies*) from north Europe right across north Russia. Height may reach 30m (100ft) in the wild but is often less in cultivation. Flowers (near right) and fruit (far right) are similar to *P. abies*, opening in May, but cones are usually smaller, about 7·5cm (3in) long. Foliage (p18) is distinguished by a single needle pointing out below the buds at a different angle to all the others.

Serbian Spruce

Picea omorika (Pančić) Purkyně
Native to a small part of Yugoslavia, of interest because it was once widely distributed through Europe before the Ice Age. Now cultivated in parks and gardens in Britain, and occasionally in north Europe for timber. Height may reach 30m (100ft). Flowers (near right) open in May, males about 1·2cm (½in) long, expanding to shed pollen, females slightly larger. Cones (far right) are about 2·5–5cm (1–2in) long with broad, rounded scales. Foliage (p18) is distinctive as the needles are flattened rather than 4-sided, with 2 white bands underneath. Bark is reddish-brown breaking into plates and papery flakes.

Oriental Spruce or Caucasian Spruce

Picea orientalis (L.) Link
Native to the Caucasus and Asia Minor, grown for ornament in Europe and eastern states of N. America and sometimes for timber in Belgium, Italy and Austria. Height to about 30m (100ft). Flowers (near right) open in late April, males about 1·2cm (½in) long, females twice as long and slender greenish purple or violet. Cones (far right) are about 5–9cm (2–3½in) long, ripening to shiny brown. Foliage (p18) is easily recognised as the needles are much shorter than on any other spruce, about 0·5–1cm (1/5–2/5in). Bark is pinkish brown, breaking into small rounded flakes.

Tiger-tail Spruce

Picea polita (Sieb. & Zucc.) Carr.
Native to Japan, cultivated in Europe and eastern N. America for ornament. Height to over 30m (100ft), but may be rather smaller in cultivation. Flowers (near right) open in May, males about 2cm (4/5in) long, females larger, about 2·5cm (1in). Cones (far right) are usually about 10cm (4in) long and ripen to dark brown, the scales rounded with a pale edge. Needles (p18) are 4-sided, hard and sharply pointed. Bark is pinkish-brown with large rough plates.

Colorado Spruce

Picea pungens Engelm.
Native to the Rocky Mountains in western N. America, particularly at the south end of the range. Grown for ornament and sometimes for timber in northern and central Europe. Height to about 30m (100ft) but may reach 45m (150ft) in favourable conditions. Flowers (near right) open in May, males about 2cm (4/5in) long, females twice that. Cones (far right) are a distinctive pale colour, with wavy toothed scales. They are about 7·5–10cm (3–4in) long. Needles (p18) are 4-sided with whitish-blue buds on each face. They are spine tipped when young, becoming blunter with age. Bark is purplish-grey, breaking into coarse plates.

Blue Spruce

Picea pungens Engelm. forma *glauca* (Reg.) Beissn.
The blue-leaved form of Colorado Spruce (*P. pungens*), perhaps more commonly grown in European parks, gardens and collections than the type. Flowers and cones (near and far right) are similar to Colorado Spruce. Foliage (p18) differs from Blue Engelmann Spruce (*P. engelmanni glauca*) in having harder spiney needles and leaf buds having scales curved outwards. Many named cultivars of this form are available for planting.

Red Spruce

Picea rubens Sarg.
A native of eastern N. America, where it was once used, along with its ally the Black Spruce (*P. mariana*), to make a spruce-beer. Its timber has been put to use for flooring and suchlike in north-eastern states of America, and also made into paperpulp. Height to about 25m (80ft) or more. Flowers (near right) open in May, male and female both about 2–3cm (¾–1¼in) long. Cones (far right) are up to 5cm (2in) long with rounded scales, very similar in size and shape to *P. mariana* but these fall from the tree as soon as they open, whereas *P. mariana* cones persist for many years. Needles (p18) are 4-sided with light bands on each face and a more yellow-green than those of *P. mariana*. Bark is dark purplish-brown, breaking into small curved plates.

Sitka Spruce

Picea sitchensis (Bongard) Carr.
An important timber tree, native to the coast of western N. America, now widely planted in western, northern and central Europe as a plantation tree, as its timber is quickly produced and of high quality. It thrives in areas of high rainfall, making it suitable for north-western Europe. Height to 50m (160ft) or more. Flowers (near right) open in May, males about 2·5–3·7cm (1–1½in) long, females a bit longer, usually red or pinkish green. Cones (far right) are distinctive with wavy edged scales, and feel soft when squeezed. They are about 5–10cm (2–4in) long, ripening from green to brown. Needles (p18) are 4-sided, and spined at the tip making foliage prickly. Upper needles lie flat pointing down the shoot. Bark (p218) is dark purplish grey or brown and breaks into coarse irregular plates which fall away.

Morinda Spruce or West Himalayan Spruce

Picea smithiana (Wall.) Boiss.
Native to west Himalaya, named after Sir James Smith who was the first president of the Linnean Society. Height to about 36m (120ft) but sometimes twice as much, with a weeping appearance, as *P. breweriana*, but less marked than in that species. Flowers (near right) open in early May, males about 2cm (4/5in) long; females longer. Cones (far right) may be 10–18cm (4–7in) long, ripening to shiny brown from light green. Scales become toothed as the cone dries. Needles (p18) are longer than other spruces, pointing outwards on all sides of the shoot. Bark is purplish-grey, and breaks into shallow, rounded plates.

Sikkim Spruce or East Himalayan Spruce

Picea spinulosa (Griff.) Henry
Native to eastern Himalaya, where it grows to more than 60m (200ft). In cultivation however it has not attained this height. Flowers (near right) open in May, males about 2·5cm (1in) long, females slightly longer. Cones (far right) are about 6–9cm (2¼–3½in) long, green with purple edges, ripening to brown. Needles (p18) are 2-sided, point forwards and have sharp points. Bark is light grey and breaks into round plates and shallow cracks.

Picea wilsonii Mast.
Native to China, cultivated elsewhere only in botanical collections and large gardens. Height to about 21m (70ft). Flowers (near right) open in May, males about 2cm (4/5in) long, females larger. Cones (far right) are about 3·7–7·5cm (1½–3in) long with rounded scales and may persist on the tree for several years. Needles (p18) are 4-sided, green on all faces, and are sharply pointed. Bark is pinkish-grey, breaking into thin flakes.

Pinus family Pinaceae, **Pine**
Evergreen coniferous trees and shrubs. Leaves are needle-like, long and slender in clusters of 2–5, rarely single or up to 8 together which when pressed together form a thin cylindrical shape. Male and female flowers are separate on the same tree, males clustered at base of new shoots, females at the tips. Fruit is a woody cone which usually takes 2 years to ripen.

Whitebark Pine

Pinus albicaulis Engelm.
A small tree, native to western N. America, at altitudes between 1,500–3,000m (5,000–10,000ft) forming a tree of about 15m (50ft) or a low shrub about 3m (10ft) in exposed sites. The edible sweet seeds were collected for food by American Indians. Flowers open in June, males red and clustered, females (near right) red, about 1·2cm (½in) long. Cones (far right) are about 3·7–7·5cm (1½–3in) with thick scales bearing sharp spines and ripening from purple to brown. They fall from the tree, eventually breaking up to release unwinged, edible seeds, about 1·2cm (½in) long. Needles (p21) are in bundles of 5, sometimes 6, or rarely 8, with pale lines on all surfaces, 5–6cm (2–2¼in) long. Leaf-buds are dark reddish-brown, with scales closely pressed. Bark of mature trees is rather white in appearance.

Bristle-cone Pine

Pinus aristata Engelm.
Native to mountains of Colorado, Arizona and New Mexico at altitudes above 2,500m (8,000ft). Height to about 15m (50ft), though may be smaller in exposed sites. Flowers open in June, males dark red, females (near right) red purple, about 0·6cm (¼in) long. Cones (far right) are about 7·5cm (3in) long and have distinctive long bristles on each scale. They also show white patches of resin which may be found all over the leaves and stem. Needles (p21) are in bundles of 5, rather short and stout, with paler inner surfaces. They all bunch together pointing forwards on the shoots to give the appearance of a bottle brush or a foxtail.

Picrasma

Picrasma quassioides (D. Don) Bennett, family Simaroubaceae
Deciduous tree, native to Japan, Korea, China and Himalaya. Very decorative but little cultivated in other areas. Height up to about 12m (40ft). Flowers (far left) open in June, each about 0·5cm (1/5in) across in a loose cluster. Fruits (near left) are about 1cm (2/5in) long, and ripen red in September or October. Leaves (p55) colour orange and scarlet in the autumn. They have 9–13 pairs of leaflets.

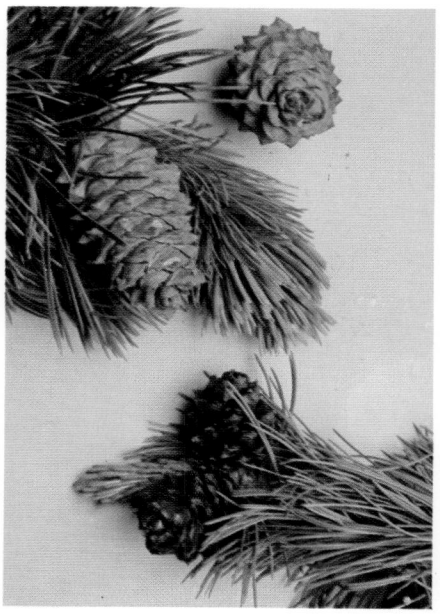

David's Pine

Pinus armandii Franch.
Named after the French missionary Père Armand David, a great naturalist, who discovered this pine in its native China. Also found in Burma and Formosa. Cultivated in botanical collections. Height to about 22·5m (75ft). Flowers (near right) open in June, males yellow and often sparse, female is reddish purple developing to cone (far right) about 7·5–15cm (3–6in) long, with thick scales and ripening from green to light brown. Foliage (p22) is made up of long needles in bunches of 5 which are often strongly bent or crinkled near the base. They are bright green on the outside with a pale band on inside. Twigs are often bare for much of their length and covered with drops of resin.

Knobcone Pine

Pinus attenuata Lemm.
Native to western N. America from Oregon through California. Height is usually around 9m (30ft) but may grow to 30m (100ft) in the wild. Flowers open in May, males orange brown in large clusters at the base of new shoots, females (near right, shown on a leading shoot) about 1·5cm (3/5in) long, usually borne in whorls. Cones (far right) are about 10–12·5cm (4–5in) long, scales more developed into knobs on outer sides, and bearing small sharp spines. They persist for a long time on the tree, sometimes for 30 or 40 years, only releasing seed after fire or the death of the tree. (The white patches in the photograph are dried resin.) Needles (p21) are in clusters of 3 and buds are cylindrical and resinous. Bark (p218) is dark grey with fine flakes, often covered with dried resin.

Mexican White Pine

Pinus ayacahuite Ehrenb.
Native to Guatemala and Mexico, where it grows in mountain valleys at altitudes 2,500–3,000m (8,000–10,000ft). Height to about 30m (100ft) or more in the wild. Flowers (near right) open in June, males yellow in clusters at base of new growth, females red, about 1cm (2/5in) long. Cones (far right) grow to about 15–30cm (6–12in), turning pale brown and opening as they ripen, scale tips usually resinous and the lowest scales curve back. Seeds have wings at least 2·5cm (1in) long with a seed about 0·6cm (¼in). Needles (p22) are slender in clusters of 5.
P. ayacahuite var. *veitchii* Shaw
A variety from Mexico which has often been confused with the species in gardens and collections. It has larger seeds, about 1·2cm (½in) long with shorter, broader wings. Cones may reach 38cm (15in) in length.

Jack Pine

Pinus banksiana Lamb.
Native to Canada and north-eastern United States, cultivated for timber on poor sandy soils in central Europe. Height to about 21m (70ft) though may be shrubby in cultivation. Flowers (near right) open in May, males yellow or reddish yellow, clustered at base of new growth, females red and prickly, about 0·5cm (1/5in) long. Cones (far right) are about 3·7cm (1½in) long, very tapered and usually curved. They ripen from green to light brown and although some cones open on the tree, most remain closed until triggered by the heat of a fire. Seeds therefore become viable after a forest fire so Jack Pine is often one of the first trees to colonise burnt areas. Needles (p19) are short, 2–4cm (¾–1½in), flattish and grouped in pairs.

Lacebark Pine

Pinus bungeana Zucc.
Native to east and central China, cultivated in botanical collections and some gardens. Height may reach around 30m (100ft), the trunk usually divided into several stems low down, sometimes bushy. Flowers (near right) open in late May, males yellow and clustered at base of new growth, females yellowish green, about 1cm (2/5in) long, developing to round cones about 5–7·5cm (2–3in) long, each scale having a short spine. Seeds are hard, about 0·8cm (⅓in) long with a short wing. Needles (p21) are shiny and hard, grouped in 3s. The bark (p218) is perhaps the most noteworthy feature, being more like a plane than a pine. On old trees it becomes almost white but this is rarely seen in cultivation.

Arolla Pine or Swiss Stone Pine

Pinus cembra L.
Native of the Alps and Carpathians, growing at altitudes up to 3,000m (10,000ft), cultivated in collections and gardens for ornament in Europe and north-eastern United States, and occasionally for timber in Scandinavia. Height to about 25m (80ft) or more. Flowers (near right) open in late May, males clustered at base of new growth, females at the tips, about 1cm (2/5in) long. Cones (far right) are round or egg-shaped, about 5–7·5cm (2–3in) long, ripening from dark purple to light brown and falling from the tree in their third year. The scales do not open, the seeds being released as the cones rot on the ground or are broken up by birds or animals in search of food. Needles (p22) are in clusters of 5, which only partially open and are green on outer surface and bluish grey on the inner surface. Twigs are clothed by an orange down.

Pinyon,
Mexican Nut Pine or
Mexican Stone Pine

Pinus cembroides Zucc.
Native to Arizona, California and Mexico where the seeds are harvested and sold as nuts. Height to about 12m (40ft) in the wild. Flowers open in late May, males yellow in dense clusters, females (near right) red, about 1cm (2/5in) long. Cones (far right) are round, about 5cm (2in) across becoming flat and flower-like as the scales ripen and open to release the large, about 1·2cm (½in) long, wingless seed. Needles (p21) are usually in 3s, but sometimes pairs, each needle curved inwards. Three other pinyons occur in south-west United States. These are considered varieties of this Mexican species, differing in the leaf thickness and the number of leaves in a cluster.

Shore Pine or
Beach Pine

Pinus contorta Loud.
Native to the coast of western N. America, from Alaska to California, an important forestry tree in Britain especially on peaty soils in the west. Also planted in central and northern Europe. Height to about 25m (80ft). Flowers (near right) open in May, males abundant, yellow, about 2cm (4/5in) long, females red, about 0·6cm (¼in) long. Cones (far right) are usually curved, about 5cm (2in) long, and each scale bears a sharp spine, which gradually wears off. Scales open to release winged seeds. Needles (p19) are often twisted and are grouped in pairs. Twigs are also twisted. The bark is usually reddish brown, and deeply cracked into square plates, or long narrow plates on old trees.

Lodgepole Pine

Pinus contorta var. *latifolia* S. Wats.
Native to the Rocky Mountains from Alaska to Colorado, this is the inland form of Shore Pine (*P. contorta*), and intermediate types may be found at the boundary of their ranges. Planted as a forestry tree in Britain, particularly on high ground. Height may reach 25m (80ft), making a more slender tree than *P. contorta*. Flowers (near right) open in late May. Cones (far right) are usually more reddish brown than *P. contorta*, also shorter and more rounded. Although some cones open each year, many remain closed and persist on the tree. Needles (p19) are in pairs and are longer, broader and paler than *P. contorta* leaves. A thin, smoother bark also distinguishes it.

Big-cone Pine

Pinus coulteri D. Don
Native to California, where the Indians used to harvest the seeds for food, and to north-western Mexico. Cultivated in botanical collections and gardens. Height may reach about 30m (100ft). Flowers (near right) open in early June, males dark purple then yellow and females red, about 1·5cm (3/5in) long. Cones (far right) are the heaviest of all pines. They may grow to about 30cm (12in) long and weigh about 2·27kg (5lb) when fresh, but generally found much smaller. The scales are hard and bear a sharp incurved claw-like spine. Seeds are also large, about 1·2cm (½in) with a wing twice as long. Most cones remain closed and persist on the tree, but some open to release seeds in autumn. Needles (p21) are long and narrow in clusters of 3 together.

Limber Pine

Pinus flexilis James
Native of the Rocky Mountains from Canada south to California and New Mexico. Height to about 18m (60ft). Flowers (near right) open in early June, males yellow or reddish yellow, females often clustered, red, about 0·6cm (¼in) long. Cones (far right) are up to 15cm (6in), or more in America, similar in appearance to cones of *P. albicaulis*, but longer and opening to release seeds when ripe. They are solitary or 2 or 3 together. Needles (p22) are in clusters of 5, and each is the same colour on each face. The edges are usually smooth, rather than finely toothed as in most 5-needle pines, though may be toothed near the tip.

Aleppo Pine

Pinus halepensis Mill.
A native of south Europe from Spain around the Mediterranean to Asia Minor. It is particularly common on drier soils on mountains and by the coast. Its wood has little value, but the resin yields oil of turpentine and is also used in making the Greek wine, retsina. Height to about 15m (50ft) though may be taller. Flowers open in May, females (near right) about 1cm (2/5in) long. Cones (far right) are about 7·5cm (3in) long, usually borne in pairs or threes and persist on the branches for several years. Needles (p19) are in pairs, growth buds are free of resin and have scales curving back.

Bosnian Pine

Pinus heldreichii Christ var. *leucodermis* (Ant.) Markgraf ex Fitschen, synonym *Pinus leucodermis* Ant.
Native to northern Italy, Yugoslavia and the Balkans and is more common than *P. heldreichii* itself. Height to about 28m (90ft) but usually much smaller. Flowers (near right) open in late May, males abundant, yellow, females dark red-purple about 0·8cm (⅓in) long developing into a dark purple cone (far right) about 2cm (4/5in) long which expands and ripens in its second year to pale brown (also far right), about 5–7·5cm (2–3in) long. The specimen in the cone photograph has some of its needles cut away to show the young cones more clearly. Needles (p19) are dark green, spine tipped and arranged in pairs.

Holford's Pine

Pinus × holfordiana A. B. Jacks
A hybrid raised at Westonbirt, England, from seed of a Mexican White Pine (*P. ayacahuite*) which had been pollinated by a Himalayan Pine (*P. wallichiana*) standing nearby. It may be found in British collections and large gardens. Height has reached about 28m (90ft) so far. Flowers (near right) open in June, males yellow and clustered around the base of new shoots, females dark red and narrow, about 2cm (4/5in) long. Cones (far right) ripen in the second year from green to woody orange brown, about 20–30cm (8–12in) long. Cone scales open to release winged seeds. Needles are in clusters of 5 (p22) and are shining green on outer surface, pale grey-blue on inner surface. Compare with *P. ayacahuite* and *P. wallichiana*.

Jeffrey Pine

Pinus jeffreyi Balf.
Native to southern Oregon, to lower California, at altitudes to 1,000m (3,500ft) in the north and 3,000m (10,000ft) in the south. Cultivated as an ornamental in European gardens and in eastern states of N. America. Height to 60m (200ft) in the wild but usually half this. Flowers (near right) open in early June, males reddish, then yellow, females dark purple, about 0·8cm (⅓in) long. Cones (far right) are up to about 20cm (8in) long when ripe. Each scale bears a narrow sharp spine and opens to release winged seeds. Needles (p21) are in bundles of 3, and are rather long and slender, producing a strong lemon smell when crushed. Bark is smooth, with a few deep cracks and is very dark brown.

Western White Pine or Mountain White Pine

Pinus monticola D. Don
Native to western N. America, where it produces a light timber used in house interiors. Cultivated in eastern N. America and Europe, but is susceptible, like other 5-needled pines from America, to a fungal disease, white pine blister-rust, which has been responsible for killing the oldest ornamental specimens. Height to about 50m (160ft) but often much less. Flowers (near right) open in early June, males pale yellow in clusters, females red, about 0·5cm (¼in) long. Cones (far right) are 12·5–25cm (5–10in) long, usually slightly curved and covered with resin. (In Britain they usually reach 15cm (6in).) Needles (p22) are rough to the touch and are in groups of 5. Inner surfaces are paler than outer. Young shoots are downy which easily distinguishes this from Weymouth Pine (*P. strobus*).

Bishop Pine

Pinus muricata D. Don
Native to the coast of California, occasionally felled for timber. Cultivated in Europe as an ornamental and found to be particularly useful as a shelter-tree in seaside areas as it withstands salt spray. Height to around 15m (50ft) but may grow to nearly twice as much. Flowers (near right) open in late May, the male in long spikes rather than short clusters, females red, about 0·6cm (¼in) long, in whorls of 3–5. Cones (far right) are about 7·5cm (3in) long, and each scale bears a sharp spine. They persist on the tree for at least 25 years, releasing seed only after a fire has forced the scales to open. Needles (p19) are hard, deep glossy green and arranged in pairs.

Austrian Pine

Pinus nigra Arnold
Native to Austria, Italy, Yugoslavia and Greece. Planted in Britain for shelter and for ornament. Height may reach over 30m (100ft) in the wild, with a shorter trunk and more branches, covered with thick foliage, than Corsican Pine (*P. nigra* var. *maritima*). Flowers (near right) open in late May, males golden yellow, females red, about 0·5cm (¼in) long. Cones (far right) are 5–7·5cm (2–3in) long and the scales open to release winged seeds. Needles (p19) are stiffer and usually shorter and straighter than on *P. n. caramanica* and *P. n. maritima*. They are arranged in pairs in dense clusters separated by bare lengths of twig.

Crimean Pine

Pinus nigra var. *caramanica* (Loud.) Rehd.
Native to Asia Minor, the Caucasus, Crimea, the Balkans and Carpathians. Height to around 30m (100ft). Flowers (near right) open in late May, and are similar to those of the Austrian Pine (*P. nigra*). Cones (far right) are similar to *P. nigra* and *P. n. maritima* but may be larger. They open to release seeds when ripe, but are often difficult to find as birds and squirrels soon break them up. Only the unripe conelets are shown in the photograph. Needles (p19) are longer than *P. nigra* and straighter than *P. n. maritima*. They are arranged in pairs. Young shoots are orange.

Corsican Pine

Pinus nigra var. *maritima* (Ait.) Melville
Native to Corsica, southern Italy and Sicily, now one of Britain's most important forestry trees for sandy soils and heathland in the south. It yields a strong timber. Also planted for shelter and in parks, gardens and railway banks. Height to about 45m (148ft) with a more slender appearance than Austrian Pine. Flowers (near right) open in late May, males yellow and females red, about 0·5cm (¼in) long. Cones (far right) are about 5–7·5cm (2–3in) long, opening when ripe to release winged seeds. Needles (p19) are usually longer than either *P. nigra* or *P. n. caramanica* and are slightly twisted. They are grouped in pairs and arranged rather sparsely on the branches, not in distinct whorls as in *P. nigra*. Bark is shown on p218.

Japanese White Pine

Pinus parviflora Sieb. & Zucc.
Native of Japan, grown as an ornament in gardens. The most common form is thought to be a Japanese cultivated variety and forms a rather low tree to about 10m (33ft). The wild type can grow to about 25m (80ft) or more and is less drooping in appearance. Flowers (near right) open in early June, the males in spikes along base of new shoots, pale purple or white turning to yellow when shedding pollen. Females are deep pink about 1·2cm (½in) long and often produced in abundance. Cones (far right) are about 5cm (2in) long, opening to release seeds and persisting on the tree for some years. Needles (p22) are slightly twisted with pale inner surfaces. They are clustered in groups of 5.

Macedonian Pine

Pinus peuce Griseb.
Native of the Balkans, planted in collections and large gardens. Height to about 36m (120ft) in the wild. Flowers (near right) open in early June, males pale yellow in a cluster, females dark red, about 1·2cm (½in) long. Cones (far right) are about 12·5cm (5in) long with drops of resin. The scales open wide to release winged seeds. Needles (p22) have dark green outer surfaces and pale inner ones. They are in clusters of 5 which point strongly forwards on young shoots.

Maritime Pine or Cluster Pine

Pinus pinaster Ait.
Native to the western Mediterranean and north Africa, now naturalised in Portugal and France, and cultivated in California and Britain. It is sometimes felled for timber, but its greatest value lies in its resin which yields a high quality oil of turpentine. The trunk is tapped by making a diagonal slit through which the resin slowly flows or is sprayed with dilute sulphuric acid which causes the resin to exude. Height to about 36m (120ft). Flowers (near right) open in late May, males golden, females dark red, about 1·8cm (¾in) long. Cones (far right) may reach about 15cm (6in) long and persist on the tree for many years in whorls or clusters. Needles (p20) are in pairs and are longer than on any other 2-needled pine. Bark (p219) is reddish brown, or dark deeply cracked into plates.

Stone Pine or Italian Stone Pine

Pinus pinea L.
Native to south-west Europe around the Mediterranean to Greece and Asia Minor. The seeds are eaten raw, roasted like peanuts or added to stews and ragouts, a traditional Italian dish. Remains of husks have been found in Roman camps in Britain, indicating a long history of their use. Height may reach 30m (100ft) but in the open it forms a much lower umbrella-shaped tree. Flowers (near right) open in June, males golden and clustered, females pale yellowish green, about 1·2cm (½in) long. Cones (far right) are large, about 12·5cm (5in) long and heavy. They remain closed for 3 years. When harvesting the seeds the cones are left in direct sun which forces them open. Needles (p20) are dark green, thick, slightly twisted and pointed. They are in pairs and often rather sparse. Bark (p219) is reddish brown with deep dark cracks forming long plates.

Western Yellow Pine

Pinus ponderosa Laws.
Native to western N. America from British Columbia south to Mexico, and variable in length of needles and size of cones throughout its range. Planted for timber in N. America and central Europe, and for ornament in large gardens and collections. Height may be more than 60m (200ft) in the wild. Flowers (near right) open in May, males red, about 3cm (1¼in) long, females also red. Cones (far right, some needles have been cut to show the cone clearly) are about 7·5–15cm (3–6in) long, ripening from purple to dark brown and opening to release winged seeds. Each scale bears a tiny bristle. Needles (p21) are in clusters of 3 and may be 12·5–25cm (5–10in) long. They are hard and curved and densely set around twigs.

Monterey Pine

Pinus radiata D. Don
Native to a coastal part of Monterey, California. Cultivated for ornament in most Pacific states, in western and southern Europe, particularly for shelter by the sea and for timber in Australia, New Zealand and South Africa. Height to 35m (115ft) but may be much taller; over 60m (200ft) has been recorded in New Zealand. Flowers (near right) open in early April, males bright yellow in large clusters, females dark purple red, about 1·8cm (¾in) long. Cones (far right) are about 10cm (4in) long, with scales much more developed on one side. They are borne in whorls and may remain closed on the tree for 30 years or more. Needles (p21) are in bunches of 3, rarely 2, shiny, bright green.

Red Pine

Pinus resinosa Ait.
Native to south-eastern Canada, the Lake States and north-eastern United States on dry rocky or sandy soils and planted in northern parts of N. America for timber and as an ornamental in parks and gardens. Found in Europe in botanical collections and large gardens. Height to 30m (100ft) in the wild. Flowers open in late May, males dark purple in clusters, females (near right) reddish purple about 1cm (2/5in) long. Cones (far right) are about 5cm (2in) long. Scales do not bear spines and open in autumn of their second year to release winged seeds (some needles have been cut off to show the cone more clearly). Needles (p20) are long and slender and grouped in pairs, densely packed on branches. They snap easily when bent in two. Shoots are orange and give off a strong lemon smell when broken. Bark of upper trunk in crown is orange red.

Northern Pitch Pine

Pinus rigida Mill.
Native to eastern N. America. Its wood has been used for fuel and occasionally for timber, and it is of little ornamental value, but found in collections and large gardens. Height to 25m (80ft). Flowers (near right) open in late May, males red in clusters, females also pinkish red, about 1cm (2/5in) long in whorls around shoots. Cones (far right) are about 3–6cm (1¼–2¼in) long and may persist in their clusters for some time. Each scale bears a sharp prickle. Needles (p21) are in groups of 3, dark green and twisted and shorter and thicker than other 3-needled pines. The trunk usually bears leafy growth sometimes on short twigs.

Weymouth Pine or White Pine

Pinus strobus L.
Native to eastern N. America. Planted for its light timber in central Europe and occasionally in the United States. Also planted in gardens and parks for ornament, but is susceptible in Britain to a fungal disease called blister-rust which has destroyed many old specimens. Height to 30m (100ft), or much more in the United States. Flowers (near right) open in early June, males yellowish green in a dense cluster, females pinkish green, about 1cm (2/5in) long. Cones (far right) are slender, about 12·5–15cm (5–6in) long, ripening from green to brown. Scales do not bear spines or prickles and open wide to release winged seeds. Needles (p22) are in bundles of 5 and are shorter than most other 5-needled pines, dark green on outsides and pale on inner surfaces. Young shoots may have tufts of short hair below the base of leaf bundles.

Scots Pine

Pinus sylvestris L.
Native to western and northern Europe and Russia, once more widespread through central Europe but now restricted by competition from other trees. A few native stands remain in Scotland, but not now elsewhere in Britain. Much planted in Europe and N. America for timber and ornament. Height to 36m (120ft). Flowers (near right) open in May, males round and yellow clustered or scattered along weaker shoots, females red, about 0·5cm (1/5in) long. Cones (far right) are about 2·5–6cm (1–2½in) long, ripening in their second year from green to brown or reddish brown. Scales do not bear prickles and open to release winged seeds. Needles (p20) are about 5cm (2in) long, blue-green, twisted and set in pairs. They may be 7cm (2¾in) on young vigorous trees. Scots Pine is recognised by orange flaky bark on the upper trunk (p219) and branches, and short needles.

Chinese Pine

Pinus tabuliformis Carr.
Native to China and Korea, cultivated in botanical collections. Height to 25m (80ft) in the wild. Flowers (near right) open in May, males pale yellow, oval, in a spike, females, dark purple 0·5cm (1/5in) long. Cones (far right) are about 5–6cm (2–2½in) long, ripening from a shiny green conelet to pale or dark brown, each scale bearing a very tiny prickle. They may persist on branches for many years. Needles (p20) are dark shiny green, usually set in pairs, but sometimes in threes.

Japanese Black Pine or Kuro-matsu

Pinus thunbergii Parl.
Native to Japan, cultivated in gardens and botanical collections. Height to about 30m (100ft) or more in the wild. Flowers (near right) open in early June, males red, turning to yellow, grouped in clusters, females purplish red, about 0·5cm (1/5in) long. Cones (far right) may be up to 6cm (2½in) long, each scale with a small spine. They are produced in large numbers, up to 100 on a shoot, even on young trees. Needles (p20) are thick, pointed and slightly twisted. They are grouped in pairs.

Mountain Pine

Pinus uncinata Mirb., synonym *P. mugo* var. *rostrata* (Ant.) Hoopes
Native to the Pyrenees east to the Alps. A good timber is produced in Spain and Mountain Pine is used in France for reafforestation on poor soils. Height to about 25m (80ft). Flowers (near right) open in early June, males dark pink or yellow in thick clusters, females dark reddish purple, about 0·5cm (1/5in) long. Cones (far right) are about 2·5–5cm (1–2in) long. Lower scales bear short downcurved spines. Needles (p20) are stiff, with grooves on inner surfaces. They are set in pairs.

Scrub Pine

Pinus virginiana Mill.
Native to eastern N. America, sometimes grown in botanical collections. Height to about 15m (50ft). Flowers (near right) open in May, males red turning yellow, females reddish white, about 0·5cm (1/5in) long and spiky in appearance. Cones (far right) may be long and narrow, about 5–6cm (2–2½in) long or short and oval, 3cm (1¼in) long. Each scale has a distinct bristle. Needles (p20) are set in pairs. They are short, thick and twisted with a paler inner surface. Young shoots have a pale greyish bloom.

Himalayan Pine or Bhutan Pine

Pinus wallichiana A. B. Jacks
Native to Himalaya, sometimes grown for timber in Europe and for ornament in parks, gardens and old churchyards in Britain. Height to 45m (150ft) in the wild. Flowers (near right) open in June, males reddish in loose groups at base of new shoots, females pale pinkish green or purple, about 2cm (¾in) long. Cones (far right) are usually in bunches and may be 15–30cm (6–10in) long when completely ripe and usually covered with resin. Needles (p22) are long and slender and are set in groups of 5, the whole bunch crinkled and bent. They are soft and droop from branches. Bark is orange-brown, and may be cracked into plates.

Kohuhu

Pittosporum tenuifolium Gaertn., family Pittosporaceae
An evergreen tree, native to New Zealand, grown in gardens and for its foliage which is commonly used by florists, especially in winter. Height to 9m (30ft). Flowers (far left) are about 1·8cm (¾in) across, open in May and have a strong sweet scent, most apparent in the evening. Fruits (near left) are about 1·2cm (½in) across and become dry and wrinkled as they ripen. Leaves (p27) are pale green, glossy and have a wavy edge. There are several cultivated varieties with leaves purple, golden or variegated.

London Plane

Platanus acerifolia (Ait.) Willd.
synonyms *P.* × *hispanica* Muenchh., *P. hybrida* Brot., family Platanaceae
A deciduous tree, thought to be a hybrid between Oriental Plane (*P. orientalis*) and Western Plane (*P. occidentalis*). Grown in town and city streets, parks and gardens in most of central and western Europe. Its wood is fine grained and makes a good veneer. Height to over 30m (100ft). Flowers (near right) open in May, male and female in separate round clusters, females larger and reddish growing at the tip of the shoot and males yellow, growing further back on old wood. There are usually 2–4 fruit clusters on one stem (far right). They are about 2·5cm (1in) across and turn brown in the autumn, breaking up in late winter, often blocking drains and gutters with debris. Leaves (p46) can be extremely variable, even on the same tree, with deeper lobes, more teeth, and of different sizes. They colour yellow and orange in autumn (p188). The bark (p219) is distinctive, peeling off in flakes leaving lighter smooth bark exposed and producing a mottled effect.

Oriental Plane

Platanus orientalis L.
Deciduous tree, native to Greece, Bulgaria, Yugoslavia and Albania. Long planted for shade in southern Europe and the Middle East, particularly in villages where it provides a shady meeting place. Less common in Britain than the London Plane (*P. acerifolia*), but distinguished by being shorter and thicker. Flowers (near right) open in May with separate male and female clusters. Fruit clusters are also similar to London Plane fruits but usually 3–6 balls on each stem. Leaves (p46) are also distinctive, as they are more deeply cut with narrow central lobes and more teeth. Bark peels off in flakes, but is more rough looking and knobbly.

Plum-fruited Yew or Chilean Yew

Podocarpus andinus Endl., family Podocarpaceae
Evergreen tree, native to Chile and Argentina. Found in botanical collections. Height to about 15m (50ft) in the wild and, so far, much taller in cultivation. Flowers (far left) open in June, male and female on separate trees: males are yellow in clusters about 2·5cm (1in) long, females tiny and green. Fruits (near left) are about 1·8cm (¾in) long and ripen to yellow. They have a sweet edible flesh surrounding a stone containing a nut which was eaten by Indians. Leaves (p13) on older trees and side shoots are narrow and pointed, dark dull green above, with 2 bluish bands on undersides. They are set all round the shoots.

Populus family Salicaceae, **Poplar**
Deciduous trees, with alternate broad leaves. Male and female flowers are in catkins usually on separate trees. Fruits are small capsules containing seeds tufted by cottony down.

White Poplar or Abele

Populus alba L.
Native to western and central Europe and central Asia. Cultivated in Europe and N. America for ornament in streets, parks and gardens, and found to be useful for shelter near the sea as it withstands salt spray. Height to 30m (100ft), but much less in Britain. Flowers open in April before leaves unfold, males reddish crimson and hairy about 7·5cm (3in) long; females (near right) greenish-yellow about 5cm (2in) long. Fruit catkins release white cottony seeds in June. Leaves (p47) are lobed and covered entirely by thick white down when first open, but becoming dark glossy green on upper surface and pure white underneath. Bark (far right) is smooth, white or grey with diamond-shaped marks and becomes black and rough at the base.

Balsam Poplar or Tacamahac

Populus balsamifera L.
Native to a large area across the north of N. America, occasionally planted for ornament in European collections and gardens. Height to 30m (100ft) in the wild, often half this in Britain. Flowers open in March, male (near right) bright red, about 7·5cm (3in) long, females greenish 10–12·5cm (4–5in) long. Fruit capsules have 2 valves and form a cluster 20–30cm (8–12in) long. Leaves (p40) are round or slightly heart-shaped at the base, round-toothed and pointed, dark green above, paler beneath. Commonly forms many suckers, and winter buds are covered by a thick resin which has a balsam smell. Bark is shown far right.

Hybrid Black Poplar

Populus × *canadensis* Moench, synonym *P.* × *euramericana* Guinier
A group of hybrids from the European Black Poplar (*P. nigra*) and Cottonwood (*P. deltoides*) of N. America, planted throughout Europe as the hybrids proved to be more vigorous and easily propagated than either parent. Many named clones are now available (see 2 of these below).

Railway Poplar

Populus × *canadensis* 'Regenerata'
This is a female clone which arose in France in 1814; it became widely planted in France and Britain particularly near railways as a screen. Now little planted, as it is susceptible to a bacterial disease. Height to about 30m (100ft). Flowers (near right) open in March and April and the fruit (far right) is ripe in June but is usually sterile. Leaves are shown p40.

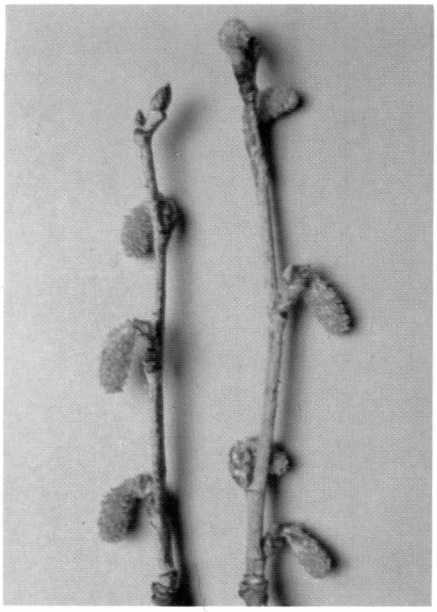

Populus × *canadensis* 'Robusta'
This is a vigorous, male clone, which arose in France at the end of the 19th century. Widely planted in Britain for shelter, screening, ornament and timber. Height to around 35m (116ft) so far. Flowers (near right) are bright red, about 6cm (2½in) long and open in March. Leaves (p40) are also a fine sight in spring, as they unfold a bronzy colour, turning to blue-green through the summer. (Catkin shown far right is *P. canescens*).

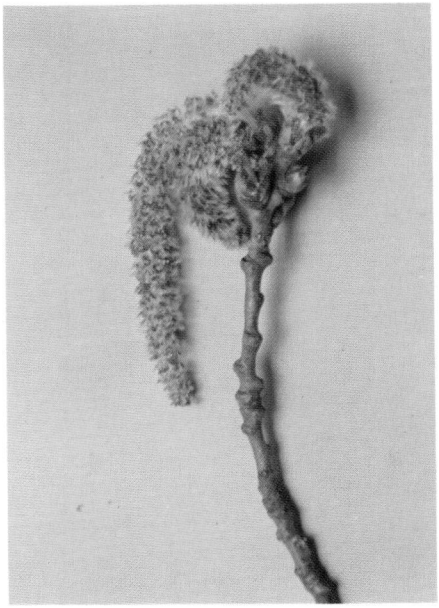

Grey Poplar

Populus canescens (Ait.) Sm.
Native to south, central and western Europe, probably including Britain. Commonly grown for ornament and shelter, especially by the sea. Height to 30m (100ft). Flowers open in March, males (above right) red and silky grey, about 5–10cm (2–4in) long, females (near right) greenish and silky about 2–5cm (¾–2in). Fruiting catkins (far right) are about 10cm (4in) long and release cottony seeds in June. Leaves (p40) are at first covered with a white down which falls away remaining only on undersides and sometimes only faintly. Some consider this to be a hybrid between White Poplar (*P. alba*) and Aspen (*P. tremula*). Bark is dark greyish-brown and ridged, but in the crown (p219) it is white with black streaks and diamonds.

Cottonwood or Necklace Poplar

Populus deltoides Marsh
Native to eastern N. America. Planted in central Europe by roads and for timber, and in eastern states of America for shelter and ornament. Height to 30m (100ft) or more in the wild. Flowers open in March, males (near right) red, up to 5cm (2in) long, females greenish, up to 10cm (4in) long. Fruit capsules have 3 or 4 valves and release cottony seeds in June. Leaves (p40) have finely hairy edges and glands at join with leaf stem. Buds and leaves have a strong balsam fragrance.

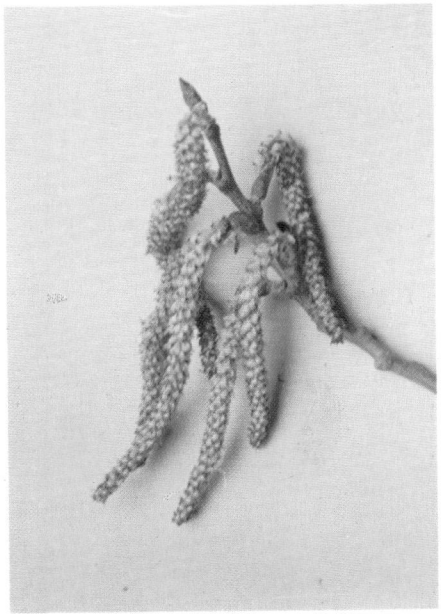

Big-toothed Aspen

Populus grandidentata Michx.
Native to eastern N. America. Height to about 21m (70ft). Flowers open in March, males red with grey silky hairs about 5cm (2in) long, females (far right) greenish also about 5cm (2in) long. Fruit catkins are about 12·5cm (5in) with 2-valved capsules and ripen in May or June. Leaves (p40) look similar to the American Aspen (*P. tremuloides*) but are more deeply toothed.

Chinese Necklace Poplar

Populus lasiocarpa Oliver
Native to central China, cultivated for interest in collections and large gardens. Height to about 18m (60ft). Flowers (near right) open in late April or May, males reddish up to about 10cm (4in) in length, females yellowish-green about 10cm (4in) long. Many trees have catkins with the lower, stalked end male and the top either female or bisexual. Fruiting catkins (far right) may reach about 20cm (8in) and release their cottony seeds in July. Leaves (p42) are remarkably large, 25cm (10in) or even more. They usually have thick red stems.

Black Poplar

Populus nigra L.
The true Black Poplar is native to Europe and western Asia, not often found, but its many cultivars and varieties are widespread. Many of these are superior timber trees though may not be so attractive. Two are described below.

Downy Black Poplar

Populus nigra L. var. *betulifolia* (Pursh) Torr.
Native to northern and central Europe. Planted by roads, and in parks and gardens. Height to about 30m (100ft). Flowers open in March, males (near right) red, about 5cm (2in) long, females greenish about the same length. Fruiting catkins are about 7·5cm (3in) long and shed white cottony seeds in June. Leaves (p40) have forward-pointing teeth and flattened stems. Young shoots, leaf stalks, main veins and flower stalks are downy but on the true Black Poplar they are hairless. Bark (far right) is dark brown, ridged and characteristically has thick bosses all over it.

Lombardy Poplar

Populus nigra cv. 'Italica'
A male clone, propagated by cuttings from a tree in Lombardy, N. Italy, early in the 18th century. Grown in Europe and N. America on roadsides, for shelter and for ornament. Height to about 30m (100ft) or more. Flowers (near right) open in March or April, up to about 5cm (2in) long. Leaves (p40) look similar to those of Black Poplar (*P. nigra*) with hairless stalks and shoots. Bark is greyish and usually fluted and cracked and often bears twiggy shoots (far right). The tree shape is perhaps its most distinctive feature.

Aspen or European Aspen

Populus tremula L.
Native to Europe (including Britain), north Africa and Asia. Commonly forms thickets in the wild as it suckers easily. Height to about 15m (50ft). Flowers open in February, male catkins pinkish with grey silky hairs, about 5–10cm (2–5in) long, females (near right) also grey and silky. Fruiting catkins (far right) are about 10–12·5cm (5–6in) long and shed white woolly seeds in May. Leaves (p40) are almost round with wavy edges but on suckers may be wedge-shaped. They have stems flattened which causes them to quiver in the wind. They have pairs of glands where the blade meets the stem and turn clear yellow in autumn. Bark is smooth and greyish with horizontal lines.

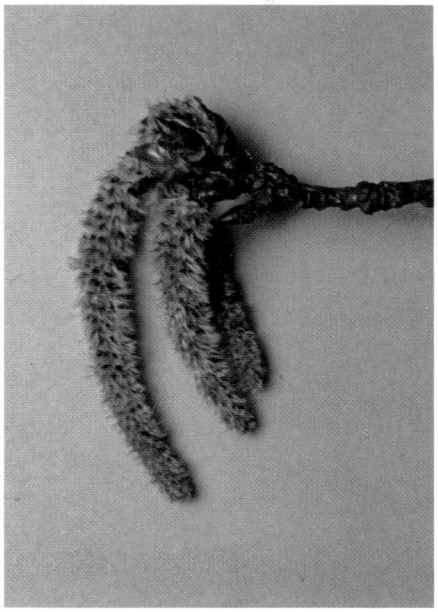

American Aspen or Quaking Aspen

Populus tremuloides Michx.
Native to a large area of N. America, in Canada south of the tundra, and western United States from Mexico northwards. Occasionally cultivated in Europe. Height to 30m (100ft) in the wild but usually half that in cultivation. Flowers open in February and March, male catkins pinkish with long silvery hairs about 5cm (2in) long and more slender than those of Aspen (*P. tremula*); females (near right) also with silvery hairs also about 5cm (2in) long. Fruiting catkins are about 15cm (6in) long and release white cottony seeds in May. Leaves (p40) are almost circular and have fine teeth on their edges (not wavy edges as *P. tremula*). They have flattened stems causing them to quake in the wind. Bark is paler and yellower than *P. tremula* and bark on young trees has horizontal dark marks.

Western Balsam Poplar or Black Cottonwood

Populus trichocarpa Hook.
Native to western N. America from Alaska south to California. It yields a timber which has been used as a veneer and for paper pulp. Commonly planted in Britain by roads, for shelter and in gardens. Height to as much as 60m (200ft) in the wild but usually much smaller. Flowers open in March, males (near right) stout and red, about 5cm (2in) long. Female catkins are greenish and may be 15cm (6in) long when ripe. They bear 3-valved downy capsules which release white cottony seeds in June. Leaves (p40) are variable in size usually about 5cm (2in) long or up to 25cm (10in) on young vigorous shoots. The buds and young leaves give off a strong balsam fragrance. Bark (far right) is greenish grey and smooth when young, becoming shallowly cracked on mature trees.

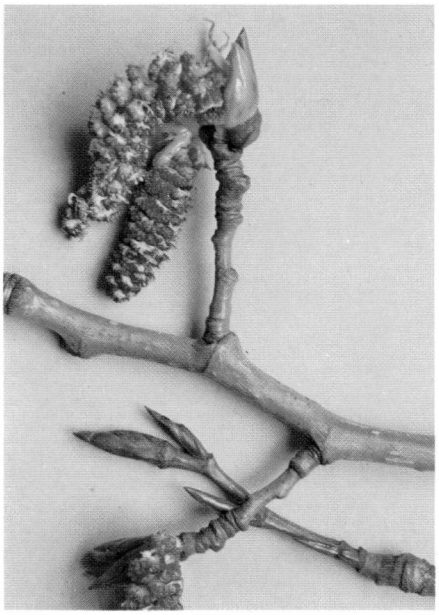

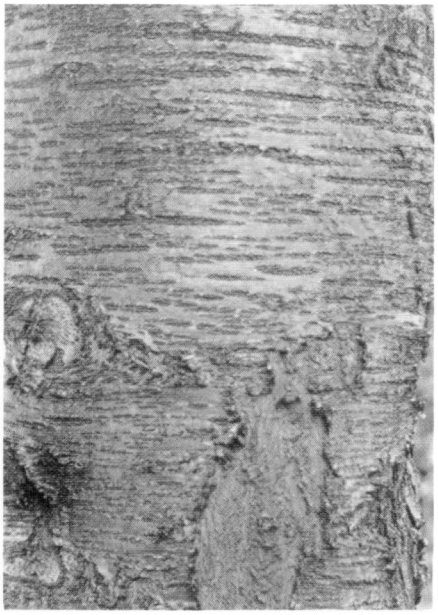

Prunus family Rosaceae
A large group of trees and shrubs, usually bearing clusters of white or pink 5-petalled flowers and a single-celled fruit containing one seed. Much cultivated for either blossom or fruit.

Prunus 'Accolade'
An ornamental garden cherry, believed to be a hybrid between *P. sargentii* and *P. subhirtella*, making a small tree with spreading branches. Flowers (far left) open in March about 4cm (1½in) across with 12–15 petals. Leaves (p30) are deciduous, deeply toothed and colour red and yellow in autumn.

American Red Plum

Prunus americana Marsh.
A deciduous tree or bush, native to eastern United States. It has given rise to many named varieties and is cultivated in eastern states for its fruits. Height to 9m (30ft). Flowers (near left) open in April and are 1·2–2·5cm (½–1in) across. Fruit are round, about 2·5cm (1in) across, ripening from yellow to bright red, with yellow flesh. Leaves (p31) have tufts of down on midrib and vein axils beneath and downy stems.

Gean, Wild Cherry or Mazzard

Prunus avium L.
Deciduous tree, native to Europe, including Britain. Its fruits trend to be bitter but it is one of the parents of most European cultivated cherries. The wood is reddish-brown with a very straight grain, and used in cabinet making, and for anything requiring a straight bore such as pipes and musical instruments. To be found in hedges and woods, gardens and parks in most of Europe, also cultivated and naturalised in eastern N. America. Height to 18m (60ft) or more. Flowers (far left) open in mid April, each about 2·5cm (1in) across in clusters on previous year's growth. Fruits (near left) are about 2cm (¾in) across and may be light or blackish red, sweet or bitter. Leaves (p31) have stems red above and yellowish beneath with 2 or more glands or lumps near the base of the leaf blade and colour yellow and red in autumn. Bark (near left below) is reddish brown and clearly marked by lenticels in horizontal lines and broken by large cracks.

Prunus avium cv. 'Plena'
Double flowered cultivar planted in gardens and streets, often with pink Japanese cherries. Height to about 12m (40ft), the largest white double cherry. Flowers (far left) open in great profusion in early May. Each is about 4cm (1½in) across with 30–40 petals. Fruit is rarely set. Leaves and bark similar to those of *P. avium*.

Cherry Plum or Myrobalan

Prunus cerasifera Ehrh.
Deciduous tree, native to the Balkans, cultivated in central Europe for its fruits, found in Britain in hedgerows and by roads. Height to about 9m (30ft). Flowers (far left) are 2cm (¾in) and open in early March before Sloe (*P. spinosa*) with which it is often confused. Fruits are about 2·5cm (1in) across, ripening yellow to red in late summer. Leaves (p31) are deep glossy green above, paler beneath with a pinkish grooved stem.

Purple-leaved Plum or Pissard Plum

Prunus cerasifera cv. 'Pissardii', synonym *P. cerasifera* var. *atropurpurea* Dipp.
Often grown in streets, parks and gardens. Flowers (near left) open in early March, about 2cm (¾in) pale pink among red leaves, usually profuse but in country areas the buds are eaten by bullfinches so that flowers may be sparse. Fruit is about 2·5cm (1in) across, purple. Leaves (p31) darken through the summer.

Almond

Prunus dulcis (Mill.) D. A. Webb, synonyms *P. amygdalus* Batsch, *P. communis* (L.) Arcang., not Huds.
Deciduous tree, probably native to south-west Asia and the Balkans, cultivated for its blossom and nuts, and naturalised in most of Europe. Also cultivated in California, Australia and South Africa. Height to about 9m (30ft). Flowers (far left) open in March and April, up to 5cm (2in) across. Fruit is 3·7–6cm (1½–2½in) long with a green downy skin and little flesh which splits to release the oval pitted nut. Leaves are narrow, widest below the middle.

Prunus 'Hillieri'
Ornamental deciduous cherry. Height to about 10m (33ft). Flowers (near left) open in mid-April, about 3cm (1¼in) across on long stems (not yet developed in photograph). Leaves (p31) are double toothed and bronzy coloured when young. *Prunus* 'Spire' came from the same cross and has similar flowers but a narrow shape, about 3m (10ft) wide at the base and 8m (26ft) high.

Holly-leaved Cherry

Prunus ilicifolia (Hook. & Arn.) Walp.
An evergreen tree or shrub, native to California, cultivated as an ornamental in western and southern Europe. Height to 9m (30ft) in the wild. Flowers (far left) open in May in California but later in Britain. Each is about 0·8cm (⅓in) across in spikes about 4–8cm (1½–3in) long. Fruits (near left) ripen in November and December. They are about 1·2cm (½in) across with a pointed tip, and ripen from green to red to dark purple. Leaves (p36) are holly-like dark and glossy with prickle pointed teeth.

Cherry Laurel

Prunus laurocerasus L.
Evergreen shrub, native to eastern Europe near the Caspian Sea, cultivated throughout Europe from the 16th and 17th centuries onwards as an ornamental. Height to over 6m (20ft). Flowers (far left) open in April, each about 0·8cm (⅓in) across in spikes 7·5–12·5cm (3–5in) long. Fruits (near left) are about 1·2cm (½in) long, ripening to black from green and red in September. Leaves (p26) are glossy green and leathery with a few minute teeth on the edges. Many cultivated varieties are available with different growth habits, leaf sizes and colours.

Portugal Laurel

Prunus lusitanica L.
Evergreen shrub, native to Spain and Portugal, cultivated for ornament in gardens in most of Europe. Height to about 6m (20ft) but may be twice as tall. Flowers (far left) open in June in profusion each about 1·2cm (½in) across in spikes 15–25cm (6–10in) long. Fruits (near left) are cone-shaped, about 0·8cm (⅓in) long, ripening to dark purple in October. Leaves (p26) are smaller than Cherry Laurel (*P. laurocerasus*), and softer, glossy green above and shallowly toothed.

Manchurian Cherry

Prunus maackii Rupr.
Deciduous tree, native to Manchuria, Korea and neighbouring parts of Russia, cultivated for ornament in gardens. Height to 12m (40ft). Fragrant flowers (far left) open in early May each about 1·2cm (½in) across in spikes 5–7·5cm (2–3in) long. Leaves (p31) have tiny dots on undersides and downy stems. Bark (p219) is shiny brown or golden, and peels in thin strips.

St Lucie Cherry

Prunus mahaleb L.
Deciduous tree, native to central and southern Europe, cultivated in gardens for its blossom and naturalised in eastern N. America. Height to about 12m (40ft). Fragrant flowers (near left) open in late April or early May about 1·2cm (½in) across. Fruits are oval, about 0·6cm (¼in) long, ripening black. Leaves (p31) are rather small. The main vein is hairy on the underside and the stem usually bears 2 glands.

Bird Cherry

Prunus padus
Deciduous tree or shrub, native to Europe (including Britain) and Asia. Often planted in streets and gardens. Height to 15m (50ft). Flowers (far left) are fragrant about 1·2cm (½in) across and open in late May in spikes 7·5–15cm (3–6in) long. Fruits (near left) are about 0·6cm (¼in) across, black and bitter to taste, but may be used to flavour brandy and wines. They ripen in July and August. Leaves (p31) are finely toothed, may have tufts of down in vein axils and glands on stems. Bark is smooth, dark greyish-brown and has a strong unpleasant smell. Two cultivars which are popular for gardens and streets are:
P. padus cv. 'Plena'. Has larger double flowers which are open for a longer time.
P. padus cv. 'Watereri'. Flowerheads are in spikes, up to 20cm (8in) and the leaves have noticeable tufts of down in vein axils underneath.

Pin Cherry or Wild Red Cherry

Prunus pensylvanica L. f.
Deciduous, native to northern N. America from the Atlantic coast to the Rockies. Short-lived but provides useful shelter to other young trees. Height to about 12m (40ft). Flowers (far left) open in late April or May, 1·2cm (½in) across. Fruit is round, about 0·6cm (¼in) and ripens to red. Leaves (p25) are finely toothed with a hairless stalk.

Peach

Prunus persica (L.) Batsch
Deciduous tree, believed to be native to China, but cultivated for so long its origins are obscure. Grown in China, Europe and eastern N. America for its sweet fleshy fruit. Height to 6m (20ft). Flowers (near left) open in April, 2·5–3·7cm (1–1½in) across. Fruits are round and fleshy, about 5–7·5cm (2–3in) across with velvety skin, sweet yellow flesh and a ridged stone. Leaves (p25) are narrow widest at or above the middle.

Sargent Cherry

Prunus sargentii Rehd.
Deciduous tree, native to northern Japan and Sakhalin, cultivated by roads and in gardens in Europe and N. America. Height to 25m (80ft) in the wild. Flowers (far left) open in early or mid April about 3–4cm (1¼–1½in) across in closely set pairs. Fruits are round, black, about 0·8cm (⅓in) wide and rarely produced. Leaves (p31) have a long narrow tip, coarse teeth and glands at blade base. They colour dazzling orange and red in late September while other trees are still green (near left).

Black Cherry or Rum Cherry

Prunus serotina Ehrh.
Deciduous tree, native to N. America where its fruit has been used to flavour brandy and rum and its wood used by cabinet makers. Grown in central Europe for timber and other parts for ornament in larger gardens. Fruits have been used in cough mixture. Height to about 30m (100ft) in best conditions. Flowers (far left) open in late May or early June about 0·8cm (⅓in) across in spikes 10–15cm (4–6in) long. Fruits (near left) are 0·8cm (⅓in) and ripen in September. Leaves (p31) are dark green and glossy on upper surface, paler beneath with hairs on the main vein. They have pairs of tiny glands on the stem at the base of the leaf-blade. The bark has a strong, bitter fragrance.

Tibetan Cherry

Prunus serrula Franch.
A deciduous tree, native to western China, cultivated in gardens for its attractive bark. Height to about 15m (50ft), usually much smaller. Flowers (far left) are about 1·6cm (⅔in) across and open in April in clusters of 2 or 3. Fruits are red, oval, about 1·2cm (½in) long. Leaves (p25) are narrow and fine toothed. Bark (near left) is shining red-brown and peels in thin strips.

Japanese Cherry

Prunus serrulata Lindl.
Probably of Chinese origin, cultivated in Japan and now rather uncommon. Many cherries with decorative blossom have been produced in Japan and it has become usual to group them under this species, although the origins of most are obscure. In Japan they are known as Sato Zakura – domestic cherries. A few are shown below:

Prunus 'Amanogawa'
A very narrow deciduous tree to 8m (26ft), ideal for small gardens. Fragrant flowers (far left) open in early or mid-April, about 2·5cm (1in) across with about 9 petals. Leaves (p30) are bronzy when they first unfold, and turn yellow in the autumn.

Prunus 'Hokusai'
Deciduous tree to 7·5m (25ft). Flowers (near left) are about 5cm (2in) wide with about 12 petals and open in late April through May. Leaves (p30) are bronzy at first, becoming green, and colouring orange and red in the autumn.

Prunus 'Kanzan', synonym 'Sekiyama'
The names 'Kanzan' and 'Sekiyama' are derived from the Chinese character representing a sacred mountain; the first name is also sometimes spelt 'Kwanzan'. A popular cherry for gardens and streets. Height to 12m (40ft). Flowers (far left) open in late April or early May, each about 5·5cm (2¼in) across with about 30 petals. Leaves (p30) have long teeth and are dark reddish when they first appear at flowering time and remain so for some time. They colour golden or sometimes red in the autumn. Bark is shown near left.

Prunus 'Mikurama – gaeshi'
Small deciduous tree, useful for small gardens and hedges because of its upright shape. Flowers (far left) have a light apple fragrance and open in mid-April. Each is about 5cm (2in) across, usually single with 5 petals and they cover the otherwise gaunt looking branches. Leaves (p30) have short teeth, are bronzy at first, soon green, and turn dark red and yellow in the autumn.

Prunus 'Pink Perfection'
A hybrid between 2 other Japanese cherries. Height to 7·5m (25ft). Flowers (near left) open in mid or late April. They are similar to those of *P.* 'Kanzan' but are darker in bud and a purer less purple pink, fading to a pale pink. Leaves (p30) are a paler bronze when they unfold.

Prunus 'Shirofugen'
A deciduous tree, which may reach 7·5m (25ft). Flowers (far left) open late in the season, in mid or late May. They are about 5cm (2in) across with around 30 petals, pink at first fading to white and pink. Leaves (p30) are purple bronze at first with red stems and turn deep copper-brown in the autumn.

Prunus 'Shirotae'
A deciduous tree, to 9m (30ft). Flowers (near left) are semi-double, about 5cm (2in) across with a light fragrance. They open in early or mid-April. Leaves (p30) are pale green at first and have teeth with long hair-like tips, giving a fringed appearance.

Great White Cherry

Prunus 'Tai-Haku'
An ancient Japanese cherry which had become extinct in Japan but has now been revived from a single specimen found in a garden in Sussex. Height to 12m (40ft). Flowers (far left) are single, up to 6cm (2½in) across and open in mid or late April. Leaves (p30) are bronzy when young, green in the summer, colouring yellow and orange in the autumn. They have a fringed edge.

Prunus 'Ukon'
A deciduous tree, popular for its unusual flowers (near left) which have a pale green or yellowish tinge. They are semi-double, about 5cm (2in) across and open in late April. Leaves (p30) are light bronzy green and colour red, and purplish brown in the autumn.

Sloe or Blackthorn

Prunus spinosa L.
A deciduous prickly shrub or small tree, native to Europe (including Britain) and N. Asia, cultivated and naturalised in eastern N. America. Its fruits are gathered from hedgerows and may be used to colour and flavour gin. The wood has been used for the teeth of hay rakes. Height to 4·5m (15ft) as a shrub but may be 6m (20ft) as a tree. Flowers (far left) open before the leaves in March or early April, about 1·2cm (½in) or more across. Fruits (near left) are about 1·2cm (½in) across and have a strongly astringent taste. Leaves (p31) are small with pointed teeth and hairs on the main vein beneath. Twigs bear hard sharp spines.

Spring Cherry or Rosebud Cherry

Prunus subhirtella Miq.
Deciduous tree, native to Japan, cultivated in gardens. Height to 9m (30ft). Flowers (far left) open in late March to mid-April, about 1·8cm (¾in) across. Fruits are black, round, 0·8cm (⅓in) across. Leaves (p31) are irregularly toothed with downy stem and main vein on underside.
P. subhirtella cv. 'Autumnalis', **Autumn Cherry**
This has semi-double pink flowers which open in November and December and sometimes again in the spring.

Choke Cherry

Prunus virginiana
A deciduous tree or shrub, native to eastern and central United States, occasionally planted and naturalised in central and western Europe. Height to 4·5m (15ft). Flowers (near left) are 0·8cm (⅓in) across in spikes 7·5–15cm (3–6in) long and open in late May. Fruit is round, red, 0·8cm (⅓in) across. Leaves (p31) have conspicuous tufts of down in vein axils beneath.

Yoshino Cherry

Prunus × *yedoensis* Matsum.
A deciduous tree, thought to be a hybrid between the Spring Cherry (*P. subhirtella*) and the Oshima Cherry (*P. speciosa*). Commonly planted in Japanese cities, in N. America, and sometimes in Europe. Height to 15m (50ft). Fragrant flowers (far left) open in late March or early April, about 2·5cm (1in), pale pink or white on red stems. Fruits (near left) are about 1cm (2/5in) across and ripen black in August. They are bitter to the taste. Leaves (p30) are doubly toothed glossy on upper surface with hairy veins below.

Pseudotsuga family Pinaceae, **Douglas Fir**
Evergreen coniferous trees, with flat narrow leaves narrowed at the base and leaving a slightly raised scar when they fall off. Cones have 3-pronged bracts protruding from each scale.

Large-coned Douglas Fir

Pseudotsuga macrocarpa (Torr.) Mayr, synonym *P. douglasii* var. *macrocarpa* (Torr.) Engelm.
Native to California, occasionally planted in gardens and collections. Height to 9–28m (30–90ft). Flowers (near right) appear in April, males yellowish, about 1·2cm (½in) long, females reddish green about 5cm (2in) long. Cones are 9–12·5cm (3½–5in) long and may be even larger. They have short protruding bracts. Leaves (p16) are set around the shoot, and slightly curved glossy green above with 2 pale bands beneath. Bark (far right) is blue-grey with wide orangey brown cracks.

Douglas Fir or Green Douglas Fir

Pseudotsuga menziesii (Mirbel) Franco, synonyms *P. douglasii* (Lindl.) Carr., *P. taxifolia* (Lamb.) Sudw.
Native to western N. America from Canada south to California. Cultivated throughout Europe for its high quality timber, known as Oregon or Columbian Pine. Also grown for ornament in eastern states of N. America and Europe. Height to 60–90m (200–300ft). Flowers (near right) open in late March and April, males yellow on underside of shoot and females yellowish green or pinkish green at tips of old growth, about 1·8cm (¾in) long. Cones (far right) ripen from green to brown in the autumn and are about 7·5cm (3in) long with bracts pointing straight. Leaves (p16) are densely set, needle-like with blunt tips and have a strong fruity fragrance. Bark on old trees is grey and rough with deep wide cracks.

Blue Douglas Fir

Pseudotsuga menziesii var. *glauca* (Mayr) Franco, synonym *P. douglasii* var. *glauca* Mayr
Native to the eastern Rocky Mountains from Montana south to Mexico. Occasionally grown for ornament in eastern states and in Europe. Height to 25m (80ft). Flowers open in late March, early April, males (near right) dull pinkish purple about 0·8cm (⅓in), females dark red, about 1·8cm (¾in) long. Cones (far right) are smaller than *P. menziesii* cones, about 5cm (2in) with bracts protruding and bent at right angles. Leaves (p16) are blue-grey above, with 2 blue-grey bands below, rounded tips and little fragrance when crushed. Bark is dark grey and scaly.

Hop Tree or Stinking Ash

Ptelea trifoliata L., family Rutaceae
Deciduous tree, native to southern Canada and eastern United States, planted in gardens and sometimes naturalised in central Europe. Height to 7·5m (25ft), often shrubby. Flowers (far left) may be almost white and open in June and July, each about 0·8cm (⅓in) in round clusters about 5–7·5cm (2–3in) across. Fruits (near left) are up to 2·5cm (1in) across, eventually ripening to a pale straw colour. Leaves (p50) have 3 leaflets, and like the bark and unripe fruits give off a strong aromatic smell when crushed.

Caucasian Wing-nut

Pterocarya fraxinifolia (Lam.) Spach, family Juglandaceae
Deciduous tree, native to the Caucasus and northern Iran, occasionally planted for timber or ornament in Europe. Height to 30m (100ft) with a short thick trunk. Flowers (near right) open in April, male catkins thick and green, 7·5–12·5cm (3–5in) long, females longer with more scattered flowers bearing red styles developing into fruiting catkins 30–50cm (12–20in) long with nuts surrounded by green wings about 1·8cm (¾in) across. Leaves (p54) may be over 60cm (2ft) long, but usually less with 7–27 stalkless leaflets, hairless on upper surface with tufts of hairs beneath. The common stalk is round and smooth.

Hybrid Wing-nut

Pterocarya × rehderiana Schneid.
A hybrid between the Caucasian Wing-nut (*P. fraxinifolia*) and the Chinese Wing-nut (*P. stenoptera*) first raised in the United States towards the end of the 19th century. Deciduous tree to about 25m (80ft). Flowers (near right) open in late April or early May, male catkins thick and dense, about 7·5cm (3in) long, females slender with scattered flowers and may be twice as long. Fruiting catkins may be as long as on *P. fraxinifolia* but each nut has slightly smaller rounder wings. Leaves (p54) have 5–25 leaflets and the common stalk has narrow wings (the Chinese parent has strongly winged leaf stems).

Pyrus family Rosaceae, **Pear**
Deciduous trees with simple toothed leaves, and distinctively shaped fruits, with gritty flesh.

Almond-leaved Pear

Pyrus amygdaliformis Vill.
Native to southern Europe, particularly around the Mediterranean, sometimes grown in other parts of Europe for ornament. Height to about 12m (40ft) but may be shrubby. Flowers (far left) open in April about 2·5cm (1in) across in clusters of 8–12, sometimes massed together. Fruits (near left) are spherical rather than pear-shaped, slightly wider than long, about 2·5cm (1in) across. They ripen yellowish brown in October. Leaves are variable, usually narrow, about 3·7–6cm (1½–2½in) long, 1·2–1·8cm (½–¾in) wide with pale hairs at first but becoming hairless and shiny on upper surface and almost hairless beneath.

Common Pear

Pyrus communis L.
Probably of hybrid origin, arising from cultivated varieties mingling with wild species. Found wild in most of Europe, including Britain and many cultivated varieties are grown in orchards and gardens. Height to about 12m (40ft), occasionally more. Flowers (far left) open in late April, early May about 2·5–3·7cm (1–1½in) across in clusters. Fruits (near left) may be almost round, up to about 10cm (4in) long, ripening yellowish with sweet flesh. Leaves (p37) are variable, but usually oval or almost round, becoming hairless or starting hairless. Bark (p219) is dark brown and broken into small thick square plates.

Quercus family Fagaceae, **Oak**
Male and female flowers are separate on the same tree, males in slender catkins, females single or a few together developing into acorns, the most important common feature. Many species are deciduous but there are also a lot of evergreen and semi-evergreen oaks.

Californian Live Oak or Encina

Quercus agrifolia Née
An evergreen, native to California, otherwise only found in oak collections. Height to 25m (80ft) although it is often shrubby with stems prostrate or only a few feet high. Flowers (near right) open in May with the appearance of the young leaves. The sessile or nearly sessile acorns are a long conical shape 3·7cm (1½in) long, often deeply enclosed in the cup (far right). They ripen in one year and fall in October. Leaves (p29) are 2·5–5cm (1–2in) long, dark and shiny above and have tufts of down in the vein axils below.

White Oak

Quercus alba L.
Deciduous, native to central and eastern N. America, where the strong heavy wood has been used in shipbuilding, cabinet making, railway sleepers, cooperage and extensively as fuel. Height to 30m (100ft), sometimes more, at altitudes to 1,400m (4,500ft) but at this altitude it is a low bush. Flowers appear with the young leaves (near right) at the end of May. The acorns (far right) are 1·8cm (¾in) long, usually sessile but not always, and fall in early October. The leaves (p48) grow up to 12·5–22·5cm (5–9in) long, the upper surface is dark glossy green, the lower downy at first. When they open they are tinted a violet colour and turn deep red in autumn, often staying on the tree all winter.

Willow-leaved Pear

Pyrus salicifolia Pall.
Native of the Caucasus and Asia Minor to the south and south-west of the Caspian Sea. Cultivated for ornament in European gardens. Height to around 6m (20ft). Flowers (far left) open in April, each about 1·8cm (¾in) across. Fruit is about 2·5cm (1in) long and is not pleasant to eat. Leaves (p24) begin life covered in silvery silky hairs, but eventually become dark green on upper surface (compare flower and fruit photographs). *P. salicifolia* 'Pendula' is often cultivated and has more weeping branches than the type.

Swamp White Oak

Quercus bicolor Willd.
Deciduous, native to south-eastern United States. The wood is hard and heavy and has been used in construction, cabinet-making, railway sleepers and fencing. Height to 21m (70ft). Acorns (near right) are 2·5cm (1in) long, a third enclosed by cup. They mature in one year and fall in October. Leaves (p49) are about 7·5–17·5cm (3–7in) long, dark green above, felty below.

Mirbeck's Oak or Algerian Oak

Quercus canariensis Willd., synonym *Q. mirbeckii* Durieu
Deciduous, native to north Africa also found in Spain. Height to 35m (120ft). Acorns (far right) ripen in one year to 2·5cm (1in). Leaves (p49) are 9–15cm (3½–6in) long, the underside usually has touches of flock on the midrib often concentrated near the base. They remain on the tree until well after Christmas.

Chestnut-leaved Oak

Quercus castaneifolia C. A. Mey.
Deciduous, native to the forests south and south-west of the Caspian Sea. Although a striking tree it is fairly rare in collections. Height to 30m (100ft). The flowers (near right) appear with the young leaves at the end of April or early May, the female flowers are seen in the terminal axils of the new shoots. The acorns (far right) which ripen in the second year are about 2·5cm (1in) long and fall in October. Leaves (p26) are 7·5–19cm (3–7½in) long, dark glossy green above, dull grey downy beneath.

Turkey Oak

Quercus cerris L.
Deciduous, native to southern and central Europe from south-east France through the Alps and Apennines to the Carpathian Mountains of Rumania. Common in gardens and parks elsewhere and naturalises quickly in woods and hedges. Grows to a height of 40m (130ft). The timber is inferior in quality compared to most oaks, but it is useful as an ornamental tree as it is elegant and quick-growing. The flowers (near right) appear in May, the females are in the leaf axils at the tip of the shoot. Acorns (far right) have big woolly cups and fall in October; they grow to 2·5cm (1in) or more long. Leaves (p49) are 6–12·5cm (2½–5in) long, covered in down both above and below and can be very diverse in shape. Bark is shown on p219.

Canyon Live Oak
or
Maul Oak

Quercus chrysolepis Liebm.
Evergreen, native to the west coast of N. America from southern Oregon along the coastal ranges of California at altitudes to 2,800m (9,000ft). The strong hard wood has been used for making agricultural tools. Rare in collections. A small tree or shrub not normally reaching more than 18m (60ft) in height, but spreading to as much as 45m (150ft) in width. Flowers (near right) appear in late May, the females are in the young leaf axils. The acorns (far right) grow up to 3·7cm (1½in) long. The specimens shown are not fully ripe; the acorns will grow much longer and extend further from the cup. The leaves may have smooth margins as in the flower photograph or holly-like as in the acorn photograph (see also p24). They are 2·5–9cm (1–3½in) long.

Scarlet Oak

Quercus coccinea Muenchh.
Deciduous, native to north-eastern United States at altitudes to 1,500m (5,000ft). Widely planted in gardens and parks for its stunning autumn colour. Height to 25m (80ft). The flowers (near right) appear with the bright yellow young leaves, the females are in the axils of the new leaves. The acorns (far right) are about 2cm (¾in) long and ripen in October. Leaves (p48) are green through the summer then turn bright red (p188) about 6 weeks before they fall. They are 7·5–15cm (3–6in) long, lustrous green above and paler beneath.

Daimio Oak

Quercus dentata Thunb.
Deciduous, native to Japan, Korea and China and grown in a few collections. Height to 18m (60ft). Flowers open in May. Acorns (near right) are 1·2–1·8cm (½–¾in) long in cups bearing long narrow scales and drop in October. Leaves (p49) turn brown in autumn and often remain on the tree during winter. They are among the largest of all the oak leaves, sometimes over 30cm (1ft) long, both sides downy at first with the upper surface becoming smooth.

Hungarian Oak

Quercus frainetto Ten.
Deciduous, native to southern Italy, the Balkans and Rumania, grows well in cultivation. Height to 30m (100ft). Flowers open in May and the acorns (far right), 1·2–1·8cm (½–¾in) long, fall in October. Leaves (p49) grow to 20cm (8in) long; the upper surface soon becomes dark green the lower surface downy and greyish green.

Lucombe Oak

Quercus × hispanica Lam. 'Lucombeana'
A natural hybrid between *Q. cerris* and *Q. suber* occurring in south Europe and found in many gardens and collections. Semi-evergreen, in the autumn the leaves turn partly brown, but they do not fall until the new leaves grow in the following June except in extremely hard winters. Height to 30m (100ft). Flowers (near right) open at the end of May. The females are in the leaf axils at the tip of the new growth. The fertile acorns (far right) are produced in two years. Note the brown edged semi-evergreen leaves in the flower photograph. Leaves (p48) may be 5–12·5cm (2–5in) long, the upper surface glossy green, the lower covered with grey felt. The bark can be more or less corky like the parent *Q. suber*, the Cork Oak.

Holm Oak or Holly Oak

Quercus ilex L.
Evergreen, native to the Mediterranean region, common in parks and gardens and roadsides, it makes a good solid healthy looking tree as wide as it is tall with a dense dark appearance due to the abundance of its foliage. It thrives with clipping. The wood is hard and durable, used for joinery, vine props and makes good charcoal. Height to as much as 28m (90ft). Flowers (near right) appear with the new leaves in June, female flowers are in the new leaf axils. The acorns (far right) up to 1·8cm (¾in) long, fall in October; after good summers there is usually a very heavy crop. The leaves (p29) are variable in size, 3·7–7·5cm (1½–3in) long, and may have spine-tipped teeth or be untoothed. Young leaves have down on both surfaces but this soon falls away from the upper surface, leaving it dark glossy green. The bark (p219) is nearly black and cracked into small squares.

Shingle Oak

Quercus imbricaria Michx.
Deciduous, native to central and eastern United States where it is found on rich hillsides and fertile damp bottom land. Sometimes planted as an ornamental tree in N. America, but it is rare in collections in Europe. Pioneers used its timber for clapboards and shingles, a type of roof tile, hence the name Shingle Oak. A small tree to about 15m (50ft) in the wild, but may reach 25m (80ft) in cultivation. Flowers (near right) appear in late May or early June, the females are in the leaf axils of the new growth. The acorns (far right) grow to 1·8cm (¾in) long and almost as wide; the specimens shown are not yet fully grown. The young leaves are a lovely yellow and remain so until mid June; a mature leaf (p28) is normally 10–17·5cm (4–7in) long and usually unlobed but occasionally three-lobed near the base.

Californian Black Oak

Quercus kelloggii Newberry
Deciduous, native to the valleys and coastal mountain ranges of California and Oregon to an altitude of 2,000m (6,500ft). Grown in botanical collections in Europe. The acorns were once the staple diet of the Californian Indians and the brittle wood used for fuel. Height to 25m (80ft) or more. The flowers (near right) can be seen in early May with the new leaves, the females are in the leaf axils. The acorns (far right) are 3·7cm (1½in) long, deeply enclosed in the cup, take two years to form and fall around October. Leaf (p48) 7·5–15cm (3–6in) long, dark shining green above, paler below.

Laurel Oak

Quercus laurifolia Michx.
Semi-evergreen, native to a wide belt along the southern coast of N. America, including Florida, otherwise rare, grown only in collections. Height to 30m (100ft). The flowers are seen at the end of May. Acorns (near right) have shallow hairless cups. Leaves (p24), normally 7·5–10cm (3–4in) long, occasionally lobed near the apex. Those shown with acorns are atypical as they are usually more narrowed at the base.

Lea's Hybrid Oak

Quercus × leana Nutt.
Deciduous, a natural hybrid between *Q. imbricaria* and *Q. velutina* found in south-eastern N. America with the parents, also in a few European collections. Height to 20m (65ft). Flowers not shown. Acorns (far right) fall in October. Leaves (p49) are variable in shape and pubescence.

Lebanon Oak

Quercus libani Olivier
Deciduous, native to Syria, Lebanon and Asia Minor. A fine tree, not as common as it might be in collections. Height to 21m (70ft). The flowers (near right) are seen with the bright yellow young leaves as early as the end of March, the females can be seen in the leaf axils. The acorns (far right) 2·5cm (1in) long fall in October. The distinctive leaves (p26) are 5–10cm (2–4in) long.

Ludwig's Oak

Quercus × ludoviciana Sarg.
Deciduous, a natural hybrid between *Q. phellos* and probably *Q. falcata* var. *pagodifolia* Elliott. found in Louisiana. Leaves are very variable up to 18cm (7in) long (p48).

Caucasian Oak

Quercus macranthera Fisch. & Mey.
Deciduous, native to the Caucasus and northern Iran. Uncommon, found only in collections. Height to 25m (80ft). Flowers in May. Acorns (near right), up to 2·5cm (1in) long, fall in October. Leaves (p49) are up to 15cm (6in) long.

Burr Oak or Mossy Cup Oak

Quercus macrocarpa Michx.
Deciduous, native to eastern N. America from the deep south to the far north. The wood is strong and durable. Height to 50m (160ft) in the wild. Flowers in May. Acorns (far right) are very variable in size but in the south may reach as much as 5cm (2in) long. Leaves (p49) are 10–25cm (4–10in) long.

Black Jack Oak

Quercus marilandica Muenchh.
Deciduous, native to south-eastern and eastern United States, a ragged tree of poor soils growing to 10m (30ft) in height. The wood is hard and good for fuel and charcoal. Flowers (near right) at the end of May with females in the new leaf axils. The acorns are small, 1·8cm (¾in) long. Leaves (p49) are distinctive, 7·5–17·5cm (3–7in) long.

Bamboo-leaved Oak

Quercus myrsinifolia Blume
Evergreen, native of south China and Japan, rare, grown only in collections. Height to 15m (50ft) in the wild but shrubby in cultivation. The young leaves are a rich purplish red. Acorns (far right) are small, up to 1·8cm (¾in) long in unusual cups with concentric rings. Leaf p26.

Water Oak

Quercus nigra L.
Deciduous, native to south-eastern United States. Height to 25m (80ft) in the wild. The leaves may be broad at the apex like *Q. marilandica* or long and narrow like *Q. phellos*. They stay quite fresh on the tree until January.

Pin Oak

Quercus palustris Muenchh.
Deciduous, native to north-eastern United States. Successful in cultivation in Europe but found mainly in some botanical collections. The wood is hard and strong, used for construction and clapboards. Height to about 25m (80ft), or more. Flowers (near right) in early May with the young bright yellow leaves, the females are in the new leaf axils. Acorns (far right) mature after 2 years, about 1·2cm (½in) long and one third covered by their cup. Those shown are in their first year. Leaves (p48), deeply lobed, grow to 7·5–12·5cm (3–5in) long, with conspicuous tufts of brown hairs on the vein axils underneath and turn scarlet and deep red in autumn (p189).

Sessile Oak or Durmast Oak

Quercus petraea (Mattuschka) Lieblein
Deciduous, native to Europe and west Asia. This and *Q. robur* are the common British oaks. The wood has been widely used in joinery and shipbuilding. Height to 30m (100ft) but can grow taller. Very long lived. Flowers (near right) appear in May, the females are in the leaf axils on the end of the new shoot. Acorns (far right) are sessile which is the main difference between this oak and *Q. robur* where the acorns are on long stalks. The acorns grow to as much as 3cm (1¼in) long, with more scales on the cup than on *Q. robur*. Leaves (p48) have a stalk whereas *Q. robur* has sessile leaves, they are 7·5–12·5cm (3–5in) long.

Willow Oak

Quercus phellos L.
Native to south-eastern United States, usually deciduous but in the south of its range it is almost semi-evergreen. It grows in low wet lands generally near streams and swamps. Height to 20–30m (70–100ft). Flowers (near right) in May, the females in the new leaf axils. Acorns (far right) are not well formed in the photograph. When mature the cup will cover less than half of the acorn which will be roundish in shape about 1·2cm (½in) long. Leaves (p24) are long, up to 10cm (4in), and willow-like giving this oak its common name, they are yellow at first then bright green colouring golden yellow in the autumn (p189) to make a superb show.

Pontine Oak or Armenian Oak

Quercus pontica K. Koch
Deciduous, native to the Caucasus and north-east Anatolia. A shrub or small tree to a height of 8m (25ft). Remarkable for its large, 10–20cm (4–8in), leaves (p29) which resemble chestnut leaves. Acorns are 2·5–3·7cm (1–1½in) long and they ripen to a deep mahogany red. The leaves colour yellow in the autumn (p189).

Basket Oak or Chestnut Oak

Quercus prinus L.
Deciduous, native to eastern United States, often found on dry rocky soils and sometimes also called Rock Oak. The wood, which is hard and easily split, has been used for construction, cooperage, wheels, fences, fuel and basket making. Height to 30m (100ft). The flowers (near right) appear with young leaves in April, earlier than most oaks. The acorns (far right) are 2·5–3·7cm (1–1½in) in length and fall in October. Leaves (p49) resemble the leaves of the Sweet Chestnut (*Castanea sativa*) which gives this oak its alternative common name. They are 15–20cm (6–8in) long, evenly lobed, dark green above and silvery white and densely pubescent below. The bark is nearly black and deeply ridged.

Downy Oak

Quercus pubescens Willd.
Deciduous, native to southern Europe, west Asia and the Caucasus. A rapid grower to a height of 20m (70ft). Flowers (near right) at the end of May, the females are to be seen in the leaf axils on the new growth. Acorns (far right) are 2·5cm (1in) long and fall in October. Leaves (p48) are downy when young but during the summer the upper surface becomes smooth and hairless; they are 5–9cm (2–3½in) long. Please note the leaf shown on p48 is not typical; those shown with the flower and acorn pictures are more normal. The winter buds and new shoots are covered in down which, with the downy leaves, gives this oak its common name.

Pyrenean Oak

Quercus pyrenaica Willd.
Deciduous, native to south Europe and Morocco, sometimes grown in collections. Height to about 18m (60ft). Does not flower till June, but then profusely, with the young, very downy leaves (near right), the females are in the new leaf axils. Acorns (far right) are found on a downy erect stalk. (Those shown are dried specimens.) Leaves (p48) are variable, often fairly large, up to 20cm (8in) long and deeply cut, covered with felt at first, later only felted on the greyish underside.
Q. pyrenaica 'Pendula'. This form is more common in gardens and collections than the type.

English Oak or Pedunculate Oak

Quercus robur L.
Deciduous, native to Europe (including Britain), east Russia, south-west Asia and north Africa. This is the more common of the two native British oaks and is extremely long lived, possibly up to 800 years or more. Valuable for timber, especially in the past when much of Britain was covered in oak forests. Height to more than 30m (100ft). Flowers (near right) in May, the female flowers can be seen on the end of the new growth. Acorns (far right) are on long stalks or peduncles, hence the alternative common name which separates it from *Q. petraea*, the Sessile Oak. The acorns are 1·8–3cm (¾–1¼in) long and fall in October. The leaves 10–12·5cm (4–5in) are sessile (p48). There are many varieties of interest, two of which are:
Q. robur cv. 'Filicifolia' **Cut-leaved Oak**. Leaf p48.
Q. robur forma *purpurascens* (DC.) K. Koch **Purple English Oak**. Leaf p48.

Sweet Gum
Liquidamber styraciflua (p132)
Scarlet Oak
Quercus coccinea (p182)
Yellow Buckeye or
Sweet Buckeye
Aesculus flava (p80)
Tulip-tree,
Yellow Poplar or
Whitewood
Liriodendron tulipifera (p133)
London Plane
Platanus acerifolia (p165)

Hers's Maple
Acer grosseri var. *hersii* (p70)
Norway Maple
Acer platanoides (p74)
Pontine Oak or
Armenian Oak
Quercus pontica (p186)
Pin Oak
Quercus palustris (p185)
Willow Oak
Quercus phellos (p186)
Shumard Oak
Quercus shumardii (p190)

Red Oak

Quercus rubra L., synonym *Q. borealis* Michx. f. Deciduous, native to the eastern half of N. America from central Florida and Texas to northern Canada. This is the best growing oak introduced from N. America to Europe; young trees may grow at the rate of 2·5m (8ft) per year. The wood, though hard, is not durable and has been used mainly for fire-wood and the bark, rich in tannin, is used in tanning leather. Height to 18–25m (60–80ft). Flowers (near right) appear in May, the red females can be seen in the axils of the new leaves. Acorns (far right) 1·8cm (¾in) long, take two years to mature and fall in October. Leaves (p48) are 10–22·5cm (4–9in) long are a lovely bright yellow for the first three weeks; the autumn colour is a deep red to brown.

Shumard Oak

Quercus schumardii Buckl.
Deciduous, native to south-eastern United States. In the Mississippi valley it is used for lumber and considered the most valuable oak. Height to 30m (100ft) or more. Flowers (near right) with the lovely yellow new leaves in May, females can be seen in the leaf axils. Acorns (far right) about 2·5cm (1in) long. The leaves (p48) can be distinguished from *Q. rubra* and *Q. coccinea* by the tufts of pale hairs on the underside; they are 7·5–9cm (3–3½in) long, and colour red in the autumn (p189).

Cork Oak

Quercus suber L.
Evergreen, native of the west Mediterranean countries, found in collections and now grown for its bark in California and other southern states. The remarkable feature of this oak is the thick cork bark (p220). In Spain and Portugal it is stripped off every ten years to provide most of the world's cork. Height to 20m (65ft), but in its rocky native environment it is often smaller and more stunted. Flowers (near right) are found at the end of May or beginning of June, the females are in the lead axils of the new growth. Acorns (far right) form in one year and fall in October, 1·2–3cm (½–1¼in) long. The leaves (p29) are dark glossy green above and clothed in grey felt below, 2·5–6·2cm (1–2½in) long.

Macedonian Oak

Quercus trojana Webb, synonym *Q. macedonica* A.DC.
Evergreen, native to south-east Italy and the Balkans. A small tree growing in cultivation to as much as 20m (65ft). The flowers (near right) appear with the young fresh green leaves in May, the females are in the new leaf axils. Acorns (far right) 1·8–3cm (¾–1¼in) long fall in October. The leaf shown on p49 is not up to scratch; those shown with the acorns are much better, note the distinctive veining. Both leaf surfaces are smooth and hairless in the mature leaf, 3–7cm (1¼–2¾in) long.

Turner's Oak

Quercus × turneri Willd.
Deciduous or semi-evergreen, a hybrid between *Q. ilex* and *Q. robur* raised in the 18th century by Spencer Turner in Essex. Much planted in gardens and collections in Europe as it makes a well formed and decorative tree to a height of 16m (55ft). Flowers (near left) at the end of May or early June, the females are in the new leaf axils. Acorns (far right) are similar to *Q. ilex*, about 1·8cm (¾in) long on long stalks and fall in October. The leaves (p49) are 6–11cm (2½–4½in) long and stay on the tree until February at least and sometimes until after the new leaves are formed, note the flower photograph.

Black Oak or Quercitron Oak

Quercus velutina Lam.
Deciduous, native of eastern N. America. The bark is used as a source of quercitron, a yellow dye, and also for tannin. Height to about 23m (75ft) but may occasionally be much taller. Flowers (near right) are found with the young leaves in late May or early June, note the females in the leaf axils. Acorns (far right) fall in October, and are up to about 1·8cm (¾in) in length. The leaves are very variable; the specimen shown on p48 is not typical and should look more similar to *Q. coccinea* (p182) and (p48), though less deeply cut away. They are usually about 12·5cm (5in) long but may reach as much as 30cm (1ft) in length. The upper surface is dark shiny green, the lower surface is scattered with a thin scurf and has tufts of down in the vein axils.

Stag's Horn Sumac

Rhus typhina L., family Anacardiaceae
Deciduous tree or shrub, native to eastern N. America, commonly grown in gardens in central and northern Europe. Height to 7·5m (25ft), but may reach 12m (40ft) in the wild. Flowers (far left) open in late June and July, male and female on separate trees. Females form a dense downy head 10–20cm (4–8in) long, males form larger looser clusters. Fruit (near left) is in a cluster 10–20cm (4–8in) long, crimson and velvety. Leaves (p58) are also covered with soft velvety hairs. They colour bright orange in autumn and this, combined with crimson fruits on female bushes, make a stunning display for any garden.

Varnish Tree

Rhus verniciflua Stokes
Deciduous tree, native to Himalaya and China, cultivated in other parts of east Asia and sometimes in Europe. A poisonous juice is extracted from the stem to make the black varnish used in making black lacquer in China and Japan, and an oil from the fruits was used in candle-making in China. Height to 18m (60ft) in China. Flowers (far left) open in July in large open clusters up to 25cm (10in) long. Fruits (near left) are 0·6cm (¼in) across, ripening yellowish brown. Leaves (p58) are 30–60cm (1–2ft) long with 7–13 shortly stalked leaflets, which are softly downy underneath.

False Acacia or Black Locust

Robinia pseudoacacia L., family Leguminosae
Deciduous tree, native to eastern and mid-western United States, cultivated for ornament in eastern states and throughout Europe, and naturalised in south-western Europe. Common in city streets and parks. Height to 25m (80ft), often forming thickets by suckering. Flowers (near right) have a sweet fragrance and open in June in clusters 10–20cm (4–8in) long. Fruit pods (far right) are 5–10cm (2–4in) long containing kidney-shaped seeds. Leaves (p57) are about 15–20cm (6–8in) long and usually have 13–15 rounded leaflets, each with a notched and spined tip. Bark (p220) is dark brown and deeply furrowed with a network of ridges. Twigs bear short stout spines.
R. pseudoacacia cv. 'Frisia'. A cultivated variety with golden-yellow leaves.

Clammy Locust

Robinia viscosa Vent.
Deciduous tree, native to Carolina and naturalised in many parts of eastern U.S.A. Cultivated for ornament in most temperate countries. Height to about 12m (40ft). Flowers (near right) have little perfume and open in June in clusters about 12·5cm (5in) long. Fruit are pods, 5–9cm (2–3½in), containing reddish brown seeds and covered with sticky hairs. Leaves (p57) are 17·5–30cm (7–12in) long with 13–21 leaflets on a sticky and hairy main stem. Young shoots are also stickily hairy and bear some thorns.

Salix family Salicaceae, **Willow**
Mostly deciduous trees and shrubs, with simple alternate usually narrow leaves, male and female flowers on separate trees. Fruits are tiny capsules enclosing seeds.

White Willow

Salix alba L.
Native to Europe (including Britain), northern Asia and northern Africa. Grows wild on riversides. Height to 25m (80ft). Catkins open in late April and May, males (far left) yellow about 3·7–5·5cm (1½–2¼in) long, females green about the same length ripening to form fruiting catkins (near left) which split to release white tufted seeds in June. Leaves (p25) are light green at first, becoming dark green with white silky hairs above and thick white down beneath, giving the tree a pale greyish white appearance.

Weeping Willow

Salix babylonica L.
Native to China, planted in gardens and parks by lakes and rivers in Europe and N. America. Superseded in Britain by the Golden Weeping Willow (*S.* × *chrysocoma*). Height to 10m (33ft). Catkins open in mid-May, males (far left) yellow, females green, up to 1·8cm (¾in) long. Leaves are narrow about 7·5–15cm (3–6in) long, hairless, dark green above and paler beneath. Young shoots are brown and hang down.

Goat Willow, Pussy Willow or Great Sallow

Salix caprea L.
Small tree or shrub, native to Europe (including Britain) and north-east Asia. Height to about 10m (33ft) but often shrubby. Catkins (near left) open on bare twigs in March and April, males grey and silky turning yellow, females green, both up to 3cm (1¼in). Female flowers develop into green capsules which release white tufted seeds in May. Leaves (p32) are broad for a willow on a red downy stem. Often rather wrinkled and with soft grey hairs underneath. Shoots have grey hairs at first and become shiny red brown.

Golden Weeping Willow

Salix × chrysocoma Dode, synonym *S. alba* 'Tristis' Gaud.
A hybrid, commonly cultivated in parks and gardens by water and on dry ground. Height to 20m (65ft). Catkins (far left) open in April, usually male, about 7cm (2¾in) curving upwards, sometimes with both male and female flowers on the catkins. Leaves (p25) are narrow and have silky hairs on both sides, paler than *S. babylonica*. Branches and shoots are golden.

Grey Sallow

Salix cinerea L.
Small tree or shrub, native to Europe (including Britain) and north-east Asia. Height may reach 10m (33ft) but usually shrubby. Catkins (near left) open in March and April, similar to *S. caprea* but more slender. Fruit capsules release seed in May. Leaves (p25) are similar in texture to *S. caprea* but narrower and less wrinkled. Young shoots are covered with brown down. Often forms hybrids with *S. caprea*.

Crack Willow or Brittle Willow

Salix fragilis L.
Native to Europe (including Britain) and west Siberia south to Iran, growing on riverbanks. Twigs snap off easily at their bases when knocked, hence the common names. This allows it to spread along a river as they root and form new plants when washed ashore. Height to 25m (80ft). Catkins open in April, males (far left) yellow about 1·8–5cm (¾–2in) long. Female catkins are green developing to fruiting catkins (near left) about 10cm (4in) long which release white fluffy seeds in May. Leaves (p25) are narrow and coarsely toothed, slightly hairy at first but turning glossy green and hairless when mature.

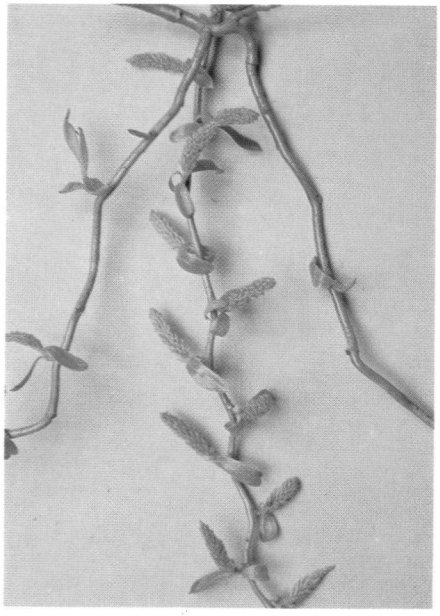

Contorted Willow

Salix matsudana Koidz. cv. 'Tortuosa'
A cultivated variety of the Pekin Willow (*S. matsudana*) which is a rare Chinese species. Planted in streets and gardens. Height to 12m (40ft). Catkins (far left) are female and open in April, about 2·5cm (1in) long. They develop into fruiting catkins which release white cottony seeds in June. Twigs and leaves (p25) are curiously twisted and curled.

Black Willow

Salix nigra Marsh.
Native to eastern N. America, where it yields a light timber used in making boxes. Height to 12m (40ft). Catkins open in April, males (far left) yellow about 2·5–5cm (1–2in) long, females green, about the same length, releasing seeds in May and June. Leaves (far left) are narrow often slightly curved, pale shining green when mature.

Bay Willow or Laurel-leaved Willow

Salix pentandra L.
Native to central and northern Europe (including Britain) and Asia Minor. Grows by rivers and is sometimes cultivated in gardens. Height to 20m (65ft). Catkins (near left) open in late April or May, males yellow, about 1·8–6cm (¾–2¼in) long, females green, more slender and shorter. Fruiting catkins (below left) may be 10cm (4in) long and release cottony seeds in June. Leaves (p25) are dark shiny green and broader than most willows.

Almond-leaved Willow or French Willow

Salix triandra L.
Small tree or shrub, native to Europe (including Britain). Height to 10m (33ft). Cultivated in Europe for basket making. Catkins open in March or April, males slender and yellow, females green. Seeds released in May and June. Leaves (p25) are narrow and shiny. Recognised by its flaky, peeling bark.

Osier

Salix viminalis L.
Shrub or small tree to about 10m (33ft), native to central and western Europe (including Britain). Often coppiced and used in making baskets and fences. Catkins open in April and May before the leaves unfold, males (near left) grey and silky with yellow anthers, about 1·8cm (¾in) long, females green, releasing seeds in June. Leaves (p24) are narrow with inrolled margins, dark green above and covered with silky hairs underneath.

Elder

Sambucus nigra L., family Caprifoliaceae
Deciduous shrub or small tree, native to Europe (including Britain), north Africa and western Asia. Grows wild in woods and scrub and waste places. Often thought of as a weed and the flowers and fruits are used in wine-making. May grow to 10m (33ft). Flowers (near right) open in June, each about 0·6cm (¼in) across in bunches 10–20cm (4–8in) across. Fruits (far right) ripen in August and September, each about 0·6cm (¼in) across. They are especially rich in vitamin C. Leaves (p53) usually have 5 or 7 toothed leaflets which have a distinctive, unpleasant smell.

Sassafras albidum (Nutt.) Nees,
family Lauraceae **Sassafras**
Native to eastern United States. Bark and roots produce a fragrant oil and Choctaw Indians used its leaves to make a soap. Height to 21cm (70ft). Male and female flowers on separate trees, small and yellowish in clusters. Fruit oval, bluish, about 0·8cm (⅓in) long. Leaves (p47) are 2 or 3-lobed or entire, colour yellow and orange in autumn and have a sweet, tangy smell.

Prince Albert's Yew

Saxegothaea conspicua Lindl.,
family Podocarpaceae
Evergreen coniferous tree, native to Chile and Argentina. Sometimes bushy or forms a slender drooping tree to about 18m (60ft) high, or less in S. America. Flowers (far left) open in May, males deep pinkish purple, about 0·2cm (1/10in) long; females on same tree, pale blue-green and developing into cones of the same colour (near left) about 1·2cm (½in) long. Leaves (p13) are flat, hard and curved with a sharp tip. They have 2 whitish bands on underside.

Umbrella Pine

Sciadopitys verticillata (Thunb.) Sieb. & Zucc.,
family Taxodiaceae
Evergreen coniferous tree, native to Japan, cultivated in large gardens. Height to about 21m (70ft) or less in cultivation but up to 36m (120ft) in native habitat. Flowers (near right) open in April and May, males yellow about 1·2cm (½in) long in clusters at shoot tips, females dark. Cones (far right) ripen over 2 years from green to brown, about 5–7cm (2–2¾in) long. The scales open to release seeds and are loosely attached – the cone usually breaks up easily when handled. Leaves (p18) are distinctively arranged in whorls along the branches. They are narrow and shining green with a deep groove both above and below. Bark is reddish brown, peeling in long strips.

Coast Redwood

Sequoia sempervirens (D. Don)
Endl., family Taxodiaceae
Evergreen coniferous tree, native to the Pacific coast from Oregon south through California. Grown for timber in N. America and sometimes in Europe in large gardens, parks and estates for ornament. Thought to be the tallest tree in the world, one having reached over 111m (367ft) in California. Flowers (far left) open in February, males yellow or brown about 0·6cm (¼in) long at tips of shoots, females about the same size, green. Cones (near left) ripen from a hard green conelet to woody brown cone about 1·8cm (¾in) long in one year. Foliage (p13) consists of scale-like leaves pressed closely to the stem and flat needle-like leaves in 2 rows on each side of the shoots. Bark (p220) is bright orange-red, soft and fibrous.

Wellingtonia or California Big Tree

Sequoiadendron giganteum (Lindl.) Buchholz, synonym *Sequoia gigantea* (Lindl.) Decne., family Taxodiaceae
Evergreen conifer, native to western slopes of the Sierra Nevada, California. Cultivated for ornament in eastern states and in western and southern Europe. Some of the tallest trees in the word have been Wellingtonias, some recorded at 110m (365ft) and 4,000 years old. In Europe it may reach about 50m (165ft). Male and female flowers (near right) appear on same tree. Males appear in October, then turn yellow and shed pollen in March. Females are tiny green conelets about 1·2cm (½in) long with spine tipped scales. Cones mature in 2 years from green conelets (far right) about 7·5cm (3in) long to dark brown. They may remain on the tree for up to 20 years. Seeds are winged. Foliage (p12) consists of scale-like leaves and have an aniseed-like smell when crushed.

Sophora japonica (L.) **Pagoda Tree,** family Leguminosae. Native to China. Height to 25m (80ft). Clusters of white flowers in August.

Sorbus family Rosaceae, **Whitebeam** and **Rowan**
Deciduous trees of 3 forms, 2 of which are commonly found: the Whitebeams with simple, sometimes lobed leaves; and the Rowans with pinnate leaves. Flowers are small, in clusters, and fruits are berry-like.

American Mountain Ash

Sorbus americana Marsh.
Native to eastern N. America, cultivated there and sometimes in Europe for attractive fruit and autumn colour. The fruit has a sharp flavour, is rich in vitamins and has been used in herbal remedies. Height to about 9m (30ft), often low and shrubby. Flowers (far left) open in May, about 0·3cm (⅛in) across in flat clusters 7·5–10cm (3–4in) across. Fruit (near left) are about 0·6cm (¼in). Leaves (p56) have 11–17 leaflets, on a dark red or green stem, and colour bright yellow in autumn.

Whitebeam

Sorbus aria (L.) Crantz.
Native to central and southern Europe (including Britain), growing on chalk and limestone. Planted in parks, gardens and streets, along with its many cultivated forms. Height to 25m (80ft). Flowers (far left) open in May, each about 1·2cm (½in) across in heads 5–7·5cm (2–3in) across. Fruits (near left) are up to about 1·2cm (½in) across and ripen red from green in September, quickly taken by birds. Leaves (p34) are irregularly toothed and covered with thick white down when they first emerge. The upper surface loses this down but the lower one remains white and felty. They colour yellow and brown in the autumn.

Rowan,
Mountain Ash or
European Mountain Ash

Sorbus aucuparia L.
Native to Europe (including Britain), N. Africa and Asia Minor. Once planted by houses in the Scottish Highlands as a protection against witchcraft, and still popular in gardens, parks and streets, and now widely planted in N. America. The wood is hard and useful for small items such as tool handles and spinning wheels, and the berries, rich in vitamin C, make a delicious jelly; and have also been used in herbal remedies. Height to about 15m (50ft). Flowers (far left) open in May in clusters about 10–15cm (4–6in) across. Fruits (near left) ripen from green in September, and are quickly eaten by birds. Leaves (p56) have 9–15 leaflets, untoothed at their bases, smaller than the American Mountain Ash (*S. americana*). Leaf buds are long, slender, dark purple and hairy. The bark (p220) is shiny grey-brown, with dark dots, or lenticels.

Japanese Rowan

Sorbus commixta Hedl.
Native to Japan, Korea and Sakhalin, sometimes grown in gardens and streets. Height to about 15m (50ft). Flowers (far left) open in May in clusters about 7·5cm (3in) across. Fruits are about 0·8cm (⅓in) across and ripen bright orangey-red in August and September. The leaves (p56) have 11–15 leaflets, dark green above and whitish beneath. They colour deep purple then red in October and November. A good distinguishing feature is the pointed shining red leaf bud, about 1cm (½in) long.

Service Tree

Sorbus domestica L.
Native to southern Europe, north Africa and west Asia, often planted in central Europe for ornament and for its fruit, which is very sour, but edible when over-ripe or frosted, and used in making a type of beer. Height to about 15m (50ft). Flowers (far left) open in May, about 1·2cm (½in) across in rounded clusters up to about 10cm (4in) across. Fruits (near left) are about 2·5cm (1in) long, pear-shaped or rounded, green tinged red to brownish when ripe. Leaves (p56) have 11–21 leaflets, softly downy beneath and may be rather yellowish above. Their buds are oval, bright green and resinous. Bark is dark brown and orange, broken into small cracks and plates.

Chinese Scarlet Rowan

Sorbus 'Embley', synonym *S. discolor* Hort.
Of Chinese origin, now grown in parks, gardens and streets. Height to about 15m (50ft). Flowers (far left) open in late May. Fruits are orange red, ripening in September. Leaves (p56) have 11–15 leaflets which are hairless beneath. In late October they colour (near left) scarlet red then dark purplish, in opposite sequence to *S. commixta*, and remain longer on the tree. Leaf buds are about 1·2cm (½in) or more long, pointed deep red.

Hupeh Rowan

Sorbus hupehensis Schneid.
Native to western China, planted in European parks and gardens. Height to about 15m (50ft). Flowers (far left) open in May about 0·8cm (⅓in) across with pinkish purple anthers in rounded heads 7·5–15cm (3–6in) across. Fruits (near left) are about 0·6cm (¼in) across, ripening to white or pink in September and persisting on the tree late in winter. Leaves (p56) have 11–13 dark bluish green leaflets, toothed only round their tips on a red grooved central stem. They turn red in autumn.

Swedish Whitebeam

Sorbus intermedia (Ehrh.) Pers.
Native to Scandinavia, the U.S.S.R., around the Baltic Sea, and north-east Germany. Planted in northern Europe in streets and parks, particularly useful in cities and towns as it withstands atmospheric pollution. Height to about 10m (33ft). Flowers (far left) open in late May, each about 1·2cm (½in) across with pale pink anthers in heads 7·5–10cm (3–4in) wide. Fruits (near left) are about 1·2cm (½in) shiny green, ripening to orange-red or reddish-brown in September. Leaves (p47) have 3–7 toothed lobes on each side, becoming shallower and reduced to teeth towards the tip. Leaf buds are green or dark reddish-brown with greyish down.

Sorbus 'Joseph Rock'
An ornamental tree from China, sometimes planted in gardens. Height to about 10m (33ft). Flowers open in May, fruits (far left) ripen to golden yellow and remain on the tree through winter. Leaves (p56) have 15–19 leaflets and colour orange-red and purple in autumn (near left).

Service Tree of Fontainebleau

Sorbus latifolia (Lam.) Pers.
Native to western and central Europe. Thought to be derived from a hybrid between the Wild Service Tree (*S. torminalis*) and one of the whitebeams. Height to 18m (60ft). Flowers (far left) open in May on downy stalks, fruits (near left) ripen brownish with speckles in September. Leaves (p47) are broader than other whitebeams with shallow lobing near the middle. They are dark green above and white felty below with a downy stem. Bark is dark brown, shaggy and peeling.

Pyrenean Whitebeam

Sorbus mougeotii Soy.-Will. & Godr.
Native to the western Alps and Pyrenees, on high mountain slopes where it may be a shrub or a small tree. Flowers (far left) open in May each about 1·2cm (½in) across. Fruits (near left) ripen in September and have a few sparse speckles. Leaves (p47) are narrower than *S. latifolia* but have more deeply cut lobes. They are dark shining above and whitish felty below.

Sargent's Rowan

Sorbus sargentiana Koehne
Native to western China, planted in parks and gardens, often grafted onto Rowan (*S. aucuparia*). Height to about 10m (33ft). Flowers (far left) open in June in clusters up to 15–20cm (6–8in) across (the one shown is much smaller). The flower stems have white hairs. Fruits (near left) are 0·6cm (¼in) across produced in huge clusters. Leaves (p55) are larger than Rowan (*S. aucuparia*) to 35cm (14in) with 7–11 leaflets. They colour bright scarlet and orange in the autumn. Leaf buds are deep red and shiny covered with drops of resin.

Bastard Service Tree

Sorbus × thuringiaca (Ilse) Fritsch
A hybrid between *S. aria* and *S. aucuparia*, sometimes planted in gardens and streets. Height to about 12m (40ft). Flowers (far right) open in May, each about 1·2cm (½in) across in flowerheads 6–10cm (2¼–4in) across with downy stems. Fruits (near left) are about 1·2cm (½in) across and ripen in September, sometimes with a few brown speckles. Leaves (p47) reflect the parent trees, deeply lobed with 1–4 pairs of free leaflets at the base. They are dark green above and white felty below. Leaf bud is about 0·8cm (⅓in) long, dark red-brown. Bark is smooth dull grey with shallow cracks.

Wild Service Tree

Sorbus torminalis (L.) Crantz
Native to Europe (including Britain), Algeria, the Caucasus and Middle East. The fruits are very acid but edible when over-ripe; they used to be sold in south England under the name of Chequers and have been used in medicine. Height to 25m (80ft). Flowers (far left) open in late May, each about 1·2cm (½in) across in loose heads about 10cm (4in) across with downy stems. Fruits (near left) are about 1·2cm (½in) long, covered with speckles, ripening in September. Leaves (p47) are unlike other *Sorbus* and this tree can easily be mistaken for a maple (*Acer*). They have 3–5 pairs of lobes, shiny bright green on both sides and colour deep reds in the autumn. The leaf buds are round and shining green. Bark is dark brown or grey, cracked into scaly plates.

Sorbus 'Wilfred Fox'
A hybrid between Whitebeam (*S. aria*) and the Himalayan Whitebeam (*S. cuspidata*), named after the creator of Winkworth Arboretum, Surrey, and who made a special study of *Sorbus* species. Height to about 12m (40ft). Flowers (far left) open in May, about 1·8cm (¾in) across with deep pink anthers in heads about 7·5cm (3in) across. Fruits are large, about 1·8cm (¾in) across, ripening golden brown in September. Leaves (p34) have shallow lobes and 12–15 pairs of veins. They become almost hairless, dark green above, remain light and felty below. Leaf buds are oval, green and brown. Bark is dark purplish grey with fine scales.

Japanese Stewartia or Deciduous Stewartia

Stewartia pseudocamellia Maxim., family Theaceae
Deciduous tree, native to Japan, sometimes grown in gardens. Height to 20m (65ft), usually less. Flowers look similar to *S. sinensis*, about 5cm (2in) across with clusters of bright yellow anthers and broad wavy-edged petals. The flower buds are set between two red-tipped bracts and open in late July and August. Leaves (p26) may be wavy edged and are dull green above and shiny underneath with downy tufts in the vein axils. They colour yellow and scarlet in the autumn (near right). Bark is orange brown and peels away to leave lighter orange new bark (far right).

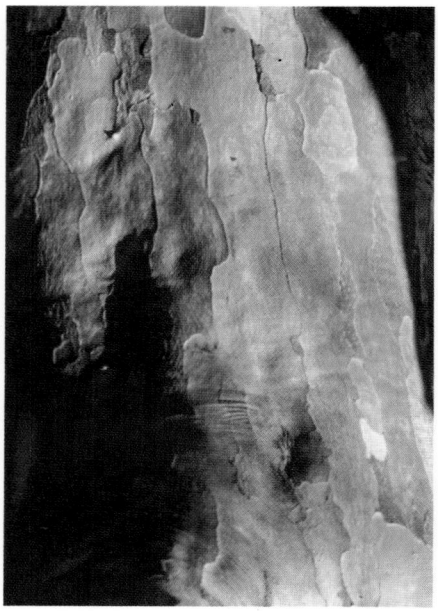

Chinese Stewartia

Stewartia sinensis Rehd. & Wils.
Deciduous tree, native to central China, grown in botanical collections. Height to about 10m (33ft). Fragrant flowers (near right) open in late July and are about 3·7–5cm (1½–2in) across and their buds are surrounded by a 5-lobed bract, each lobe tinged red at the tip. Leaves (p26) are larger than *S. pseudocamellia* and are bright green in both surfaces. They have red hairy stems and colour red and crimson in the autumn (far right). Bark (p220) is dark coppery brown and peels away leaving large areas of smooth light grey, green or creamy bare stem.

Snowbell Tree

Styrax japonica Sieb. & Zucc., family Styracaceae
Deciduous tree, native to China and Japan, grown as an ornamental in gardens. Height to about 11m (36ft). Flowers (far left) are often produced in great abundance, the undersides of each branch densely packed with clusters of 3–4 flowers (only one cluster is shown). They open in July and are about 2·5cm (1in) across. Fruits (near left) are about 1·2cm (½in) long. Leaves (p35) have a few tiny teeth and a short stem. They are shiny above and less so beneath, with tufts of down in the vein axils.

Big Leaf Storax

Styrax obassia Sieb. & Zucc.
Deciduous tree, native to Japan, grown in gardens but less popular than *S. japonica*. Height to about 14m (45ft). Fragrant flowers (far left) open in June about 2·5cm (1in) across in flowerheads up to 20cm (8in) long, hanging from branch tips. Fruits (near left) are about 1·8cm (¾in) long covered with soft brown down. Leaves (p39) are almost round with a pointed tip on mature trees and rather hairy on the upper surface. Young trees may have leaves with teeth near the tips or with flat tips.

Taiwania cryptomerioides Hayata, family Taxodiaceae
Evergreen conifer, native to Formosa, China and Burma. Height to about 14m (45ft) in cultivation. Cones (not shown) look similar to those of *Cunninghamia lanceolata*. Foliage (p12) is similar to *Cryptomeria japonica* but needles are bluer and taper from a broader base to a sharp spiny point.

Swamp Cypress or Bald Cypress

Taxodium distichum (L.) Rich., family Taxodiaceae
Deciduous conifer, native to swamps of south-eastern United States. When near water their roots form 'knees' which stick up above the water level. Grown in gardens and parks in Europe and N. America. Height to 45m (150ft) in the wild. Male flowers appear in late autumn, turn yellow and shed pollen (near right) in April when the clusters are 10–30cm (4–12in) long. Female flowers are tiny green conelets about 0·2cm (1/10in) long shown in photograph (near right) at the base of male catkins. Cones (far right) are about 2·5cm (1in) across, and ripen from green to brown. Leaves (p13) are soft and flat, evenly arranged in two rows. They turn a dull orange in the autumn and fall with their branchlets. Branchlets are arranged alternately or not quite opposite. Bark (p220) is reddish brown and ridged or peeling and fibrous, often fluted at buttressed base. Compare with Dawn Redwood (*Metasequoia glyptostoboides*).

Taxus family Taxaceae, **Yew**
Evergreen trees or shrubs. Male and female flowers on separate plants, and seeds are held in fleshy cups. Leaves are flat and narrow.

Common Yew or English Yew

Taxus baccata L.
Native to Europe, Iran and Algeria. Planted for shelter ornament and topiary. Leaves and seeds are poisonous and the wood is hard and durable. Height to 25m (80ft). Flowers (far left) open in March or April, males yellow, about 0·6cm (¼in), females tiny and green. Fruit (near left) are about 1·2cm (½in). Leaves (p14) are comb-like above and below, pointing well forward. Bark (p220) is dark brown and reddish peeling in thin strips.

Irish Yew

T. baccata cv. 'Fastigiata'
A cultivated yew with upright growth habit. Often planted in churchyards and sometimes called the Churchyard Yew. Most are female.
T. baccata cv. 'Fastigiata Aureomarginata', **Golden Irish Yew** A form of Irish Yew with golden new growth (p14). Only male flowers are produced, no fruit.
T. baccata cv. 'Fructo-luteo', **Yellow-berried Yew** A form with orange yellow fruits (far left).

Taxus brevifolia Nutt., **Pacific Yew or Western Yew** Native to the Pacific coast of N. America. Height to 12m (40ft). Flowers similar to *T. baccata* and fruit has a red fleshy cup with a green seed protruding. Leaves (p14) dark, green above, paler below.

Chinese Yew

Taxus celebica (Warburg) Li
Native to China, sometimes grown in botanical collections. Height to 8m (26ft). Male flowers (near left) are about 0·2cm (1/10in) across, scattered along the undersides of shoots, and shed pollen in late February and March. Fruit is sparse, about 0·6cm (¼in) across, green with a darker green protruding seed and which rarely ripens to red in cultivation. Leaves (p14) are yellowish green on both sides and are sparse, giving this yew a rather straggly appearance.

Japanese Yew

Taxus cuspidata Sieb. & Zucc.
Native to Japan, grown in botanical collections. A bushy tree or shrub to 15m (50ft). Male flowers (far left) are about 0·2cm (1/10in) across and shed pollen in late February and March. Females are tiny and greenish, similar to those of *T. baccata*, and develop into distinctive fruits (near left), about 0·8cm (⅓in) across, with dark greyish green seed protruding. Leaves (p14) are curved or stick straight upwards. They are hard, dark shiny green above, yellowish green beneath with a sharp tip.

Spur Leaf

Tetracentron sinense Oliv., family Tetracentraceae
Deciduous tree, native to China, grown in botanical collections and some large gardens. Height to about 15m (50ft). Flowers are in catkins 9–15cm (3½–6in) long which appear in the spring and gradually expand and open through the summer. The photograph near right shows the catkin in May, far right in August. Leaves (p42) look similar to *Cercidiphyllum japonicum* but are arranged alternately. They are distinctive since they arise singly from spurs of branches and twigs.

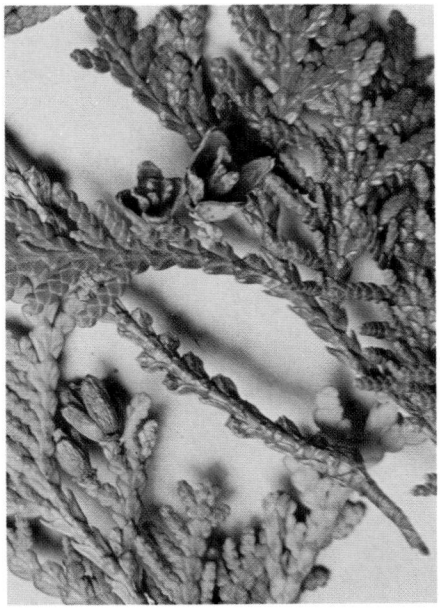

Thuja family Cupressaceae, **Arbor-vitae**
Evergreen coniferous trees and shrubs with scale-like leaves pressed closely to the stem. Male and female flowers on the same tree. Cones are small with few scales and winged seeds.

White Cedar or American Arbor-vitae

Thuja occidentalis L.
Native to eastern N. America, grown in N. America and Europe for ornament or hedging. Cultivated dwarf forms are more common in Europe than the type. Height to about 15m (50ft). Flowers (far left) open in March and April, males dark red, females dark brownish yellow (bottom right of photograph), both about 0·1cm (1/20in) across. Cones (near left) ripen from yellowish-green the following autumn, about 1·2cm (½in) long with 8–10 scales. Leaves (p10) are dark green above, yellowish beneath and when crushed give off a smell of apples.

Chinese Cedar or Chinese Arbor-vitae

Thuja orientalis L.
Native to China, Manchuria and Korea, grown, with its numerous cultivated varieties, in Europe and N. America. Height to 18m (60ft). Flowers (far left) open in March, males dark yellow, females dull bluish-green about 0·1cm (1/20in). Cones (near left) about 1·8cm (¾in) across, usually with 6 hooked scales. They ripen from bluish-green to brown in the autumn, opening to release winged seeds. The specimen in cone photograph is of the cultivar 'Elegantissima'. Leaves (p10) are dark green on both sides and have no smell when crushed.
T. orientalis cv. 'Elegantissina'. A small cultivated variety with upswept branches. Leaves are golden tipped in the summer, fading to green in the winter. A good tree for small gardens or for growing in pots.

Western Red Cedar or Giant Arbor-vitae

Thuja plicata Donn ex D. Don
Native to western N. America where it is an important timber tree. Grown in Europe for timber, shelter, in gardens and often as hedging. Height to 40m (135ft) or more. Flowers (far left) open in March, males dark red, pale yellow when shedding pollen, females yellowish green, both about 0·2cm (1/10in) long. Cones (near left) are about 1·2cm (½in) long with 10–12 scales, ripening from yellowish green to brown and opening slightly to release winged seeds. Leaves (p10) are dark and glossy above and paler beneath with some light whitish marks. They emit a strong fruity smell even without being crushed.

Japanese Thuja or Japanese Arbor-vitae

Thuja standishii (Gord.) Carr.
Native to central Japan, grown in botanical collections and gardens. Height to about 20m (65ft) in cultivation. Flowers (far left) open in March, males dark reddish turning yellow when shedding pollen, females brownish green, both about 0·1cm (1/20in) across. Cones (near left) are about 1·2cm (½in) with 10–12 scales, ripening from bright green to dark brown in the autumn. Leaves (p10) are dull yellowish green or greyish above with patches of grey at leaf bases beneath. The shoots are often curved at the tip and have a lemony smell when crushed.

Hiba or Hiba Arbor-vitae

Thujopsis dolabrata (L.f.) Sieb. & Zucc., family Cupressaceae
Evergreen conifer, native to Japan, grown for ornament in large gardens. Height to about 20m (65ft) in cultivation. Flowers open in late April or May, males dark blackish green, females bluish green, both about 0·1cm (1/20in) long. Cones (far right) are 1·2–1·8cm (½–¾in) long, with 6–10 scales, ripening to dark bluish brown from bluish green, and opening to release seeds. Leaves (p11) are larger than on *Thuja* species, dark green and glossy above with 2 white bands on underside. Bark (near right) is dark reddish brown and peels in strips.

Tilia family Tiliaceae, **Lime, Linden or Basswood**
Deciduous trees with broad toothed leaves, small fragrant clustered flowers, with a long leafy bract attached to the stem, and small round, usually one-seeded fruits.

American Lime, American Linden or Basswood

Tilia americana L.
Native of eastern N. America, cultivated for shade or ornament in north-eastern states and occasionally in Europe. Important in N. America as a source of nectar for honey bees. Height to about 21m (70ft) or more in the wild. Flowers (far left) open in early July, each about 1·2cm (½in) on downy stems, with a rounded bract up to 10cm (4in) long. Fruits are about 0·3cm (⅛in) across, smooth and hairless. Leaves (p41) are large, about 20cm (8in) long, light green on both surfaces, and hairless except for tiny downy tufts in the axils of the veins underneath. Bark (near left) is dark greyish brown and rough, ridged and furrowed.

Small-leaved Lime

Tilia cordata Mill.
Native to Europe (including Britain), the Caucasus and Siberia, planted in parks and gardens and by roads, particularly useful in towns and cities. Height to about 30m (100ft). Flowers (far left) are about 1·2cm (½in) across and open in early July, usually in spreading clusters of 5–10 with a strong sweet fragrance. Fruits (near left) are about 0·6cm (¼in) wide. Leaves (p41) are smaller than most limes, about 3·7–7cm (1½–2¾in) long, dark green above and paler beneath with rust-coloured tufts of down in the vein axils and at leaf base. Bark is smooth and grey ageing to dark grey with large cracks and flakes.

Caucasian Lime or Crimean Lime

Tilia × euchlora K. Koch
Thought to be a hybrid between *T. cordata* and another from the Caucasus. Planted in Europe in parks, streets and some gardens. Height to about 20m (65ft). Flowers (far left) open in late July, larger and more yellow than other limes with 3–7 in a cluster. They have a narcotic effect on bees, which may be found lying on the ground under the trees. Fruits (near left) are elliptic and downy, about 1·2cm (½in) long. Leaves (p41) are dark glossy green above and paler beneath with conspicuous tufts of pale brown hairs in the vein axils. Bark is smooth dull grey with some deep cracks.

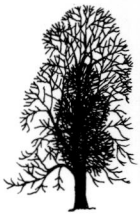

Common Lime or European Linden

Tilia × europaea L., synonym *T.* × *vulgaris* Hayne
A hybrid between *T. cordata* and *T. platyphyllos* which probably occurred naturally. Planted in north-western Europe for shade and ornament, more commonly found than either parent. Height to about 39m (130ft). Fragrant flowers (far left) open in early July in drooping clusters of 4–10, and fruits (near left) are about 0·8cm (⅓in) long and downy. Leaves (p41) are bright green and hairless except for pale downy tufts in the vein axils beneath. They are often covered with a shiny resin or honey-dew exuded by aphids which amass on these trees. A good distinctive feature are the numerous suckers produced at the base and forming dense burrs on the trunk. Leaves on suckers can be large and should not be confused with larger-leaved species.

Oliver's Lime

Tilia oliveri Szysz.
Native to central China and sometimes grown in European gardens and collections. Height to about 24m (80ft). Flowers (far left) open in early July, with large bright green bracts about 10cm (4in) long. Fruits (near left) are about 1·2cm (½in) across, soft downy surfaced. Leaves (p41) are dull green and smooth above with silvery undersides. Bark is smooth and grey with thin dark streaks and triangular folds at old branch scars.

Weeping Silver Lime or Weeping White Linden

Tilia petiolaris DC.
May be native to the Caucasus or of garden origin. Grown in gardens, parks and town streets. Height to about 24m (80ft). Strongly scented flowers (far left) open in late July, and have a narcotic effect on bees. Fruits are slightly ridged, about 1·2cm (½in) long and are rarely fertile. Leaves (p41) are dark green above, white and downy beneath with long downy stems, and are borne on hanging shoots. Bark is dark grey with narrow ridges and furrows.

Large-leaved Lime

Tilia platyphyllos Scop.
Native to Europe (including Britain), the Caucasus and Asia Minor, planted in European streets, parks and avenues. Height to 41m (135ft). Flowers (near left) open in late June, each about 1·2cm (½in). Fruits are downy, about 1·2cm (½in) long with 3–5 ridges. Leaves (p41) are dark above and paler, usually hairy on the lower surface, especially the midrib, vein axils and the stem. Bark is dark grey with narrow cracks or ridges.

Silver Lime

Tilia tomentosa Moench.
Native to south-eastern Europe and south-west Asia, planted in European parks and gardens. Height to about 24m (80ft) or more. Strongly scented flowers (far left) open in late July, and have a narcotic effect on bees. Fruit (near left) is about 0·6–1·2cm (¼–½in) long, downy with 5 ridges. Leaves (p41) are dark and wrinkled on upper surface and grey and downy underneath and on the stem. Bark of mature trees is dark grey and ridged.

California Nutmeg

Torreya californica Torr., family Taxaceae
Evergreen, native to California grown for ornament in western Europe. Height to about 21m (70ft) or more in the wild. Male flowers (near right) are about 0·8cm (⅓in) long, turn yellow and shed pollen in June. Females, on separate plants, are tiny and green at the base of new shoots. Fruits (far right) about 3·7cm (1½in) long, shining green with purple streaks and containing a large brown seed. Those shown in the photograph are preserved specimens. Leaves (p13) are dark yellowish green above with 2 whitish bands underneath and taper to a hard sharp spine.

Torreya nucifera (L.) Sieb. & Zucc. **Japanese Nutmeg**
Native to Japan. Height to 9m (30ft). Male flowers oval, light green, about 0·2cm (1/10in), females tiny and green. Fruits about 2·5cm (1in) similar to *T. californica*. Leaves (p13) are dark shiny green above with 2 white bands underneath. They emit an strong tangy smell.

Tsuga family Pinaceae, **Hemlock**
Evergreen coniferous trees with small flat leaves and small woody cones.

Eastern Hemlock or Canadian Hemlock

Tsuga canadensis (L.) Carr.
Native to north-eastern United States and Canada, cultivated in northern states and in western Europe in gardens and botanical collections, and occasionally for its timber, although of poor quality. The inner bark has been important in leather tanning. Height to about 30m (100ft). Flowers (far left) open in May, males about 0·3cm (⅛in) across, greenish yellow, females slightly larger and greenish. Cones (near left) are 1·2–2·5cm (½–1in) long, ripening from green to brown in October. Leaves (p14) are in rows on either side of the shoot with an extra row along the top flattened to the shoot and with the white underside uppermost, a useful feature for recognition.

Carolina Hemlock

Tsuga caroliniana Engelm.
Native to south-eastern United States, grown occasionally for ornament in northern states and in western Europe. Height to about 15m (50ft). Flowers (far left) are open in late April, males dark crimson, females pale pinkish lilac, both about 0·6cm (¼in) long. Cones (near left) are about 2·5cm (1in) long, opening when ripe. Leaves (p14) point out irregularly to the sides and above the shoot, narrower than other *Tsuga* species, with bright white bands beneath.

Chinese Hemlock

Tsuga chinensis (Franch.) Pritz.
Native to central and western China, grown in botanical collections. Height to about 12m (40ft) and may be rather bushy. Flowers (far left) open in late April, males yellow tinged purple, females dark pinkish purple, both about 0·6cm (¼in). Cones (near left) are up to about 2·5cm (1in) long, dark purplish ripening to brown. Leaves (p14) are similar to *T. heterophylla* but are lighter green above and greener below.

Northern Japanese Hemlock

Tsuga diversifolia (Max.) Mast.
Native to central and northern Japan, grown in botanical collections and some gardens. Height to about 24m (80ft). Flowers (far left) open in April, males dark crimson, females pink, about 0·3cm (⅛in). Cones (near left) are about 1·8cm (¾in), ripening from green to brown. Leaves (p14) are densely set, dark green above with 2 bright white bands underneath and have notched tips.

Western Hemlock

Tsuga heterophylla (Raf.) Sarg.
Native to north-western N. America, planted for its strong timber in northern and western Europe. Also cultivated for ornament in gardens and estates. Height to about 45m (148ft) and sometimes more, with a distinctively drooping leading shoot. Flowers (far left) open in late April or May, males dark crimson, females reddish purple, both about 0·3cm (⅛in) long. Cones (near left) are about 2·5cm (1in) long, dark bronzy green ripening to brown. Leaves (p14) are in 2 sets but point outwards and upwards. They are of varying lengths, dark green above with 2 bluish bands below and have rounded tips. Foliage has a strong aromatic smell when crushed.

Mountain Hemlock

Tsuga mertensiana (Bong.) Carr.
Native to the mountains of western N. America from Alaska south to California, of little value for timber but occasionally grown in eastern states and western and central Europe as an ornamental in large gardens. Height to about 21m (70ft) but may be much taller in the wild. Flowers (far left) open in late April, males dark rosy purple about 0·3cm (⅛in), female dark violet (though may be yellow green), slightly longer. Cones (near left) may be 5–7·5cm (2–3in), larger than any other *Tsuga* cone. They ripen from purple (or green) to brown when they open to release their seed. Leaves (p14) are set all round the shoot, blue-green on both surfaces.

Southern Japanese Hemlock

Tsuga sieboldii Carr.
Native to southern Japan, cultivated in botanical collections and some large gardens. Height to about 30m (100ft). Flowers (far left) open in April, males dark crimson, about 0·2cm (1/10in), females pale pink or purple, about 0·4cm (1/6in) long, nodding. Cones (near left) are about 2·5cm (1in) long, ripening from green to brown. Leaves (p14) are rather broad with a notched tip and 2 whitish bands below. Their arrangement look more irregular than on Northern Japanese Hemlock (*T. diversifolia*).

Ulmus family Ulmaceae, **Elm**
Deciduous trees with fruit surrounded by a leafy wing and simple double-toothed lopsided leaves arranged alternately.

Ulmus americana L. **American Elm or White Elm**
Native to eastern N. America. Height to 36m (120ft). Flowers in March on stems 1·2cm (½in) long. Fruits oval, about 1·2cm (½in) long with a notched tip. Leaves (p33) rough above with light downy tufts in the vein axils beneath.

Wych Elm or Scotch Elm

Ulmus glabra Huds.
Native to Europe (including Britain) and western Asia. Its wood is hard, resistant to splitting and wetting. Planted for ornament in Europe and north-eastern N. America. Height to about 41m (135ft). Flowers (near right) open in early March in clusters about 1cm (½in) long. Fruits (far right) are about 2·5cm (1in) across with the seed in centre, ripen pale brown and fall in July. Leaves (p34) are rough on the upper surface and softly hairy beneath with very short stems almost concealed by a curved base on one side. Bark is smooth and grey becoming brownish grey with cracks and furrows on mature trees.

Camperdown Elm

U. glabra 'Camperdown'
Commonly planted in European city and town streets, parks and gardens and also occasionally in north-eastern N. America. Height to around 12m (40ft) with distinctive tortuous growth and mushroom shape. Flowers and fruit (near and far right) are similar to *U. glabra* but show the zig-zag hanging twigs. Leaves are larger than *U. glabra* leaves, up to 20cm (8in) long and often more lopsided.

Ulmus × hollandica Mill. 'Hollandica', synonym *U. major* Sm. **Dutch Elm**
One of a group of hybrids between *U. glabra* and *U. minor*. Height to about 35m (116ft). Flowers open in late March, fruits about 1·8cm (¾in) long with the seed touching the edge of the wing. Leaves (p34) are broad, with dark green rough upper surface and paler under surface with rough hairs on the veins. New shoots are hairy. Bark is dark grey and flaky.

Huntingdon Elm or Chichester Elm

Ulmus × hollandica 'Vegeta', synonym *U. vegeta* Lindl.
Planted in streets, parks and gardens. Height to about 35m (116ft) with a dome-shaped crown. Flowers (near right) open in early April and fruit (far right) are set by late April, about 1·8cm (¾in) long with seed in the centre, usually marked by a reddish or crimson blotch. Leaves (p34) are longer and narrower than

U. × hollandica 'Hollandica' and have longer stems, 1·2–1·8cm (½–¾in). They are smooth and shiny above with tufts of down in the axils beneath. Young shoots are bright green and only slightly hairy. Bark is grey or brown, and ridged.

European White Elm or Fluttering Elm

Ulmus laevis Pall.
Native to central Europe and western Asia, grown in botanical collections. Height to about 20m (65ft). Flowers (near right) open in March on unusually long stalks, allowing them to flutter in the wind, hence one of its common names. Fruits (far right) are set by May, about 1·2cm (½in) long with white hairs around their edges. Leaves (p34) are strongly lopsided, one side at the base having 2 or 3 extra veins. They are slightly downy above and paler and downy beneath. Bark is grey or brown with broad ridges and deep furrows and often with clusters of twiggy shoots forming burrs.

Smooth-leaved Elm

Ulmus minor Mill.,
synonym *U. carpinifolia* G. Suckow
Native to Europe (possibly including Britain), northern Africa and south-west Asia. Height to about 30m (100ft) with upright branches forming a dome-shaped crown. Flowers (near right) open in March, fruits (far right) are about 1·8cm (¾in) long with the seed near to the notched tip. Leaves (p34) are variable but always bright shiny green above with tufts of down in the axils beneath on a downy stalk. Bark is greyish brown with long ridges and furrows.
U. minor var. *cornubiensis* (Weston) Rehd., **Cornish Elm** This has a loosely conical crown, with shiny green cup-shaped leaves. To about 35m (116ft).
U. minor var. *sarniensis* (Loud.) Rehd., **Jersey Elm** or **Wheatley Elm** This has a neat conical crown and dark green leaves. To about 38m (126ft).

English Elm

Ulmus procera Salisb.,
synonym *U. campestris* Mill.
Native to Britain, once widespread in fields hedges parks and streets, but now devastated by Dutch Elm disease and being replaced by other species. Also planted in north-eastern United States. Its wood is hard and resists wetting and splitting. Height to about 30m (100ft), suckering freely to form new trees, often along a hedge. Flowers (near right) open in late February and early March and fruits (far right) are set by April and May, smaller than those of *U. glabra* with seed near the tip. Leaves (p29) are variable in shape, dark green and rough above with pale down on the main vein beneath on a short downy stalk. Bark (p220) is dark brown and cracked into small rectangular plates. Many localised forms occur in different parts of Britain.

Rock Elm or Cork Elm

Ulmus thomasii Sarg.
Native to north-eastern N. America, sometimes planted there for shade and ornament and occasionally in botanical collections in Europe. Its wood is hard and strong, once much used in N. America. Height to about 30m (100ft). Flowers (near right) open in March in long slender clusters, each flower stem about 1·2cm (½in) long. Fruits (far right) are about 1·2cm (½in) long and downy, ripening in May. Leaves (p33) are rough at first with downy undersides, becoming smooth, dark green and shiny above, paler and downy underneath. Twigs often have corky wings, though not shown in photographs. Bark is dark brownish grey, with broad flaked ridges and fissures.

California Laurel, California Bay or Headache Tree

Umbellularia californica (Hook. & Arn.) Nutt., family Lauraceae
An evergreen, native to the coastal region of California and Oregon, which has yielded a valuable timber, useful for house interiors. Sometimes grown in collections and gardens in Europe. Its foliage is strongly aromatic when crushed and is said to induce a sharp headache after inhaling it. Height to about 24m (80ft), sometimes shrubby. Flowers (far left) open in January (much later in cool climates) in 2–4 clusters of about 10. Each flower is about 0·6cm (¼in) across. Fruits (near left) are about 2·5cm (1in) long and ripen from yellowish green in August and September. Leaves (p32) are smooth, and uniformly pale green. They fade to yellow or orange before falling in their second season.

Common Prickly Ash or Toothache Tree

Zanthoxylum americanum Mill., family Rutaceae
Deciduous tree, native to eastern N. America, sometimes grown in European gardens. The North American Indians are said to have chewed the twigs and fruit to ease the pain of toothache. Height to about 8m (26ft) as a tree but usually a shrub. Flowers (near right) open in May or June. Fruits (far right) are about 0·6cm (¼in) long and ripen to black in October or November. Leaves (p55) have 5–11 leaflets, with small rounded teeth and branches bear stout sharp prickles.

Zelkova family Ulmaceae
A small group of deciduous trees, in the same family as the elms (*Ulmus*) but differing in having male and female flowers separate on the same tree and fruit in the form of small nutlets.

Caucasian Elm

Zelkova carpinifolia (Pall.) K. Koch
Native to the Caucasus mountains, planted in European parks and large gardens. Height to about 35m (116ft) with a distinctive shape (see silhouette). Flowers (far left) open in April, the males as clusters of anthers about 0·6cm (¼in) long, females smaller in the leaf axils at the tip of new growth. Fruits (near left) are about 0·6cm (¼in) long with 4 ridges. Leaves (p29) have 6–12 pairs of veins, dark green and often roughly hairy on upper surface with hairs on the main vein beneath. Bark (p220) is smooth, splitting into scales, to show exposed orange bark beneath.

Keaki or Japanese Zelkova

Zelkova serrata (Thunb.) Mak.
Native to Japan, sometimes grown in large gardens and parks in Europe. Height to about 20m (65ft) or more. Flowers (far left) open in late April or May, males in leaf axils at base of new growth, about 0·4cm (1/6in) long, females smaller and green towards the tip of the shoot. Fruit is about 0·3cm (⅛in) and green. Leaves (p29) have longer stems than *Z. carpinifolia* and have 8–12 pairs of veins. They have more pointed teeth and colour yellow, orange and red in the autumn. Bark (near left) is smooth when young, becoming brown and orange and flaky when mature.

Bark is the outer layer of a tree trunk and provides protection to the nutrient carrying vessels beneath the surface. It is produced by a one cell thick layer known as the cork cambium. In some trees this lies in overlapping plates so that the bark breaks along the joins as the trunk expands, forming ridges as in Chestnut (*Castanea sativa*), or plates as in many of the pines (*Pinus*). On other trees it is a complete sheath, continually renewing itself and peeling off the surface in thin strips, as on Paper-bark Maple (*Acer griseum*) or Paper Birch (*Betula papyrifera*). Different species, therefore, have bark characteristics which may be useful when identifying a tree. All bark varies with the environment; for example, in cities they may be blackened by exhaust fumes or in very damp places they may be covered by moss or lichen. They may also differ according to age and growth of the specimen, so that a great deal of experience may be needed before making a positive identification. However, some are distinctive and easily recognised. A few photographs and descriptions are included in the text, but the following is a selection of interesting, attractive and/or distinctive barks.

Greek Fir *Abies cephalonica* (p61)

Nikko Fir *Abies homolepis* (p62)

Red Snake-bark Maple *Acer capillipes* (p66)

Paper-bark Maple *Acer griseum* (p69)

Horse Chestnut *Aesculus hippocastanum* (p81)

Common Alder *Alnus glutinosa* (p83)

Monkey Puzzle *Araucaria araucana* (p85)

Blue Birch *Betula coerulea-grandis* (p88)

Downy Birch *Betula pubescens* (p91)

European Hornbeam *Carpinus betulus* (p93)

Sweet Chestnut *Castanea sativa* (p95)

Common Hawthorn *Crataegus monogyna* (p108)

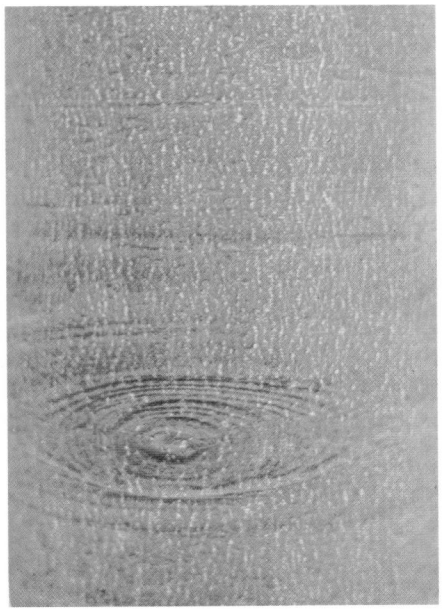

Winter's Bark *Drimys winteri* (p113)

Cider Gum *Eucalyptus gunnii* (p114)

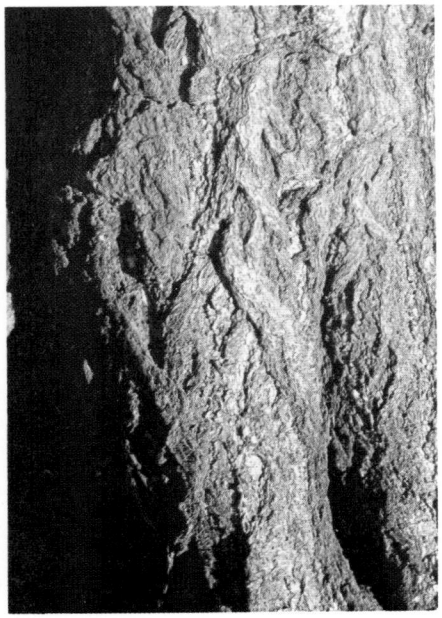

Maidenhair Tree *Gingko biloba* (p120)

Honey Locust *Gleditsia triacanthos* (p121)

Common Holly *Ilex aquifolium* (p122)

Japanese Walnut *Juglans ailantifolia* (p125)

Black Walnut *Juglans nigra* (p125)

European Larch *Larix decidua* (p129)

Roblé Beech *Nothofagus obliqua* (p142)

Persian Ironwood *Parrotia persica* (p144)

Sitka Spruce *Picea sitchensis* (p150)

Knobcone Pine *Pinus attenuata* (p153)

Lacebark Pine *Pinus bungeana* (p154)

Corsican Pine *Pinus nigra* var. *maritima* (p159)

Maritime Pine *Pinus pinaster* (p160)

Stone Pine *Pinus pinea* (p160)

Scots Pine *Pinus sylvestris* (p162)

London Plane *Platanus acerifolia* (p165)

Grey Poplar *Populus canescens* (p167)

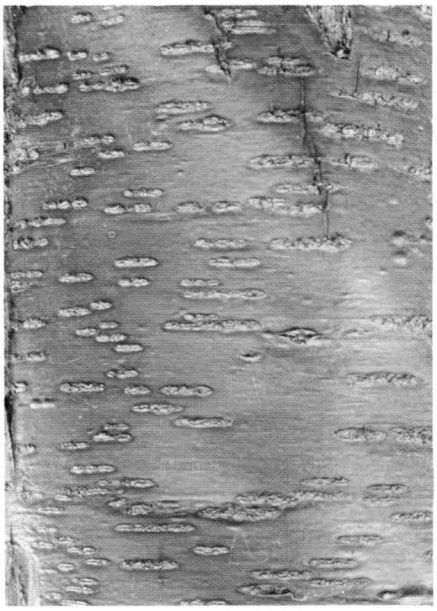

Manchurian Cherry *Prunus maackii* (p172)

Common Pear *Pyrus communis* (p179)

Turkey Oak *Quercus cerris* (p181)

Holm Oak *Quercus ilex* (p183)

Cork Oak *Quercus suber* (p190)

False Acacia *Robinia pseudoacacia* (p192)

Coast Redwood *Sequoia sempervirens* (p196)

Rowan *Sorbus aucuparia* (p198)

Chinese Stewartia *Stewartia sinensis* (p202)

Swamp Cypress *Taxodium distichum* (p203)

Common Yew *Taxus baccata* (p204)

English Elm *Ulmus procera* (p213)

Caucasian Elm *Zelkova carpinifolia* (p215)

Index of Common Names

(Note – An index of botanical names has not been included, as the text entries are arranged alphabetically. Numbers in bold refer to the main text entry.)

Abele 47, **166**
Acacia, False 57, **192**, 220
  Persian **82**
Adam's Laburnum 50, **128**
Alder, Black 39, **83**, 216
  Common 39, **83**, 216
  European 34, **83**
  Grey 34, **83**
  Italian 39, **83**
  Oregon 34, **84**
  Red 34, **84**
Aleppo Pine 19, **156**
Algerian Fir 16, **64**
  Oak 49, **181**
Allegheny Serviceberry 37, **84**
Almond **171**
Almond-leaved Pear **179**
  Willow 25, **195**
Alpine Fir 16, **63**
Alternate-leaf Dogwood 35, **103**
American Arbor-vitae 10, **205**
  Aspen 40, **169**
  Elm 33, **212**
  Holly 36, **124**
  Hornbeam 33, **93**
  Larch 23, **131**
  Larch, West 23, **131**
  Lime 41, **207**
  Linden 41, **207**
  Mountain Ash 56, **197**
  Red Plum 31, **170**
  Smoketree 32, **105**
Amur Cork-tree 55, **144**
  Maple 43, **69**
Angelica Tree 59, **84**
Antarctic Beech 29, **141**
Apple, Crab 37, **139**
  Hawthorn-leaved Crab 47, **137**
  Prairie Crab 37, **138**
  Sweet Crab 37, **137**
Arbor-vitae, American 10, **205**
  Chinese 10, **205**
  Giant 10, **206**
  Hiba 11, **206**
  Japanese 10, **206**
Arizona Ash 53, **120**
  Cypress, Rough-barked 11, **110**
  Smooth 11, **110**
Armenian Oak 29, **186**, 189
Arolla Pine 22, **154**
Ash, Arizona 53, **120**
  Common 55, **119**
  Common Prickly 55, **214**
  European 55, **119**
  Flowering 53, **119**
  Manna 53, **119**
  Narrow-leaved 55, **118**
  Oregon 53, **119**
  Red 53, **120**
  Single-leaved 33, **119**
  Stinking 50, **178**
  Velvet 53, **120**
  Weeping **119**
  White 53, **118**
Ash-leaved Maple **72**, 77
Aspen 40, **169**
  American 40, **169**
  Big-toothed 40, **167**
  European 40, **169**
  Quaking 40, **169**
Atlas Cedar 23, **97**
Austrian Pine 19, **158**
Autumn Cherry **176**
Azarole **106**

Bald Cypress 13, **203**, 220
Balearic Box 32, **92**
Balkan Maple 45, **70**
Balsam Poplar 40, **166**
  Western 40, **169**
Bamboo-leaved Oak 26, **185**
Basket Oak 49, **186**
Basswood 41, **207**
Bastard Service Tree 47, **201**
Bay 32, **132**
  Bull 27, **135**
  California 32, **214**
  Sweet 35, **136**
Bay Willow 25, **195**
Beach Pine 19, **155**
Bechtel Crab **138**
Beech, Antarctic 29, **141**
  Blue 33, **93**
  Common 33, **116**, 117
  Dawyck **117**
  Dombey's Southern 29, **141**
  European 33, **116**, 117
  Fern-leaved 47, **117**
  Oriental 33, **116**
  Purple 33, **117**
  Roblé 29, **142**, 218
  Weeping **117**
Bhutan Pine 22, **164**
Big Bud Hickory 54, **95**
Big Leaf Storax 39, **203**
Big Shellbark Hickory 54, **94**
Big Tree, California 12, **197**
Big-cone Pine 21, **156**
Big-toothed Aspen 40, **167**
Bigtooth Maple 46, **69**
Birch, Black 38, **88**
  Blue 38, **88**, 216
  Canoe 38, 77, 90
  Cherry 38, **88**
  Downy 38, **91**, 217
  Grey 38, **90**
  Himalayan 38, **91**
  Paper 38, 77, **90**
  Red 38, **89**
  River 38, **89**
  Silver 38, **90**
  Sweet 38, **88**
  Western 38, **89**
  White European 38, **90**
  Yellow 38, **89**
Bird Cherry 31, **173**
Bishop Pine 19, **158**
Bitternut 54, **94**
Black Alder 39, **83**, 216
  Birch 38, **88**
  Cherry 31, **174**
  Cottonwood 40, **169**
  Gum 35, 77, **142**
  Hawthorn 38, **106**
  Jack Oak 49, **185**
  Locust 57, **192**, 220
  Maple 44, **72**
  Mulberry 39, **141**
  Oak 48, **191**
  Oak, Californian 48, **184**
  Pine, Japanese 20, **163**
  Poplar **168**
  Poplar, Downy 40, **168**
  Poplar, Hybrid 40, **166**, **167**
  Spruce 17, **148**
  Walnut 58, **125**, 218
  Willow **195**
Blackthorn 31, **176**
Blue Beech 33, **93**
  Birch 38, **88**, 216
  Cedar 23, **97**
  Douglas Fir 16, **178**
  Engelmann Spruce 17, **146**
  Spruce 18, **150**
Bosnian Pine 19, **157**
Bottom Shellbark Hickory 54, **94**
Box, Balearic 32, **92**
  Common 32, **92**
Box Elder 53, **72**, 77
Brewer's Weeping Spruce 17, **146**
Bristle-cone Pine 21, **152**
Brittle Willow 25, **194**
Broad-leaved Cockspur Thorn 37, **109**
Buckeye, California 51, **79**
  Ohio 51, **80**
  Red 52, **81**
  Sweet 51, **80**, 188
  Yellow 51, **80**, 188
Bull Bay 27, **135**
Burr Oak 49, **185**
Butternut 58, **125**

California Bay 32, **214**
  Big Tree 12, **197**
  Buckeye 51, **79**
  Laurel 32, **214**
  Nutmeg 13, **209**
Californian Black Oak 48, **184**
  Live Oak 29, **180**
Campbell's Magnolia 28, **134**
Camperdown Elm **212**
Canadian Hemlock 14, **209**
Canoe Birch 38, 77, **90**
Canyon Live Oak 24, **182**
Cappadocian Maple 44, **66**, 76
Carolina Hemlock 14, **210**
Castor-oil Tree, Prickly 44, **128**
Catalpa, Hybrid 42, **96**
  Southern 42, **96**
  Western 42, **97**
  Yellow 42, **96**
Caucasian Elm 29, **215**, 220
  Lime 41, **207**
  Oak 49, **185**
  Spruce 18, **149**
  Wing-nut 54, **178**
Cedar, Atlas 23, **97**
  Blue 23, **97**
  Chilean Incense 11, **88**
  Chinese 10, 58, **97**, **205**
  Cyprus 23, **98**
  Incense 10, **92**
  Japanese 12, **109**
  Pencil 12, **127**
  Port Orford 10, **101**
  Smooth Tasmanian 11, **87**
  Summit 11, **87**
  Western Red 10, **206**
  White 10, **205**
Cedar of Lebanon 23, **98**
Chalk Maple 44, **71**
Cherry, Autumn **176**
  Bird 31, **173**
  Black 31, **174**
  Choke 31, **176**
  Cornelian 35, **104**
  Great White 30, **176**
  Holly-leaved 36, **171**
  Japanese 30, **174**
  Manchurian 31, **172**, 219
  Pin 25, **173**
  Rosebud 31, **176**
  Rum 31, **174**
  Sargent 31, **173**
  St Lucie 31, **172**
  Spring 31, **176**
  Wild 31, **170**
  Wild Red 25, **173**
  Yoshino 30, **177**
Cherry Birch 38, **88**
  Laurel 26, **172**
  Plum 31, **171**
Cherrystone Juniper 12, **126**
Chestnut, Common Horse 52, **81**, 216
  Golden 24, **102**
  Indian Horse 52, **81**
  Japanese Horse 52, **82**
  Red Horse 51, **80**
  Spanish 26, **95**, 217
  Sweet 26, **95**, 217
Chestnut Oak 49, **186**
Chestnut-leaved Oak 26, **181**
Chichester Elm 34, **212**
Chile Pine 13, **85**, 216
Chilean Fire Bush 24, **114**
  Incense Cedar 11, **88**
  Yew 13, **165**
Chinese Arbor-vitae 10, **205**
  Cedar 10, 58, **97**, **205**
  Crab **139**
  Fir 13, **109**
  Hemlock 14, **210**
  Juniper 12, **125**
  Necklace Poplar 42, **168**
  Pine 20, **163**
  Plum Yew 13, **99**
  Scarlet Rowan 56, **199**
  Stewartia 26, **202**, 220
  Tulip Tree 43, **133**
  Yellow Wood **103**
  Yew 14, **204**
Choke Cherry 31, **176**
Cider Gum 24, **114**, 217
Clammy Locust 57, **193**
Cluster Pine 20, **160**, 219
Coast Redwood 13, **196**, 220
Cobnut 39, **104**
Cockspur Thorn 37, **106**
  Broad-leaved 37, **109**
  Hybrid 37, **108**
Coffee Tree, Kentucky 59, **121**
Coigüe 29, **141**
Colorado Fir 15, **61**
  Spruce 18, **149**
Common Alder 39, **83**, **216**
  Ash 55, **119**
  Beech 33, **116**, 117
  Box 32, **92**
  Hawthorn 47, **108**, 217
  Holly 36, **122**, 217
  Hornbeam 33, **93**, 217
  Horse Chestnut 52, **81**, 216
  Juniper 12, **126**
  Laburnum 50, **129**
  Larch 23, **129**, 218
  Lime 41, **208**
  Mulberry 39, **141**
  Pear 37, **179**, 219
  Persimmon 27, **112**
  Prickly Ash 55, **214**
  Silver Fir 15, **60**
  Yew 14, **204**, 220
Contorted Willow 25, **194**
Coral-bark Maple **73**
Cork Elm 33, **214**
  Oak 29, **190**, 220
Cork-tree, Amur 55, **144**
Cornelian Cherry 35, **104**
Cornish Elm **213**
Corsican Pine 19, **159**, 218
Cotoneaster, Himalayan Tree- 32, **105**
Cottonwood 40, **167**
  Black 40, **169**
Cow's Tail Pine 13, **100**
Crab, Bechtel **138**
  Chinese **139**
  Hupeh **138**
  Japanese 37, **137**
  Magdeburg 37, **138**
  Oregon 37, **138**
  Purple 37, **139**
  Siberian 37, **136**
  Wild 37, **139**
Crab Apple 37, **139**
  Hawthorn-leaved 47, **137**
  Prairie 37, **138**
  Sweet 37, **137**
Crack Willow 25, **194**
Cretan Maple 43, **78**
Crimean Pine 19, **159**
Cucumber Tree 28, **134**
  Yellow 32, **134**
Cut-leaved Oak 48, **187**
Cypress, Bald 13, **203**, 220
  Hinoki 10, **101**
  Italian 11, **111**
  Lawson 10, **101**
  Leyland 10, **110**
  Monterey 11, **111**
  Nootka 10, **101**
  Patagonian 11, **118**
  Rough-barked Arizona 11, **110**
  Sawara 10, **102**
  Smooth Arizona 11, **110**
  Stinking 10, **101**
  Swamp 13, **203**, 220
Cyprus Strawberry Tree 27, **85**
  Cedar 23, **98**

Dahurian Larch 23, **130**
Daimio Oak 49, **182**
Date Plum 27, **112**
David's Pine 22, **153**
Dawn Redwood 13, **140**
Dawyck Beech **117**
Deciduous Stewartia 26, **202**
Delavay's Silver Fir 15, **61**
Deodar 23, **97**
Devil's Walkingstick 59, **84**
Dogwood, Alternate-leaf 35, **103**
  Flowering 35, **103**
  Nuttall's 35, **104**
  Pacific 35, **104**
  Table 35, **103**

Dombey's Southern Beech 29, **141**
Douglas Fir 16, **177**
Blue 16, **178**
Green 16, **177**
Large-coned 16, **177**
Dove Tree 41, **112**
Downy Black Poplar 40, **168**
Birch 38, **91**, 217
Hawthorn 38, **108**
Japanese Maple 46, **70**
Oak 48, **187**
Dragon Spruce 17, **145**
Drooping Juniper 12, **127**
Dunkeld Larch 23, **130**
Durmast Oak 48, **186**
Dutch Elm 34, **212**
Dwarf Maple 44, **69**

Ear-leaved Umbrella Tree 28, **134**
East Himalayan Spruce 18, **151**
Eastern Hemlock 14, **209**
Hop Hornbeam 33, **143**
Redcedar 12, **127**
Strawberry Tree 27, **85**
Elder 53, **195**
Box 53, **72**, 77
Elm, American 33, **212**
Camperdown **212**
Caucasian 29, **215**, 220
Chichester 34, **212**
Cork 33, **214**
Cornish **213**
Dutch 34, **212**
English 29, **213**, 220
European White 34, **213**
Fluttering 34, **213**
Huntingdon 34, **212**
Jersey **213**
Rock 33, **214**
Scotch 34, **212**
Smooth-leaved 34, **213**
Wheatley **213**
White 33, **212**
Wych 29, 34, **212**
Encina 29, **180**
Engelmann Spruce, Blue 17, **146**
English Elm 29, **213**, 220
Hawthorn 47, **107**
Oak 48, **187**
Oak, Purple 48, **187**
Walnut 54, **125**
Yew 14, **204**, 220
Eucryphia, Nyman's Hybrid 50, **115**
Euodia, Korean 53, **116**
European Alder 34, **83**
Ash 55, **119**
Aspen 40, **169**
Beech 33, **116**, 117
Hop Hornbeam 33, **143**
Hornbeam 33, **93**, 217
Larch 23, **129**, 218
Linden 41, **208**
Silver Fir 15, **60**
White Birch 38, **90**
White Elm 34, **213**
Evergreen Magnolia 27, **135**

False Acacia 57, **192**, 220
Fernleaf Maple **70**, 76
Fernleaved Beech 47, **117**
Field Maple 45, **65**, 76
Fig 44, **117**
Fir, Algerian 16, **64**
Alpine 16, **63**
Blue Douglas 16, **178**
Caucasian 16, **64**
Chinese 13, **109**
Colorado 15, **61**
Common Silver 15, **60**
Delavay's Silver 15, **61**
Douglas 16, **177**
European Silver 15, **60**
Forrest's Silver **61**
Grand 15, **62**
Greek 15, **61**
Green Douglas 16, **177**
Japanese 15, **62**
Korean **63**
Large-coned Douglas 16, **177**
Low's **61**
Momi 15, **62**
Nikko 15, **62**, 216
Noble 16, **64**
Red 16, **63**
Santa Lucia 15, **60**
Veitch's Silver 16, **65**
White 15, **61**
Fire Bush, Chilean 24, **114**
Flowering Ash 53, **119**
Dogwood 35, **103**
Fluttering Elm 34, **213**
Forrest's Maple 43, **68**
Silver Fir **61**
Foxglove-tree 42, **144**
Fraser Magnolia 28, **134**
French Willow 25, **195**
Frosted Thorn 37, **109**
Fullmoon Maple 46, **70**

Garland Tree 37, **137**
Gean 31, **170**
Giant Arbor-vitae 10, **206**
Fir 15, **62**
Glossy Privet 32, **132**
Goat Willow 32, **193**
Golden Chain 50, **129**
Chestnut 24, **102**
Irish Yew 14, **204**
Weeping Willow 25, **194**
Goldenrain Tree 57, **128**
Grand Fir 15, **62**
Great Sallow 32, **193**
White Cherry 30, **176**
Greek Fir 15, **61**, 216
Green Ash 53, **120**
Douglas Fir 16, **177**
Grey Alder 34, **83**
Birch 38, **90**
Poplar 40, **167**, 219
Sallow 25, **194**
Grey-budded Snake-bark Maple 43, **75**, 77
Gum, Cider 24, **114**, 217
Snow 24, **114**
Spinning 24, **115**

Hackamatack 23, **131**
Hackberry 29, **99**
Mississippi 27, **99**
Handkerchief Tree 41, **112**
Hawthorn, Black 38, **106**
Common 47, **108**, 217
Downy 38, **108**
English 47, **107**
Midland 47, **107**
Scarlet 38, **108**
Hawthorn-leaved Crab Apple 47, **137**
Maple 38, **67**
Hazel 39, **104**
Turkish 39, **105**
Headache Tree 32, **214**
Hedge Maple 45, **65**, 76
Hedgehog Holly 36, **123**
Heldreich's Maple 45, **70**
Hemlock, Canadian 14, **209**
Carolina 14, **210**
Chinese 14, **210**
Eastern 14, **209**
Northern Japanese 14, **210**
Western 14, **211**
Hercules Club 59, **84**
Hers's Maple 43, **70**, 189
Hiba 11, **206**
Arbor-vitae 11, **206**
Hickory, Big Bud 54, **95**
Big Shellbark 54, **94**
Bottom Shellbark 54, **94**
Little Shellbark 53, **95**
Pignut 53, **94**
Shagbark 53, **95**
Swamp 54, **94**
White Heart 54, **95**
Highclere Holly **121**
Himalayan Birch 38, **91**
Holly 36, **124**
Juniper 12, **127**
Pine 22, **164**
Spruce, East 18, **151**
Spruce, West 18, **151**
Tree-cotoneaster 32, **105**
Hinoki Cypress 10, **101**
Holford's Pine 22, **157**
Holly, American 36, **124**
Common 36, **122**, 217
Hedgehog 36, **123**
Highclere **121**
Himalayan 36, **124**
Perny's 36, **124**
Holly Oak 29, **183**, 219
Holly-leaved Cherry 36, **171**
Holm Oak 29, **183**, 219
Hondo Spruce 17, **147**
Honey Locust 56, **121**, 217
Hop Hornbeam, Eastern 33, **143**
European 33, **143**
Hop Tree 50, **178**
Hornbeam, American 33, **93**
Common 33, **93**, 217
Eastern Hop 33, **143**
European 33, **93**, 217
European Hop 33, **143**
Japanese 33, **93**
Hornbeam Maple 26, **66**
Horse Chestnut, Common 52, **81**, 216
Indian 52, **81**
Japanese 52, **82**
Red 52, **80**
Hungarian Oak 49, **182**
Huntingdon Elm 34, **212**
Hupeh Crab **138**
Rowan 56, **198**
Hybrid Black Poplar 40, **166**, **167**
Catalpa 42, **96**
Cockspur Thorn 37, **108**
Strawberry Tree 26, **85**
Wing-nut 54, **179**

Incense Cedar 10, **92**
Chilean 11, **88**
Indian Bean 42, **96**
Horse Chestnut 52, **81**
Irish Yew **204**
Golden 14, **204**
Iron Tree 32, **144**, 218
Ironwood 33, **143**
Persian 32, **144**, 218
Italian Alder 39, **83**
Cypress 11, **111**
Maple 44, **73**
Stone Pine 20, **160**, 219

Jack Pine 19, **154**
Japanese Arbor-vitae 10, **206**
Big-leaf Magnolia 28, **135**
Black Pine 20, **163**
Cedar 12, **109**
Cherry 30, **174–176**
Crab 37, **137**
Fir 15, **62**
Hemlock, Northern 14, **210**
Hornbeam 33, **93**
Horse Chestnut 52, **82**
Larch 23, **130**
Magnolia, Northern 27, **135**
Maple 46, **73**, 76
Maple, Downy 46, **70**
Maple, Purple **73**
Nutmeg 13, **209**
Plum Yew 13, **100**
Rowan 56, **198**
Stewartia 26, **202**
Thuja 10, **206**
Walnut 57, **125**, 218
White Pine 22, **159**
Yew 14, **204**
Zelkova 29, **215**
Jeffrey Pine 21, **157**
Jersey Elm **213**
Judas-tree 39, **100**
Juniper, Cherrystone 12, **126**
Chinese 12, **125**
Common 12, **126**
Drooping 12, **127**
Himalayan 12, **127**
Mexican 12, **126**
Needle 12, **127**
One-seed 12, **126**
Syrian 12, **126**
Temple 12, **127**

Katsura Tree 39, **100**
Keaki 29, **215**
Kentucky Coffee Tree 59, **121**
King William Pine 11, **87**
King-nut 54, **94**
Korean Euodia 53, **116**
Fir **63**
Koyama's Spruce 17, **147**
Knobcone Pine 21, **153**, 218
Kohuhu 27, **164**
Kuro-matsu 20, **163**

Laburnum, Adam's 50, **128**
Common 50, **129**
Scotch 50, **129**
Voss's 50, **129**
Lacebark Pine 21, **154**, 218
Larch, American 23, **131**
Common 23, **129**, 218
Dahurian 23, **130**
Dunkeld 23, **130**
European 23, **129**, 218
Japanese 23, **130**
Tibetan 23, **131**
West American 23, **131**
Western 23, **131**
Large-coned Douglas Fir 16, **177**
Large-leaved Lime 41, **208**
Laurel 32, **132**
California 32, **214**
Cherry 26, **172**
Laurel Oak 24, **184**
Laurel-leaved Willow 25, **195**
Lawson Cypress 10, **101**
Lea's Hybrid Oak 49, **184**
Lebanon Oak 26, **184**
Leyland Cypress 10, **110**
Likiang Spruce 17, **147**
Limber Pine 22, **156**
Lime, American 41, **207**
Caucasian 41, **207**
Common 41, **208**
Large-leaved 41, **208**
Oliver's 41, **208**
Silver 41, **209**
Small-leaved 41, **207**
Weeping Silver 41, **208**
Lime-leaved Maple 39, **68**
Linden, American 41, **207**
European 41, **208**
Weeping White 41, **208**
Little Shellbark Hickory 53, **95**
Live Oak, Californian 29, **180**
Canyon 24, **182**
Locust, Black 57, **192**, 220
Clammy 57, **193**
Honey 56, **121**, 217
Lodgepole Pine 19, **155**
Lombardy Poplar 40, **168**
London Plane 46, **165**, 188, 219
Low's Fir **61**
Lucombe Oak 48, **183**
Ludwig's Oak 48, **184**

Macedonian Oak 49, **191**
Pine 22, **160**
Madrona 27, **86**
Magdeburg Crab 37, **138**
Magnolia, Campbell's 28, **134**
Evergreen 27, **135**
Fraser 28, **134**
Japanese Big-leaf 28, **135**
Northern Japanese 27, **135**
Southern 27, **135**
Willow-leaved 24, **135**
Wilson's 27, **136**
Maidenhair Tree 43, **120**, 217
Manchurian Cherry 31, **172**, 219
Manna Ash 53, **119**
Maple, Amur 43, **69**
Ash-leaved 53, **72**, 77
Balkan 45, **70**
Bigtooth 46, **69**
Black 44, **72**
Cappadocian 44, **66**, 76
Chalk 44, **71**
Coral-bark **73**
Cretan 43, **78**
Downy Japanese 46, **70**
Dwarf 44, **69**
Fernleaf **70**, 76
Field 45, **65**, 76
Fullmoon 46, **70**
Grey-budded Snake-bark 43, **75**, 77
Forrest's 43, **68**
Hawthorn-leaved 38, **67**
Hedge 45, **65**, 76
Heldreich's 45, **70**
Hers's 43, **70**, 189
Hornbeam 26, **66**
Italian 44, **73**

Japanese 46, **73**, 76
Lime-leaved 39, **68**
Miyabe's 45, **71**
Montpelier 43, **72**
Mountain 45, **78**
Nikko 50, **72**, 77
Norway 45, **74**, 189
Oregon 45, **71**
Paper-bark 50, **69**, 216
Pere David's 34, **68**
Purple Japanese **73**
Red 43, **75**
Red Snake-bark 43, **66**, 216
Rock 44, **69**
Scarlet 43, **75**
Silver 46, **75**
Striped 43, **74**
Sugar 45, **78**
Sycamore 45, **74**
Tartar 39, **78**
Van Volxem's 45, **79**
Vine 46, **67**, 76
Vine-leaved 50, **67**
Maritime Pine 20, **160**, 219
Maul Oak 24, **182**
May 47, **107**
Mazzard 31, **170**
Mediterranean Medlar **106**
Medlar 26, **140**
Mediterranean **106**
Mespilus, Snowy 37, **84**
Mexican Juniper 12, **126**
Nut Pine 21, **155**
Stone Pine 21, **155**
White Pine 22, **153**
Midland Hawthorn 47, **107**
Mimosa 59, **65**
Mirbeck's Oak 49, **181**
Mississippi Hackberry 27, **99**
Miyabe's Maple 45, **71**
Mockernut 54, **95**
Momi Fir 15, **62**
Monkey Puzzle 13, **85**, 216
Monterey Cypress 11, **111**
Pine 21, **161**
Montpelier Maple 43, **72**
Moose-bark 43, **74**
Moosewood 43, **74**
Morinda Spruce 18, **151**
Mossy Cup Oak 49, **185**
Mountain Ash 56, **198**, 220
American 56, **197**
European 56, **198**, 220
Mountain Hemlock 14, **211**
Maple 45, **78**
Pine 20, **163**
Snowdrop Tree 26, **121**
White Pine 22, **158**
Mulberry, Black 39, **141**
Common 39, **141**
Paper 39, **91**
White 39, **140**
Myrobalan 31, **171**

Narrow-leaved Ash 55, **118**
Necklace Poplar 40, **167**
Chinese 42, **168**
Needle Juniper 12, **127**
Nettle-tree, Southern 25, **98**
Nettle Tree 29, **99**
Nikko Fir 15, **62**, 216
Maple 50, **72**, 77
Nirre 29, **141**
Noble Fir 16, **64**
Nootka Cypress 10, **101**
Northern Japanese Hemlock 14, **210**
Magnolia 27, **135**
Northern Pitch Pine 21, **162**
Norway Maple 45, **74**, 189
Spruce 17, **145**
Nut Pine, Mexican 21, **155**
Nutmeg, California 13, **209**
Japanese 13, **209**
Nuttall's Dogwood 35, **104**
Nyman's Hybrid Eucryphia 50, **115**

Oak, Algerian 49, **181**
Armenian 29, **186**, 189
Bamboo-leaved 26, **185**
Basket 49, **186**
Black 48, **191**
Black Jack 49, **185**
Burr 49, **185**
Californian Black 48, **184**
Californian Live 29, **180**
Canyon Live 24, **182**
Caucasian 49, **185**
Chestnut 49, **186**
Chestnut-leaved 26, **181**
Cork 29, **190**, 220
Cut-leaved 48, **187**
Daimio 49, **182**
Downy 48, **187**
Durmast 48, **186**
English 48, **187**
Holly 29, **183**, 219
Holm 29, **183**, 219
Hungarian 49, **182**
Laurel 24, **184**
Lea's Hybrid 49, **184**
Lebanon 26, **184**
Lucombe 48, **183**
Ludwig's 48, **184**
Macedonian 49, **191**
Maul 24, **182**
Mirbeck's 49, **181**
Mossy Cup 49, **185**
Pedunculate 48, **187**
Pin 48, **185**, 189
Pontine 29, **186**, 189
Purple English 48, **187**
Pyrenean 48, **187**
Quercitron 48, **191**
Red 48, **190**
Scarlet 48, **182**, 188
Sessile 48, **186**
Shingle 28, **183**
Shumard 48, 189, **190**
Swamp White 49, **181**
Tanbark 26, **133**
Turkey 49, **181**, 219
Turner's 49, **191**
Water **185**
White 48, **180**
Willow 24, **186**, 189
Oleaster 24, **113**
Ohio Buckeye 51, **80**
Oliver's Lime 41, **208**
One-seed Juniper 12, **126**
Orange, Osage 35, **133**
Oregon Ash 53, **119**
Alder 34, **84**
Crab 37, **138**
Maple 45, **71**
Oriental Beech 33, **116**
Plane 46, **165**
Spruce 18, **149**
Sweet Gum 44, **132**
Thorn 47, **107**
Osage Orange 35, **133**
Osier 24, **195**

Pacific Dogwood 35, **104**
Silver Fir 15, **60**
Yew 14, **204**
Pagoda Tree 57, **197**
Papaw 28, **86**
Paper Birch 38, 77, **90**
Mulberry 39, **91**
Paper-bark Maple 50, **69**, 216
Patagonian Cypress 11, **118**
Peach 25, **173**
Pear, Almond-leaved **179**
Common 37, **179**, 219
Willow-leaved 24, **180**
Pedunculate Oak 48, **187**
Pencil Cedar 12, **127**
Pepperidge 35, 77, **142**
Pere David's Maple 34, **68**
Perny's Holly 36, **124**
Persian Acacia **82**
Ironwood 32, **144**, 218
Walnut 54, **125**
Persimmon, Common 27, **112**
Picrasma 55, **152**
Pignut Hickory 53, **94**
Pin Cherry 25, **173**
Oak 48, **185**, 189
Pine, Aleppo 19, **156**
Arolla 22, **154**
Austrian 19, **158**
Beach 19, **155**
Bhutan 22, **164**
Big-cone 21, **156**
Bishop 19, **158**
Bosnian 19, **157**
Bristle-cone 21, **152**
Chile 13, **85**, 216
Chinese 20, **163**
Cluster 20, **160**, 219
Corsican 19, **159**, 218
Cow's Tail 13, **100**
Crimean 19, **159**
David's 22, **153**
Himalayan 22, **164**
Holford's 22, **157**
Jack 19, **154**
Japanese Black 20, **163**
Japanese White 22, **159**
King William 11, **87**
Knobcone 21, **153**, 218
Lacebark 21, **154**, 218
Limber 22, **156**
Lodgepole 19, **155**
Macedonian 22, **160**
Maritime 20, **160**, 219
Mexican Nut 21, **155**
Mexican Stone 21, **155**
Mexican White 22, **153**
Monterey 21, **161**
Mountain 20, **163**
Mountain White 22, **158**
Northern Pitch 21, **162**
Red 20, **161**
Scots 20, **162**, 219
Scrub 20, **164**
Shore 19, **155**
Stone 20, **160**, 219
Swiss Stone 22, **154**
Umbrella 18, **196**
Western White 22, **158**
Western Yellow 21, **161**
Weymouth 22, **162**
White 22, **162**
Whitebark 21, **152**
Pink Siris **82**
Pinyon 21, **155**
Pissard Plum 31, **171**
Pitch Pine 21, **162**
Plane, London 46, **165**, 188, 219
Oriental 46, **165**
Plum, American Red 31, **170**
Cherry 31, **171**
Pissard 31, **171**
Purple-leaved 31, **171**
Plum Yew, Chinese 13, **99**
Japanese 13, **100**
Plum-fruited Yew 13, **165**
Pontine Oak 29, **186**, 189
Poplar, Balsam 40, **166**
Black **168**
Chinese Necklace 42, **168**
Downy Black 40, **168**
Grey 40, **167**, 219
Hybrid Black 40, **166**, **167**
Lombardy 40, **168**
Necklace 40, **167**
Railway 40, **166**
Western Balsam 40, **169**
White 47, **166**
Port Orford Cedar 10, **101**
Portugal Laurel 26, **172**
Prairie Crab Apple 37, **138**
Prickly Ash, Common 55, **214**
Prickly Castor-oil Tree 44, **128**
Pride of India 57, **128**
Prince Albert's Yew 13, **196**
Privet, Glossy 32, **132**
Tree 32, **132**
Purple Beech 33, **117**
Crab 37, **139**
English Oak 48, **187**
Japanese Maple **73**
Purple-leaved Plum 31, **171**
Pussy Willow 32, **193**
Pyrenean Oak 48, **187**
Whitebeam 47, **200**

Quaking Aspen 40, **169**
Quercitron Oak 48, **191**
Quince 32, **111**

Railway Poplar 40, **166**
Raoul 29, **142**
Rauli 29, **142**
Red Alder 34, **84**
Ash 53, **120**
Birch 38, **89**
Buckeye 52, **81**
Cedar, Western 10, **206**
Cherry, Wild 25, **173**
Fir 16, **63**
Horse Chestnut 51, **80**
Maple 43, **75**
Oak 48, **190**
Pine 20, **161**
Plum, American 31, **170**
Silver Fir 15, **60**
Snake-bark Maple 43, **66**, 216
Spruce 18, **150**
Redcedar, Eastern 12, **127**
Redwood, Coast 13, **196**, 220
Dawn 13, **140**
River Birch 38, **89**
Roble Beech 29, **142**, 218
Rock Elm 33, **214**
Maple 44, **69**
Rosebud Cherry 31, **176**
Rough-barked Arizona Cypress 11, **110**
Rowan 56, **198**, 220
Chinese Scarlet 56, **199**
Hupeh 56, **199**
Japanese 56, **198**
Sargent's 55, **201**
Rum Cherry 31, **174**

Sallow, Great 32, **193**
Grey 25, **194**
Sargent Cherry 31, **173**
Sargent's Rowan 55, **201**
Santa Lucia Fir 15, **60**
Sassafras 47, **196**
Sato Zakura 30, **174–176**
Sawara Cypress 10, **102**
Scarlet Hawthorn 38, **108**
Maple 43, **75**
Oak 48, **182**, 188
Rowan, Chinese 56, **199**
Scholar's Tree 57
Scotch Elm 34, **212**
Laburnum 50, **129**
Scots Pine 20, **162**, 219
Scrub Pine 20, **164**
Serbian Spruce 18, **148**
Service Tree 56, **198**
Bastard 47, **201**
Wild 47, **201**
Service Tree of Fontainebleau 47, **200**
Serviceberry, Allegheny 37, **84**
Sessile Oak 48, **186**
Shagbark Hickory 53, **95**
Shellbark Hickory, Big 54, **94**
Bottom 54, **94**
Little 53, **95**
Shingle Oak 28, **183**
Shore Pine 19, **155**
Shumard Oak 48, 189, **190**
Siberian Crab 37, **136**
Spruce 18, 148
Silk Tree **82**
Silver Bell 26, **121**
Birch 38, **90**
Fir, Common 15, **60**
Fir, Delavay's 15, **61**
Fir, European 15, **60**
Fir, Forrest's **61**
Fir, Pacific 15, **60**
Fir, Red 15, **60**
Fir, Veitch's 16, **65**
Lime 41, **209**
Lime, Weeping 41, **208**
Maple 46, **75**
Wattle 59, **65**
Siris, Pink **82**
Sitka Spruce 18, **150**, 218
Sloe 31, **176**
Small-leaved Lime 41, **207**
Smoketree, American 32, **105**
Smooth Arizona Cypress 11, **110**
Tasmanian Cedar 11, **87**
Smooth-leaved Elm 34, **213**
Snake-bark Maple, Grey-budded 43, **75**, 77
Red 43, **66**, 216
Snow Gum 24, **114**
Snowbell Tree 35, **203**
Snowdrop Tree, Mountain 26, **121**
Snowy Mespilus 37, **84**
Sorrel Tree 27, **143**
Sour Wood 27, **143**
Southern Beech, Dombey's 29, **141**
Southern Catalpa 42, **96**
Japanese Hemlock 14, **211**

Magnolia 27, **135**
Nettle-tree 25, **98**
Spanish Chestnut 26, **95**, 217
Spinning Gum 24, **115**
Spring Cherry 31, **176**
Spruce, Black 17, **148**
Blue 18, **150**
Blue Engelmann 17, **146**
Brewer's Weeping 17, **146**
Caucasian 18, **149**
Dragon 17, **145**
East Himalayan 18, **151**
Hondo 17, **147**
Koyama's 17, **147**
Likiang 17, **147**
Morinda 18, **151**
Norway 17, **145**
Oriental 18, **149**
Red 18, **150**
Serbian 18, **148**
Siberian 18, **148**
Sitka 18, **150**, 218
Tiger-tail 18, **149**
West Himalayan 18, **151**
White 17, **146**
Spur Leaf 42, **205**
St Lucie Cherry 31, **172**
Stag's Horn Sumac 58, **192**
Stewartia, Chinese 26, **202**, 220
Deciduous 26, **202**
Japanese 26, **202**
Stinking Ash 50, **178**
Cypress 10, **101**
Stone Pine 20, **160**, 219
Mexican 21, **155**
Swiss 22, **154**
Storax, Big Leaf 39, **203**
Strawberry Tree 26, **86**
Cyprus 27, **85**
Eastern 27, **85**
Hybrid 26, **85**
Striped Maple 43, **74**
Sugar Maple 45, **78**
Sugarberry 27, **99**
Sumac, Stag's Horn 58, **192**
Summit Cedar 11, **87**
Swamp Cypress 13, **203**, 220
Hickory 54, **94**
White Oak 49, **181**
Swedish Whitebeam 47, **199**
Sweet Bay 35, **136**
Birch 38, **88**
Buckeye 51, **80**, 188
Chestnut 26, **95**, 217
Crab Apple 37, **137**
Gum 44, **132**, 188
Gum, Oriental 44, **132**
Swiss Stone Pine 22, **154**
Sycamore 45, **74**
Syrian Juniper 12, **126**

Table Dogwood 35, **103**
Tacamahac 40, **166**
Tamarack 23, **131**
Tanbark Oak 26, **133**
Tartar Maple 39, **78**
Tasmanian Cedar, Smooth 11, **87**
Temple Juniper 12, **127**
Thorn, Broad-leaved Cockspur 37, **109**
Cockspur 37, **106**
Frosted 37, **109**
Hybrid Cockspur 37, **108**
Oriental 47, **107**
Thuja, Japanese 10, **206**
Tibetan Cherry 25, **174**
Larch 23, **131**
Tiger-tail Spruce 18, **149**
Toothache Tree 55, **214**
Tree of Heaven 58, **82**
Tree Privet 32, **132**
Tree-cotoneaster 32, **105**
Tulip Tree 43, **133**, 188
Chinese 43, **133**
Tupelo 35, 77, **142**
Turkey Oak 49, **181**, 219
Turkish Hazel 39, **105**
Turner's Oak 49, **191**

Umbrella Tree 28, **136**
Ear-leaved 28, **134**
Umbrella Pine 18, **196**

Van Volxem's Maple 45, **79**
Varnish Tree 58, **192**
Veitch's Silver Fir 16, **65**
Velvet Ash 53, **120**
Vine Maple 46, **67**, 76
Vine-leaved Maple 50, **67**
Voss's Laburnum 50, **129**

Walnut, Black 58, **125**, 218
English 54, **125**
Japanese 57, **125**, 218
Persian 54, **125**
White 58, **125**
Water Oak **185**
Wattle, Silver 59, **65**
Weeping Ash **119**
Beech **117**
Silver Lime 41, **208**
Spruce, Brewer's 17, **146**
White Linden 41, **208**
Willow **193**
Willow, Golden 25, **194**
Wellingtonia 12, **197**
West American Larch 23, **131**
Himalayan Spruce 18, **151**
Western Balsam Poplar 40, **169**
Birch 38, **89**
Catalpa 42, **97**
Hemlock 14, **211**
Larch 23, **131**
Red Cedar 10, **206**
White Pine 22, **158**
Yellow Pine 21, **161**
Yew 14, **204**
Weymouth Pine 22, **162**
Wheatley Elm **213**
White Ash 53, **118**
Birch, European 38, **90**
Cedar 10, **205**
Cherry, Great 30, **176**
Cypress 10, **102**
Elm 33, **212**
Elm, European 34, **213**
Fir 15, **61**
Heart Hickory 54, **95**
Linden, Weeping 41, **208**
Mulberry 39, **140**
Oak 48, **180**
Oak, Swamp 49, **181**
Pine 22, **162**
Pine, Japanese 22, **159**
Pine, Mexican 22, **153**
Pine, Mountain 22, **158**
Pine, Western 22, **158**
Poplar 47, **166**
Spruce 17, **146**
Walnut 58, **125**
Willow 25, **193**
Whitebark Pine 21, **152**
Whitebeam 34, **197**
Swedish 47, **199**
Whitewood 43, **133**, 188
Wild Cherry 31, **170**
Crab 37, **139**
Red Cherry 25, **173**
Service Tree 47, **201**
Willow, Almond-leaved 25, **195**
Bay 25, **195**
Black **195**
Brittle 25, **194**
Contorted 25, **194**
Crack 25, **194**
French 25, **195**
Goat 32, **193**
Golden Weeping 25, **194**
Laurel-leaved 25, **195**
Pussy 32, **193**
Weeping **193**
White 25, **193**
Willow Oak 24, **186**, 189
Willow-leaved Magnolia 24, **135**
Pear 24, **180**
Wilson's Magnolia 27, **136**
Wing-nut, Caucasian 54, **178**
Hybrid 54, **179**
Winter's Bark 24, **113**, 217
Wych Elm 29, 34, **212**

Yellow Birch 38, **89**
Buckeye 51, **80**, 188
Catalpa 42, **96**
Cucumber Tree 32, **134**
Pine, Western 21, **161**
Wood 53, **103**
Wood, Chinese **103**
Yellow-berried Yew **204**
Yew, Chilean 13, **165**
Chinese 14, **204**
Chinese Plum 13, **99**
Common 14, **204**, 220
English 14, **204**, 220
Golden Irish 14, **204**
Irish **204**
Japanese 14, **204**
Japanese Plum 13, **100**
Pacific 14, **204**
Plum-fruited 13, **165**
Prince Albert's 13, **196**
Western 14, **204**
Yellow-berried **204**
Yoshino Cherry 30, **177**
Yulan **134**

Zelkova, Japanese 29, **215**
Zoeschen Maple 45, **79**